MONDAY to FRIDAY

Chicken

MONDAY to FRIDAY

Chicken

MICHELE URVATER

Illustrations by Tim Robinson

WORKMAN PUBLISHING • NEW YORK

For my husband, Michael, and daughter, Alessia, who showed endless patience and good humor while eating chicken almost daily for two years.

Acknowledgments

Thanks to everyone at Workman Publishing for their support and loyalty over the last twenty-five years. A super, special, heartfelt thank you to Suzanne Rafer, my editor, who takes so much care with every book she tackles.

I'd also like to thank in editorial, Kathie Ness and Carrie Schoen; in the art department, Flamur Tonuzi, Nancy Gonzalez, and Erica Heitman; in publicity, Jackie Mills; in marketing, Andrea Glickson; and of course, the sales department.

Copyright © 1998 by Michèle Urvater

Library of Congress Cataloging-in-Publication Data
Urvater, Michèle.
Monday-to-Friday Chicken / by Michèle Urvater; illustrations by Tim Robinson
p.   cm.

Includes index.
ISBN 0-7611-1318-5 (hardcover)—ISBN 1-56305-931-2 (pbk.)
1. Cookery (Chicken) I. Title.

TX750.5.C45U78   1998

641.6'65—dc21   97-52224
                                                    CIP

Cover design by Paul Hanson
Book design by Flamur Tonuzi and Nancy Gonzalez with Erica Heitman
Front cover photograph by Louis Wallach
Author photograph by Walt Chrynwski
Book illustrations by Tim Robinson

Workman books are available at special discounts when purchased in bulk for premiums and sales promotions as well as for fund-raising or educational use. Special editions or book excerpts can be created to specification. For details, contact the Special Sales Director at the address below.

Workman Publishing Company, Inc.
708 Broadway
New York, NY 10003-9555

Manufactured in the United States of America

First printing October 1998
10 9 8 7 6 5 4 3 2 1

Contents

when appetites are slight; for times when appetites are heartier, *Complete Meals* (page 133) offers recipes for Chicken and Apple Toss over Polenta and Curried Chicken over Aromatic Rice; lastly, *On the Grill* (page 164) includes beautifully charred Grilled Chicken over Red Cabbage and Mushroom-Lover's Chicken to create indoors—or out.

NO-TEND OVEN COOKING 170

For days when you have a little more time, take a few minutes to prepare the dishes featured here and relax while they cook in the oven. *Oven Meals* (page 171) like Mediterranean Casserole and Garlic Chicken with Peppers and Beans are complete meals; *Oven Entrées* (page 190), like Baked Herbed Chicken and Meltingly Marvelous Chicken, need a quick side dish to round out the dinner; and for real ease, try Zesty Herbed Chicken as featured in the *Chicken in the Microwave* section (page 197).

SUNDAY START-UPS AND QUICK FIXES 201

When you have the time on the weekend, roast two chickens and some vegetables and turn them into meals to enjoy during the rest of the week. Chicken Stew Any Way and Every Way, Southwest Turkey Casserole, Grandma Helen's Jewish Chicken Soup, and Game Hens with Pecan Rice Pilaf are just a few of the ideas included in this chapter.

HOMEMADE EXOTIC PANTRY . . .222

Homemade herb pastes and purées, sauces and stocks enliven any dish and give even the most humble chicken soup, sandwich, or salad an exotic touch. A homemade Coconut Peanut Sauce, Ancho Paste, Tomato Salsa, or Porcini Stock are great secret ingredients to have on hand.

Chicken:
The Monday-to-Friday Way

"You can never have enough chicken recipes," says friend and food writer Arthur Schwartz. He's right, of course, and his statement is supported by the fact that in this country 30 percent of the protein consumed is in the form of chicken. Why is this bird so popular? I believe it must be for all the reasons I like to cook it:

Chicken is versatile, high in protein, low in fat, and most important to the Monday-to-Friday cook, fast and easy to prepare.

But the title of this book really ought to have been Monday-to-Friday Chicken Meals rather than plain old Monday-to-Friday Chicken. Recipes, even quick ones, that center on one ingredient present a particular problem to the Monday-to-Friday cook: What else are you going to prepare to complete the meal? This book provides the answer. The recipes are not for more ways to prepare chicken on its own, but rather for delicious meals that include chicken and at least one other element—the vegetables or the starch, and in some cases both.

While I have tried to provide a balanced collection of recipes for all parts of the chicken, from the whole bird to its little wings, it's no surprise that a number of recipes feature skinless, boneless chicken breasts—the cut that is the fastest and most versatile to cook.

You'll also discover recipes for cut-up turkey and Cornish game hens. Both types of poultry are sources of good Monday-to-Friday dishes, as are ground chicken and turkey, and sausages and bacon made from poultry.

THE MONDAY-TO-FRIDAY SYSTEM

If you don't own my other "Monday-to-Friday" cookbooks, you might be wondering what this system is really about. The phrase "Monday-to-Friday" refers to the hectic workweek we all have to face these days, whether we work within the home or hold a job, whether we are single or married with children. The Monday-to-Friday way of cooking offers solutions for getting a delicious home-cooked dinner on the table no matter how stretched for time you may be.

Because people's schedules are hectic in ways unique to their particular lifestyles, my strategies are constructed to suit different schedules and individual needs. While many of my recipes can be on the table 30 minutes after you begin preparation, not all of them are that quick. Some recipes take more time, are done in larger quantities, and are designed for weekend cooking so you have leftovers for later in the week. A Monday-to-Friday meal might feature a home-cooked dish surrounded by store-bought side dishes, or a one-pot dinner created from ingredients found on the cupboard or freezer shelves. To rediscover the pleasures of the dinner hour, all you need to do is to stock your pantry, plan ahead a little, and relax. When everyone's hungry, you'll be ready.

THE PANTRY

A home-cooked meal can happen even if you begin to think about what to serve for dinner at 6 o'clock, while you're stuck in traffic and haven't yet picked up your child from the baby-sitter's. How? If you've stocked your pantry in the clever Monday-to-Friday way with fresh, frozen, canned, and dried ingredients, I promise you can create terrific meals in short order. You'll be amazed at how quickly you can get dinner on the table, and you'll be delighted at how delicious your dinner will be.

My pantry includes a whole host of foods. Some ingredients, like chicken breasts stashed in the freezer, become the main course; others, like black beans or penne pasta, become the side dishes that support the chicken; and others, like prepared pesto and canned tomatoes, are the key flavorings that guarantee that what you cook will taste delicious.

In this book I emphasize what I call my "exotic pantry," a term I use for the part of my pantry that includes a stash of highly seasoned ethnic relishes and condiments. Chicken combines beautifully with boldly seasoned ingredients, allowing you to create an outstanding dinner. If you live in a large enough town, these unusual convenience ingredients will be available in gourmet or ethnic shops. Some may even be buyable in larger, well-stocked supermarkets. If you live in a part of the country that has a limited choice of such stores, the "Exotic Pantry" chapter will show you how to make these special items yourself.

THE CALENDAR: MATCHING MEALS TO SCHEDULES

Of all the suggestions in my Monday-to-Friday books, keeping a calendar on which to jot down menu ideas is perhaps the most useful—and the one most people resist. The world is divided between planners and those who wing it. I have given up on converting the "wingers" to my way of thinking because they thrive on leaving all decision-making, including what to serve for dinner, to the last minute.

But for those of us who can tolerate some planning, I recommend keeping an erasable monthly calendar (the kind you write on with washable ink) on the fridge so you can jot down menu ideas for the upcoming week. However you decide to do it, whether on a fancy store-bought calendar or one you have fashioned on the computer, the important point is to have a calendar on which to plan a week's worth of menus. And if the idea of planning five menus is a bit overwhelming, then start slowly and plan only two or three days of meals. The menus don't have to be fully developed; in fact, they should not be.

Plan out just a sketch of a menu for each day, and flesh it out later on. What do I mean by a sketch of a menu? Well, for example on my calendar I might scribble "chicken and baked potatoes" for Monday night and then "pasta and salad" for Tuesday. If I know I am going to have a particularly hectic day on Thursday and will be coming home very late, I might plan to bring in take-out for that night.

A more specific menu is determined closer to cooking time. If I have time to shop for fresh ingredients, the Tuesday "pasta" meal becomes linguine with chopped fresh tomatoes, served with a side of steamed broccoli. If, on the other hand, I come home late and need to create a meal in a hurry, then the "pasta" meal turns into linguine with frozen corn and canned clams, fashioned entirely from ingredients I have on my pantry shelves.

Planning this way takes care of other dinnertime-related issues as well. First of all, shopping becomes more efficient, because, using this weekly menu, I draw up a shopping list and in one trip to the market have the ingredients I need to cook whatever I have planned.

Also, by writing out my dinner ideas for the week, I guarantee that I don't repeat the same type of main course two nights in a row. That's why I prefer a monthly calendar to a weekly one: I can see what I cooked the week before and avoid repeating entire menus week after week. This variety makes my household a happier one at dinnertime.

The calendar has other functions as well. If I see that I've planned to have chicken for dinner tomorrow night, then I'm reminded to move the chicken from the freezer to the refrigerator, or to stop at the market and buy it fresh. And finally, my calendar doubles as a shopping list. When my pantry is emptied of canned tomatoes, for example, I immediately jot it down on the calendar so that I won't forget the tomatoes when I am writing out my shopping list the next weekend.

A crucial part of planning the type of meal you will serve each day depends on what your weekly schedule is like. If your teenager comes home late on Tuesdays because of rehearsals for a school play, that's the night you plan on serving a stew, which she can reheat, or a main-course salad that she can eat cold. If you know all the other members of your family are eating out one night of the week, that's the night to indulge yourself and cook those soft-shell crabs no one else enjoys.

So if you've been having trouble pulling dinner together and have been relying on pizza delivery a bit too often, get yourself a calendar, and try the Monday-to-Friday way. You'll discover that you can once again enjoy delicious home-cooked meals.

A NOTE ABOUT THE RECIPES

Most Monday-to-Friday recipes can be prepared from start to finish within a 30- to 45-minute time frame. You will save time if you gather all the ingredients and saucepans you'll need before you begin any work. The recipe cooking times start with the ingredients gathered and lined up on the counter.

The recipes are written so that the time spent on cooking is used most efficiently. Lots of time can be wasted if you slice, dice, cut, and measure out all of your ingredients before you begin to cook. If a couple of ingredients need to be sautéed for 10 minutes before you add the others, make use of this time to mince the fresh herbs that go in at the end of the cooking time.

I have deliberately kept portions on the smaller side, in keeping with today's lighter approach to cooking.

Chicken Chatter

Before delving into the recipes, here's all the information you need for buying, storing, and handling chicken safely.

WHAT TYPE OF CHICKEN IS THE BEST?

What chicken tastes best? Should you buy commercially raised, kosher, or free-range chickens? The choice will be determined by your palate and your pocketbook, but here's some information to help you decide. Mass-produced chickens are the product of intensely controlled breeding and feeding environments. The birds are fed grain designed to quickly fatten them up, and they are cooped up with little space to move around so their muscles don't exercise and toughen. Kosher chickens, which are raised in similar conditions, have been slaughtered and processed following strict kosher rules dictated by Jewish dietary law.

There's no legal definition of "free-range" chickens, but in general it means that the birds have more indoor space in which to move around. This movement will toughen the bird's muscles, yielding a better-flavored bird. Some "range" birds really do roam freely every day to forage for food, but most are let out of the coop for only an hour or two per day—and there is no labeling system that distinguishes one type of free-range from the other.

Organically raised chickens means the birds are fed a diet free from hormones and antibiotics. However, as with "free-range" chickens, none of this is regulated or standardized. Organic and "free-range" chickens are, of course, more expensive than mass-produced birds. You can usually find them sold in specialty stores, butcher shops, and some supermarkets. I tested all three varieties and have to admit that the "free-range" chicken had deeper, better flavor. However, because "free-range" chickens are not as readily available, all the recipes in this book were tested with good-quality supermarket poultry.

TELL-TALE SIGNS OF QUALITY

Whether free-range, kosher, or commercially raised, the skin color of the chicken, which can range from white to deep yellow, is influenced by diet and has no bearing on the taste or tenderness. In different sections of the country, bird skin color varies with consumer preference, culture, and habit.

The freshest chicken is sold in the busiest of markets, where there is a fast turn-around of product. To buy the freshest chicken possible, check the "sell by" date on the package. This indicates the last day the chicken should be sold, so look for the date that is furthest away from the date of purchase. (The most recently packaged chicken is often at the back of the shelf—be a smart consumer and look carefully.) Look for plump, even-colored skin, without pinfeathers, bruises, or blotches.

Avoid buying packaged chicken with large amounts of liquid in the bottom of the tray. A lot of liquid in the bottom of the package means it has been sitting around for a while and the chicken has lost moisture. If, when you get it home and unwrap the chicken, it has an unpleasant odor, don't cook it; return the package and get your money back.

Refrigerate raw chicken immediately after purchasing it, and never leave it on a countertop. (See page 9 for information on storing in the refrigerator and the freezer.)

WHAT TO BUY FOR THE MONDAY-TO-FRIDAY KITCHEN

Poultry is so popular and versatile, you can buy it just about any way you like. You can buy whole birds, or get them quartered. You can buy packages of your favorite part (drumsticks, thighs, breasts, wings) or even part of your favorite part (for example, "drumettes," the meaty part of the wing). However, not all of what is available is of interest to the Monday-to-Friday cook. Here are the cuts of chicken I rely on most for my busy workweek cooking, beginning with the ones I use most frequently.

BONELESS CHICKEN AND TURKEY BREASTS

Most cookbooks start off by explaining how to buy a whole chicken and then proceed to the various parts of the bird. I, however, am beginning with a description of skinless, boneless chicken breasts because that is what I cook most frequently; no other cut of chicken offers quite as many possibilities to the Monday-to-Friday cook. Most people, even children, love its mild flavor and lack of fat.

Poultry breast, whether from the chicken or the turkey, is so immensely popular that it comes packaged in a number of ways. It is marketed whole, bone- and skin-on, or whole, skinless and boneless. The skinless, boneless breast is sold in a variety of forms. In my neighborhood, for example, I see it packaged as "sliced thin" or as "cutlets"—that is, the breast meat cut or pounded into thin slices ready to be sautéed. Sometimes the tenderloins, which are the separate muscles lodged inside the breast half, are sold separately as "tenders" (as I refer to them throughout) or chicken tenderloins and are suggested for use in stir-fries. Sometimes you find "stir-fry" chicken—pieces of skinless, boneless chicken breast or "tenders" already cut into strips.

A good rule of thumb is to buy the chicken that has been handled the least. I buy a large quantity of skinless, boneless chicken breasts (2 to 3 pounds at least) and then repackage them to suit my family's needs. This little bit of home butchering means having chicken that is handled the least by others (safer and cleaner) and lets me control the size of the chunks or strips so they cook evenly.

When I come home from the market, I remove the chicken from its original packaging and first separate the "tenders" from the larger breast pieces. I package the "tenders" whole, or cut them into strips or chunks to use in soups, stews, and sautés. Some of the breast meat I halve and leave whole for cutlets, and some of it I cut into strips and chunks. This way I can defrost exactly the amount I need. What a convenience it is to have these cut-up chicken pieces in the freezer—I can toss them into a soup or stew, even when I've forgotten to defrost them first! The juices of the soup or stew make up for whatever moisture is lost by thawing the chicken as it cooks.

For a change of texture and taste, every now and then I load up on turkey breast rather than on chicken breasts, and I break it down and repackage it just as I do the chicken breasts.

POULTRY PARTS

As I've mentioned, at the market you'll find an astonishing array of chicken packaged in parts, on and off the bone. (I rarely stock my freezer with bone-in chicken parts because I usually use them in my "Sunday start-up cooking," and I buy what I need that day or at most a day ahead.)

For moist stews or baked dishes, I like either quartered chicken or chicken cut into eight pieces. More often than not, I use the dark meat of the thigh and drumstick because it is moister and stands up better in longer-cooked dishes.

On occasion I indulge in chicken wings. I particularly like to buy packages of the meatier "drumettes." These are especially nice for families with young kids because they mimic little chicken legs and are handy for kids to hold onto.

GROUND CHICKEN AND TURKEY

Ground poultry is great for burgers, soups, stews, and sauces to serve over pasta. Whether it's chicken or turkey, ground poultry is processed from the dark meat of the bird. Ground turkey has a bit more taste and texture than ground chicken.

If you want your ground poultry to be as low in fat and calories as possible, then grind the skinless breast meat in a meat grinder or ask the butcher to do it for you. Whatever you do, don't grind it in a food processor unless you are interested in cooking with chicken paste.

Both ground chicken and ground turkey are good candidates for the freezer.

THE WHOLE BIRD

I buy whole chickens for "Sunday start-up roasts," when I want to cook in advance and

have leftovers for later in the week.

Choose whole birds, small or large, with a high plump breast, smooth, tight, unbroken skin, and short plump legs. Stay away from birds that have a lot of pinfeathers, or that look as if their skin is either wet and slimy or dry with purplish bruises.

The small whole chickens known as "broilers" or "fryers" weigh between 3 and 3½ pounds and are only 7 weeks old; as their name implies, they are best used for grilling or frying. However, because the size is convenient for a small family such as mine, I usually use them for roasting too.

"Roasters" are fatter, heavier birds, moister than the broilers and thus better for roasting. They weigh between 5 and 8 pounds. I like to roast them when I'm planning to get two meals out of a single bird.

OTHER POULTRY

Rock Cornish Hens: Every now and then I buy Rock Cornish hens, which I use to pan-fry, stew, or roast, because I like their more intense flavor. In reality they are simply miniature chickens. They are so named because they are a cross between a Cornish and a White Rock chicken. One bird, weighing between 1¼ to 1¾ pounds, is meant to feed one person, but I find that that is too much. In general, I figure on two Cornish hens for four portions.

Turkey Breast: Turkey breast is another cut I buy occasionally for "Sunday start-up cooking." I like it for a change of pace and when I want pure white meat. It's also what I choose when I want one cooking effort to yield enough meat to stretch over three meals. Turkey breasts average 5 to 6 pounds and are sold bone-in, whole or halved.

HOW MUCH TO BUY PER PERSON?

Depending upon appetites and what else is served for dinner, figure on ¾ pound to 1 pound per person for a whole bird, ¾ pound per person for poultry pieces on the bone, and from 4 to 6 ounces per person for skinless, boneless poultry.

HOW TO STORE IN THE REFRIGERATOR

Refrigerate chicken as soon as you get it home. In fact, if you are traveling some distance by car, especially on a hot day, you may want to bring a small cooler with you and keep the chicken in it. If this is not an option, in summer keep the chicken in the car rather than in the trunk so that it stays as cool as possible on the way home.

When you get home, put the chicken in the coldest part of your refrigerator (in my small re-frigerator it means the bottom, but in a fancy fridge with lots of compartments, it means the meat drawer). You can keep it in its original package if you intend to cook it the same or the following day.

Keep uncooked chicken for 2 days. Cooked chicken can be stored in the refrigerator for up to 3 days.

HOW TO STORE IN THE FREEZER

You can buy frozen chicken, but don't. The fresher the chicken, the better it will taste. If you buy chicken already frozen, you never know how carefully it was handled in transportation and storage, or whether the chicken was partially defrosted and then refrozen. When I want to have chicken stocked in my freezer—which I always do—I buy it fresh, repackage it into portions and sizes that make sense for my style of cooking, and then freeze it.

If you don't intend to cook poultry within a day or so of purchase, then you have to freeze it to extend its life. Repackage it first in moisture-resistant material such as freezer paper, a double thickness of aluminum foil, or freezer plastic bags, making sure to press all the air out of the package before sealing it.

If you are going to freeze a whole bird, first remove the giblet package and freeze it separately. Fresh giblets don't keep as well as the meat of the chicken and should be used within 1 day.

Label the package with the date you packed it, and remember that freezing food doesn't mean that time stands still. Frozen poultry will keep at 0°F for 3 to 4 months, but it tastes best if you eat it within 2 months. The giblets should keep frozen for 1 month.

You can freeze cooked chicken using the same techniques as for raw poultry. Obviously a recipe for chicken combined with sauce or soupy ingredients should be frozen in a rigid container with a tight-fitting lid; it will keep for 2 or 3 months.

Whatever the cut, be sure you thoroughly defrost the poultry before cooking. As with fresh poultry, thawed poultry should be used within a day, or 2 at most.

Thawing Tips: Under no circumstances should you thaw chicken on the counter, because room temperature provides a perfect breeding environment for bacteria. Instead, set the wrapped frozen chicken on a tray or plate (to catch the drips) and thaw it in the fridge. Allow 24 hours to thaw a 4-pound whole chicken and, depending on the size and number in the package, anywhere from 4 to 9 hours for chicken parts.

But as we know, the best-laid plans often go awry, so if you forgot to thaw the chicken and really need it, then thaw it in the microwave following the oven manufacturer's in-structions, or thaw it in cold water: Place the chicken, in its wrapping or in a watertight plastic bag, in a bowl of cold water. Change the water often; the chicken will be thawed within a couple of hours.

SAFE EATING

Salmonella, a bacteria that can cause serious illness, is found in water, soil, and in the intestinal tract of animals and birds. Most people associate salmonella with raw poultry and uncooked eggs, but in fact it can be found in meat, fish, and raw vegetables as well. While everyone should be careful about how

TO WASH OR NOT TO WASH

Just about every cookbook recommends washing chicken before cooking. Well, don't, even if your mother told you to. In fact, the National Broiler Council claims that this practice is unsafe because any water that clings to the bird after rinsing can drip on counters and floors and spread bacteria around the kitchen.

However, if you can't get out of the habit, then rinse the bird or parts over the sink. Using paper towels, pat the chicken dry over the sink so there are no drips. Throw out the paper towels and set the chicken on a cutting board.

they handle raw foods, they should not be so terrified as to overcook all their food. Salmonella is easily destroyed by heat, at 140°F, which is not all that scalding hot.

The National Broiler Council also claims that chicken is less frequently a source of salmonellosis (the illness caused by salmonella) than are other meats because chicken is not eaten raw or even rare. But, because you can't see or smell salmonella, to be safe take the following precautions:

- Always cook chicken through; make sure its juices are no longer pink inside.
- After preparing poultry for cooking, before you touch anything else, be sure to thoroughly wash your hands and all knives, cutting boards, or other utensils that you used in hot soapy water.
- The National Broiler Council recommends cutting and preparing poultry on a plastic cutting board, which is dishwasher safe and easier to sanitize (even though there is now some controversy about how safe plastic cutting boards really are). You can sanitize your cutting board by immersing it in 170°F water for 30 seconds (a dishwasher brings water up to this heat; tap water won't be hot enough) or by using a chemical disinfectant (follow label instructions).

- If cloth kitchen towels came in contact with raw poultry, or if you wiped hands that had touched raw poultry on them, set them aside to be laundered.
- Marinate poultry in the refrigerator.
- Never baste anything on the grill or broiler with a marinade that held raw poultry. If you are going to use the marinade further, boil it first for a couple of minutes.
- Don't leave raw chicken out at room temperature.
- Keep raw poultry refrigerated until ready to use, and keep cooked poultry refrigerated until ready to eat.
- Eat cooked poultry within 2 days.

The National Broiler Council recommends cooking a whole chicken to an internal temperature of 180°F, bone-in chicken parts to 170°F, ground chicken to 165°F, and boneless parts to 160°F. An "instant read" thermometer will determine the temperature. I just make sure that when I serve chicken it is no longer pink inside.

Monday-to-Friday
Pantry List

The Monday-to-Friday pantry works in two ways: When you have nary a fresh ingredient in the house, you can draw from the pantry to create a quick meal. But more often, you will use the pantry to help flavor a recipe or to round out a meal centered on fresh ingredients. This list of store-bought pantry items highlights the ingredients you need to create chicken dinners and those flavorings especially well suited to chicken. I've also included a chapter of homemade pantry items that are a little more exotic, but easy to prepare. Those recipes begin on page 222.

Poultry in the Pantry

In the freezer:

1 to 2 pounds skinless, boneless chicken or turkey breast cutlets

1 pound skinless, boneless chicken or turkey cut into ¾-inch dice, packed in 8-ounce portions

1 pound tenderloins ("tenders") or skinless, boneless chicken or turkey cut into strips, packed in 8-ounce portions

1 pound ground chicken or turkey, packed in 4-ounce patties

1 pound turkey or chicken sausage, fresh or smoked

8 ounces turkey bacon

In the refrigerator:

12 ounces smoked chicken breast or smoked turkey

Other Main Course Items

A beautifully grilled chicken breast does not a dinner make. You'll need at least one other food to round out the meal, be it a chunk of country French bread, or a side of mesclun salad, or any of a number of other side dishes that will help make the dinner really delicious.

Sometimes I incorporate these other ingredients into the recipe itself, and other times I cook them separately and serve them as an accompaniment. These sides are either robust, starchy ingredients, like pasta, rice, or beans, or leaner ones, like broccoli or frozen corn.

PASTA

1 pound each:

Thin or medium-size strand or ribbon pasta such as capellini, vermicelli, thin linguine, or spaghettini

Another strand or ribbon pasta, different from the above, such as regular spaghetti, perciatelli, or bucatini

Short-shaped, medium-size pasta such as elbow macaroni, penne, or fusilli

Tiny pasta such as orzo or couscous

GRAINS

1 pound pearl barley

Terrific with chicken in thick, robust soups; great as a simple side dish as well.

1 pound long-grain white rice (preferably converted because the grains are fluffier)
1 pound aromatic long-grain white or brown rice, such as basmati or Texmati

While there are lots of kinds of rice you can buy, you need only a couple of varieties on hand, one plain and one special "aromatic" rice. The aromatic rice is terrific because it works extra flavor into your dish without extra effort.

1 box (10 ounces) Near East or other brand wheat pilaf, or 2 cups cracked wheat from the health-food store
1 box (5¼ ounces) Near East or other brand tabouleh, or 2 cups bulgur wheat from the health-food store

Cracked and bulgur wheat are a welcome change from rice and pasta. Bulgur wheat (wheat that has been steamed and dried before cracking) is perfect for quick meals because you need only rehydrate it. Cracked wheat is terrific when you want some "chew" in your grains; it needs to be cooked but is done in 20 minutes.

1 box (about 1 pound) instant polenta

I adore the flavor of corn in all its forms— fresh on the cob, frozen in soups, dried and pulverized as cornmeal for breads and mush. Authentic cornmeal mush or Italian polenta takes too long to make during the week, so I content myself with the coarsely milled "instant" polenta imported from Italy. Because it is precooked, you can make it in 10 minutes, and because it is imported, the texture is great. Stay away from the reconstituted refrigerated polenta sold in plastic-wrapped sausagelike shapes; it is simply dreadful.

BREADS

If you have good bread in the house, you can usually skip preparing another starch. Any chicken recipe becomes a complete meal when you serve a good chunk of high-quality bakery bread alongside it. If it's hard for you to make a trip to a good bakery on a regular basis, buy several types of breads at once and freeze them. Don't forget to include tortillas and taco shells, too, for the times you want dinner all wrapped up. Alternate the type of bread you serve each week so you don't tire of one variety.

1 or 2 loaves or packages of each:
French, Italian, or sourdough
    (8 to 12 ounces)
Multigrain, pumpernickel, whole wheat, or rye (1 to 1½ pounds)
Pita bread
Flour tortillas (20 ounces burrito-style)
Corn tortillas (10 ounces)
Taco shells (4½ ounces)

LEGUMES

These are simply fabulous served as plain side dishes with grilled or roasted chicken, or as part of a stew or soup where you want lots of body. Canned beans are the obvious choice for Monday-to-Friday fare. Try stocking up on ones from the health-food store; they have better texture and cost only pennies more than beans in the supermarket.

To lend body to soups, the lentil of choice is the red one, which cooks in 10 minutes. For side dishes where you want texture, use the imported French green lentil, which takes 20 minutes to cook.

1 or 2 cans (16 to 19 ounces each) of one or more:
Black beans
Chickpeas
Small red or pink beans
White beans

1 package (16 ounces) of each:
1 bag dried red lentils
1 box imported whole green lentils

VEGETABLES

Pantry vegetables work in two ways: They can turn a chicken recipe into a chicken dinner or they can work as seasonings.

In the freezer:
1 package (10 ounces) corn kernels
1 package (10 ounces) "petite" peas
2 packages (10 ounces each) other vegetables of your choice (I like chopped spinach for soups or stews)

In the refrigerator:
1 bunch carrots
1 bunch celery
4 red or green bell peppers
Mesclun (for the fastest green salad imaginable)

DAIRY

In the refrigerator:
1 pint plain yogurt, regular or low-fat
1 pint sour cream, regular or low-fat (optional)
½ pound cheese for grating and adding to soups; extra-sharp Cheddar or imported Parmesan

On the pantry shelves:
2 cans (12 ounces each) evaporated skim milk

Pantry Supplies for Seasoning

The ingredients below are crucial to my pantry because they make every dish, not just the chicken ones, taste delicious. With so wide a range of seasonings, an endless array of chicken dinners becomes do-able.

SEASONING VEGETABLES

In the refrigerator:

1 to 2 pounds onions
1 head garlic
1 bunch scallions, or 2 bunches fresh chives
2 or 3 lemons
2 or 3 limes
1 or 2 bunches fresh parsley, preferably flat-leaf
1 or 2 bunches other fresh herb, such as basil, dill, or cilantro (optional)

On the pantry shelves:

1 can (28 ounces) Italian plum tomatoes
2 cans (14½ ounces each) stewed tomatoes
2 cans (14½ to 16 ounces each) crushed tomatoes
1 or 2 jars (6 ounces each) marinated artichoke hearts
1 or 2 jars or cans (8 to 12 ounces) eggplant caponata or eggplant ratatouille
1 or 2 jars (6 to 8 ounces each) roasted red peppers

OILS

1 bottle (16 to 32 ounces) extra-virgin olive oil
1 bottle (16 to 32 ounces) vegetable oil
1 bottle (5 ounces) Asian sesame oil (optional)
1 bottle (8 to 12 ounces) "specialty" oil, such as hazelnut or walnut (optional)

VINEGARS

1 bottle (12 ounces) red wine vinegar
1 bottle (12 ounces) white wine vinegar or tarragon vinegar
1 bottle (8 to 12 ounces) "specialty" vinegar, either balsamic, rice, or Champagne
1 bottle (16 ounces) verjus (optional).

Verjus is the juice from the first pressing of grapes, used in lieu of vinegar for its softer flavor. Because it is less astringent than vinegar, in salad dressings you can use more of it and less of oil. Look for bottles of verjus in specialty markets.

BROTH

4 cans (about 14 ounces each) chicken broth, preferably no- or low-salt

SPIRITS

2 bottles dry white wine, or 1 bottle dry white
  vermouth
2 bottles dry red wine
1 bottle Cognac or brandy
1 bottle Port or Madeira

CONDIMENTS, RELISHES, AND OTHER ASSORTED GOODIES

All the supplies listed below are in my pantry because they add flavor. They are to cooking what accessories are to an outfit: they can make all the difference. A hefty selection of seasonings, from dried porcini and great barbecue sauces to dried spices and fresh herbs, provides the means with which to create an infinite number of recipes even when the main ingredient—chicken—remains the same.

2 cans (2 ounces each) flat anchovies,
  or 1 tube (1½ ounces) anchovy paste
1 jar (3 ounces) capers, preferably
  nonpareil
1 jar (8 ounces) hoisin sauce
1 tube (about 3 ounces) garlic paste
  (optional)

1 package (2 ounces) dried mushrooms:
  porcini, cèpes, or "wild"
1 jar (8 ounces) Dijon mustard
1 can (4 ounces) walnuts, pecans, or
  blanched sliced almonds
1 jar (12 to 16 ounces) pitted "country-style"
  or Spanish green olives or pitted Kalamata
  black olives, or 1 jar (3 to 4 ounces) black
  or green olive paste (olivada) or black olive
  sauce
1 jar or tube (4 ounces) pesto sauce, or 1 tub
  (4 ounces) frozen pesto sauce
1 or 2 jars (4 ounces each) pimientos
1 jar (1 pound) smooth spaghetti sauce
1 jar (1 pound) chunky spaghetti or
  marinara sauce
1 bottle (14 ounces) ketchup
1 bottle (12 or 16 ounces) barbecue sauce
1 jar (1 quart) mayonnaise, preferably
  Hellmann's
1 tube (about 3 ounces) tomato paste
  (optional)
1 jar (8 ounces) sun-dried tomatoes, or
  1 tube (4½ ounces) sun-dried tomato paste
  (optional)
1 jar (16 ounces) dry roasted peanuts, or
  1 jar (16 ounces) chunky natural peanut
  butter
1 box (12 ounces) golden or black raisins
1 box (10 ounces) dried currants
1 jar (16 ounces) kosher dill pickles
1 bottle (5 ounces) Worcestershire sauce
1 jar (5 ounces) prepared white horseradish
1 bottle (5 ounces) light tamari or soy sauce
A selection of your favorite dried spices
  and herbs

SPICY AND BOLD SEASONINGS

This list is a mere sampling of the boldly seasoned ethnic and regional ingredients now widely available in larger supermarkets, fancy-food stores, and take-out stores. They'll let you vary your meals in more exciting ways. Never do I use a "convenience" ethnic seasoner—tandoori paste, for example—straight from the jar; it is too overwhelming. Usually I will add a spoonful or so of the flavoring to a dish to add a different, spicy, and vibrant flavor. You can make some of these ingredients yourself; see the Homemade Exotic Pantry, beginning on page 222.

1 jar (12 ounces) pickled jalapeño or "nacho" peppers

2 jars (about 12 ounces each) "mild," "medium," or "hot" salsa to taste

1 bottle (2 ounces) Tabasco or other hot sauce

2 cans (4 ounces each) chopped green chiles

1 jar (8 ounces) Chinese chile paste with garlic

1 can (15 ounces) Middle Eastern tahini

2 cans (15 ounces each) Thai coconut milk, regular or "light"

1 jar or can (6 to 10 ounces) Indian tandoori paste

1 jar (10 ounces) Indian mango, lime, or "mixed" pickles

Chicken Soups and Stews

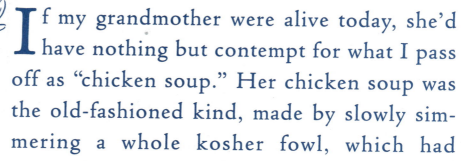

If my grandmother were alive today, she'd have nothing but contempt for what I pass off as "chicken soup." Her chicken soup was the old-fashioned kind, made by slowly simmering a whole kosher fowl, which had plenty of texture and taste. The making of the soup takes hours and is, of course, unsuitable for Monday-to-Friday no-fuss spur-of-the-moment cooking. In deference to her, I have included Grandma Helen's Jewish Chicken Soup in the Sunday Start-Ups and Quick Fixes chapter on page 221, but the soups and stews in this chapter are quick and easy to prepare, provide a complete meal (or close to one) in a single pot, and make use of a wide range of ethnic ingredients. Following are my tips for creating Monday-to-Friday chicken soups.

COMPOSING CHICKEN SOUP

My technique for making chicken soup for busy weeknight dinners goes something like this: I begin by cooking ½ to 1 cup of seasoning ingredients—onions, carrots, celery, or some combination thereof— in oil or butter. After the seasoning vegetables have softened, I add 6 to 8 cups of liquid, such as plain water, a flavorful broth, unsweetened coconut milk, or canned plum tomatoes with their juices, or a mixture. After the liquid has been introduced, along come the dried herbs or spices, which give the soup its special character. To make the soup substantial enough to serve as dinner, at this point I might add, per person, about ½ cup diced potatoes, cooked beans, or uncooked pasta, as well as ½ cup of a longer-cooking vegetable, such as fresh fennel. Small cubes of raw chicken and frozen vegetables are cooked last because they're done in 5 minutes. And finally, off the heat, I add a finishing touch such as grated cheese, a squirt of lemon juice, or a handful of chopped fresh herbs. All this comes together to serve 4.

BEST CUTS OF CHICKEN

Grandma's chicken soup was made by simmering the whole bird because the bones added depth of flavor to the broth, but during the week the best forms of chicken for quick main-course soups are fast-cooking skinless, boneless chicken breasts or thighs, poultry sausage, or ground chicken.

USING COOKED CHICKEN

To make use of leftover cooked chicken, follow the recipe as written but omit the steps that instruct you to cook the raw chicken. Instead, add bite-size pieces of cooked chicken to the finished soup at the end of the cooking time, and simmer them just long enough to reheat them. You'll find special Second-Time-Around Soup recipes on page 34.

STORING CHICKEN SOUPS

Most of these soups are perfect for do-ahead meals. Keep them in the refrigerator for 3 to 4 days, but be sure you bring them back to a full boil to destroy any bacteria. Before you reheat soups that include potatoes, rice, or pasta, be sure to add more liquid or they'll be too thick.

You can freeze these chicken soups for 3 months—with the exception of those made with potatoes or pasta. Pasta just gets too mushy and potatoes are terrible when frozen. You can reheat soup straight from the freezer, but if you do, pour ¼ inch of water into the saucepan before adding the frozen soup. This way, the solids won't burn at the bottom of the pan while the soup is thawing and reheating.

Chicken Mulligatawny Soup

MAKES: *4 servings*
TIME: *30 minutes*

In some recipes, the nuances of flavor come about only after long cooking, when the separate flavors of the individual ingredients blend together into a new harmonious whole. During the workweek, when I don't have the time for this slow development of taste, I bring bold spices into play and I use them in large enough quantities to quickly create exciting flavor. If you use low-fat yogurt in this recipe, don't stir it into the soup, because it will curdle; instead, top each portion with a spoonful of yogurt.

2 tablespoons butter
½ onion, finely chopped
2 carrots, finely chopped
2 teaspoons curry powder
½ teaspoon ground cumin
⅛ teaspoon ground cloves
2 cups (14 ounces) canned plum tomatoes with their juices
2 whole skinless, boneless chicken breasts (about 1½ pounds total)
3 cups water
1 package (10 ounces) frozen chopped or whole-leaf spinach, thawed
Salt and freshly ground black pepper
1 cup regular or low-fat plain yogurt

1. Melt the butter in a large saucepan over medium heat. Add the onion and carrots, cover the pan, and simmer over low heat until tender, about 5 minutes.

2. Add the curry powder, cumin, cloves, and tomatoes and their juices. Break up the tomatoes by mashing them against the side of the pan with a wooden spoon. Cover and simmer over low heat for 5 minutes. While this is cooking, cut the chicken into ½-inch cubes.

3. Add the water and spinach to the saucepan and bring the liquid to just under a boil. Add the chicken and bring the liquid back to just under a boil (you don't want to boil the liquid or the chicken will toughen and cloud the broth). Simmer gently over low heat until the chicken is just cooked through, 3 minutes. Season to taste with salt and pepper, and remove the soup from the heat.

4. Whisk ¼ cup of the hot soup into the yogurt to temper it. Return the tempered yogurt to the hot soup and stir until blended. Remove the soup from the heat, adjust the seasoning, and serve immediately.

VARIATION

In step 3, instead of the water, substitute 2 cups unsweetened coconut milk and 1 cup of chicken or vegetable broth. Garnish with ¼ cup chopped peanuts or cashews and ¼ cup chopped fresh cilantro leaves.

Chicken Soup with Vegetable Threads

MAKES: *4 servings*
TIME: *30 minutes*

It's obvious that in no way do these "threads" refer to clothing—they are small pieces of carrots, jicama, and mustard greens. This soup is fresh and delicious and offers a bonus: it's healthful too.

8 to 12 ounces fresh mustard greens
    or spinach
2 carrots
2 cups chicken broth
4 cups water
2 whole skinless, boneless chicken
    breasts (about 1½ pounds total)
½ jicama (8 ounces)
3 or 4 limes (to yield ½ cup juice)
Salt and freshly ground black pepper

1. Chop off the coarse stems of the mustard greens. Then pinch off the leaves on either side of the stem and tear or slice the leaves into pieces. Soak the leaves in water to cover.

2. Using a vegetable peeler, slice the carrots into lengthwise strips, discarding the skinny inner core. In a medium-size saucepan, bring the carrot strips, broth, and water to a simmer over medium heat.

3. While the liquid is coming to a boil, cut the chicken into 1 × ¼-inch strips. Peel the jicama and cut it into 1½ × ¼-inch strips. Juice the limes.

4. Add the chicken to the broth. Lift the mustard greens out of the water (leaving the grit in the bottom of the bowl), and add them to the soup. Simmer until the chicken is just cooked through, 3 minutes.

5. Remove the soup from the heat and stir in the jicama and lime juice. Season to taste with salt and pepper.

VARIATIONS

With Herb Paste: In step 5, after you stir in the lime juice, add ¼ cup Coconut Peanut Sauce or Cilantro Purée (pages 226 and 225).

With Avocado: Place strips of ripe Hass avocado in the bottom of each soup bowl, and ladle the hot soup over them.

ESPECIALLY GOOD FOR CHILDREN

Cook some vermicelli or capellini pasta. Place the noodles in the middle of each child's bowl, and moisten them with broth and chicken only. Add whatever vegetables the kids might enjoy—usually the carrots and jicama only.

Hot and Sour Soup

MAKES: *4 servings*
TIME: *30 minutes*

To develop a lot of flavor in record time, I use generous doses of big, bold seasonings in this hot and sour soup. They make a delightful contrast to the bland chicken.

2 tablespoons Asian sesame oil
1 clove garlic, minced
1 quarter-size slice fresh ginger, or ½ teaspoon ground dried ginger
2 cups chicken or vegetable broth
2 cups water
2 tablespoons rice vinegar
2 tablespoons soy sauce
½ teaspoon sugar
10 ounces mushrooms, wiped clean, trimmed, and thinly sliced
2 whole skinless, boneless chicken breasts (about 1½ pounds total)
1 can (8 ounces) sliced bamboo shoots, drained
10 ounces fresh spinach, chopped, or 1 package (10 ounces) frozen chopped spinach, thawed
Salt
Hot sauce or Asian chili paste with garlic

1. Heat the sesame oil in a large saucepan over medium heat. Add the garlic and ginger and sauté until you can smell the garlic, about 20 seconds.

2. Add the broth, water, vinegar, soy sauce, sugar, and mushrooms. Cover and bring the liquid to a boil over high heat. Reduce to a simmer and cook over medium heat until the mushrooms are tender, about 5 minutes.

3. While this is cooking, slice the chicken, along the grain, into strips about 2 inches long, ¼ inch thick, and ½ inch wide.

4. Add the bamboo shoots and chicken to the broth, bring the liquid back to a simmer, and cook over low heat until the chicken is just cooked through, about 3 minutes. Add the spinach, stir once, and immediately remove the saucepan from the heat (if you are using thawed frozen spinach, simmer for a minute or so to heat it through). Season to taste with salt, and serve the hot sauce on the side.

ESPECIALLY GOOD FOR VEGETARIANS *After step 2, remove a portion or two of the broth to another saucepan. Add sliced raw chicken to one saucepan, and for the vegetarians in the group, add diced tofu to the other. Divide the bamboo shoots and spinach and add half of each to each saucepan.*

Saffron Broth with Chicken

MAKES: *4 servings*
TIME: *35 minutes*

....

This is one of my favorite soups (another is the Coconut and Cilantro Soup on page 35). My husband and I could eat it once a week without tiring of its sophisticated flavor. It is hard to believe such a delicious dinner can be had in a mere 35 minutes! What makes it so satisfying is the counterpoint and balance of flavors between the lean saffron broth, the rich pepper mayonnaise, the sweet carrots, and the peppery turnips.

> ½ teaspoon saffron threads
> 1 tablespoon warm water
> 2 cups chicken or vegetable broth
> 2 cups water
> 2 small cloves garlic, minced
> 3 or 4 carrots, cut into ¼-inch-thick
>   rounds
> 2 white turnips, cut into 3 × ¼-inch
>   matchsticks
> 2 whole skinless, boneless chicken breasts
>   (about 1½ pounds total)
> ¼ cup bottled roasted red peppers
>   or pimientos
> ½ cup mayonnaise
> Salt
> ⅛ teaspoon cayenne pepper
> 4 slices Italian bread (¾ inch thick)

1. Dissolve the saffron in the 1 tablespoon warm water.

2. Place the broth, 2 cups water, half the garlic, the carrots, turnips, and half the saffron in a large saucepan. Bring to a boil over medium-high heat. Cover and simmer until the vegetables are tender but still crisp, about 5 minutes.

3. Meanwhile, cut the chicken into ¾-inch dice. Finely chop the red peppers, and combine them with the mayonnaise and remaining garlic and saffron. Season to taste with salt and cayenne pepper. Lightly toast the bread.

4. Add the chicken to the soup and bring the broth back to a simmer over medium heat. Cook, uncovered, until the chicken is cooked through, 2 to 3 minutes. Adjust the seasoning.

5. Spread each slice of toast with saffron mayonnaise and cut each slice on the diagonal into ½-inch fingers. Divide them evenly among 4 soup bowls. Ladle the steaming broth, vegetables, and chicken over the bread and serve immediately.

SECOND TIME AROUND

To reheat leftovers and enrich the soup, bring the soup back to a boil. Whisk 1 egg into the remaining mayonnaise, and ladle some of the hot soup into the mayonnaise to temper it. Whisk the egg mayonnaise back into the hot soup, and stir over low heat until the broth has thickened. Do not boil the liquid or the egg will curdle. Remove from the heat, adjust the seasoning, and serve immediately.

Mahogany Soup

MAKES: *4 servings*
TIME: *30 minutes*

Dried porcini mushrooms infuse this soup with a deep earthy aroma. Because the mushrooms flavor the broth so well, you won't need to waste too much time on preparing other seasonings. This, in turn, allows you an extra 5 minutes to wash some fresh spinach. The spinach wilts tenderly into the mahogany-colored soup, adding just the right touch of texture and a welcome note of color. Resist the temptation to add more Parmesan, because it would obliterate the taste of the porcini mushrooms.

1 ounce (½ cup) dried porcini
    mushrooms
1 clove garlic, minced
Salt
6 cups water
1 cup orzo or tubettini pasta
2 whole skinless, boneless chicken breasts
    (about 1½ pounds total)
1 package (10 ounces) fresh spinach
Freshly ground black pepper
¼ cup grated Parmesan cheese (optional)

PORCINI AT THE READY

It takes an hour at least to soften and re-hydrate dried porcini. I get around this timing problem by soaking 2 ounces of dried porcini in a quart of water. I store this in a covered glass jar in the refrigerator, where it keeps for 2 to 3 weeks. The porcini will soften over time in the water. For more information, see Porcini Stock, page 235.

1. Rinse the mushrooms under cold water to rid them of grit. Break them up into small pieces, and put them in a 4-quart saucepan along with the garlic, 1 teaspoon salt, and the water. Bring the liquid to a boil over high heat. Add the orzo, lower the heat to medium, and cook, partially covered, until the pasta is tender but still firm to the bite, 10 minutes. (Take care not to completely cover the saucepan because the starch in the pasta causes the water to bubble over.)

2. While the orzo is cooking, cut the chicken into ½-inch cubes. Stem the spinach and put the leaves in a large bowl. Cover the leaves with cold water. Lift the leaves out of the water to rinse them, and transfer them to a second bowl. If the water the spinach was rinsed in is sandy, repeat this process a second time.

3. Add the chicken to the saucepan and

bring the soup back to just under a boil; simmer the chicken until it is just tender, 1 to 2 minutes.

4. Add one-third of the spinach leaves to the soup, and stir until just wilted. Add half the remaining leaves and stir again until wilted; then add the remaining leaves. When all the spinach has wilted but is still bright green, remove the soup from the heat and season to taste with salt and pepper. Ladle the soup into bowls, and serve the Parmesan on the side.

ESPECIALLY GOOD FOR COMPANY

In step 1, instead of water use 4 cups chicken broth; and in step 4, before adding the spinach, add 2 cups heavy cream.

Asian Salad Chicken Soup

MAKES: *4 servings*
TIME: *25 minutes*

Much of the intriguing flavor in this delicious soup comes from the dressing in which the bean sprouts and watercress marinate. This fabulous soup is also incredibly easy and requires almost no work from the cook.

2 cups chicken, fish, or vegetable
    broth
2 cups water
2 tablespoons soy sauce
4 cups mushrooms, wiped clean,
    trimmed, and thinly sliced
2 nickel-size slices fresh ginger
¼ teaspoon dried red pepper flakes
2 whole skinless, boneless chicken
    breasts (about 1½ pounds total)
2 tablespoons rice vinegar
2 tablespoons Asian sesame oil
2 tablespoons vegetable oil
3 cups bean sprouts
4 scallions, trimmed and thinly sliced
    (white and green parts)
1 bunch watercress, rinsed and
    stemmed
Salt and freshly ground black pepper
2 tablespoons black or toasted white
    sesame seeds (optional)

1. Place the broth, water, soy sauce, mushrooms, ginger, and red pepper flakes in a large saucepan over high heat, and bring to a boil. Lower the heat and simmer, covered, until the mushrooms are tender, 10 minutes. Meanwhile, cut the chicken into 4-inch-thick slices; cut the slices into 2-inch lengths.

2. Blend the rice vinegar with the sesame and vegetable oils in a bowl, and toss this dressing with the bean sprouts, scallions, and watercress. Season to taste with salt and pepper. Divide this salad among 4 soup bowls and set aside.

3. When the mushrooms are tender, add the chicken to the soup and simmer over medium heat, uncovered, until it is cooked through, 5 minutes. Remove the ginger slices, and season to taste with salt and pepper. Ladle the hot soup over the bean sprout mixture and garnish with the sesame seeds. Serve immediately.

TASTY TOASTY SEEDS

Toasting seeds, dried herbs, and spices releases their oils and makes their flavor more intense. To toast white sesame seeds, heat a small cast-iron or other heavy skillet (ungreased) over medium heat. When the skillet is very hot, add the sesame seeds and stir them continuously until they smell toasty and begin to turn golden, about 2 minutes. Take care they do not burn.

Spinach and Chicken in Mustard Broth

MAKES: *4 servings*
TIME: *25 to 30 minutes*

A dab of mustard brings life to this dieter's dream soup. It is light and subtle yet filling, with no fat other than what occurs naturally in the ingredients. Even though this soup includes pasta, I still like serving it with a piece of warm sourdough baguette or a slice of pumpernickel bread. Tomato sandwiches are lovely with this soup and make the meal more ample.

2 whole skinless, boneless chicken
    breasts (about 1½ pounds total)
2 lemons
1½ teaspoons Dijon mustard
4 cups chicken broth
2 cups water
½ cup orzo
2 bunches (1 to 1¼ pounds)
    fresh spinach, or 2 packages
    (10 ounces each) frozen
    chopped spinach,
    thawed
6 scallions
Salt and freshly ground
    black pepper

1. Cut the chicken into ½-inch dice and place in a large bowl. Juice the lemons (you should

have ¼ cup), and pour over the chicken, tossing to coat (see Note).

2. Combine the mustard with the broth and water in a medium-size saucepan, and bring to a simmer over medium heat. Add the pasta and cook, uncovered, until tender, 5 minutes. Add the chicken and lemon juice and simmer until cooked through, 2 to 3 minutes.

3. Meanwhile, stem the spinach and soak the leaves in water to cover. Lift the leaves out of the water, leaving the grit behind. Coarsely tear the spinach leaves. Trim and thinly slice the scallions (white and green parts).

4. Add the scallions and fresh or frozen spinach to the soup (in a couple of batches, if necessary). The instant all of the spinach has wilted, remove the soup from the heat and season to taste with salt and pepper. Serve immediately.

Note: If you have some extra time, allow the chicken to marinate for up to 30 minutes before proceeding with step 2.

VARIATIONS

- Instead of spinach, in step 4 add 12 ounces chopped escarole and simmer it for 2 minutes.
- In step 4, chop 2 heads of bok choy, keeping the ribs and leaves separate. Add the ribs in step 2 when you add the chicken, and add the leaves in step 4 instead of the spinach.

Fast Chicken Minestrone

MAKES: *6 servings*
TIME: *40 minutes*

OK, so this isn't what you'd expect from a minestrone—even though in Italy a minestrone is exactly what this is—that is, a vegetable soup that can be fashioned in any number of ways. My fast version doesn't contain the expected dose of potatoes and rice, nor does it take 3 hours to simmer into a melting mass of vegetables. But believe me, it tastes delicious, and on a cold winter night, it comforts as well as any classic rendition.

¼ cup olive oil
1 onion, sliced into thin half-moons
2 large carrots
2 cups shredded cabbage
2 cups canned, chopped plum
*   tomatoes with their juices*
4 cups water
1 to 1¼ pounds skinless, boneless
*   chicken (breasts or thighs)*
2 zucchini (1 pound)
2 cans (15 ounces each) red kidney
*   beans, drained and rinsed*
½ cup (packed) fresh parsley or basil
*   leaves, or a combination of herbs*
Salt and freshly ground black pepper
1 cup freshly grated Parmesan cheese

1. Heat the olive oil in a large saucepan over medium heat. Add the onion, and sauté until it takes on some color, 4 to 5 minutes. While the onion is cooking, slice the carrots into ½-inch rounds.

2. Add the carrots and cabbage to the onion, cover the saucepan, and cook until they begin to wilt down, 5 minutes. (Add some water if they begin to stick to the bottom of the pan.)

3. Add the tomatoes with their juices and the water. Bring the liquid to a boil over high heat, then lower the heat and simmer, covered, until the vegetables are tender, 10 minutes. While the vegetables are cooking, cut the chicken and zucchini into ½-inch cubes.

4. Add the chicken, zucchini, and beans to the pan, cover, and simmer to cook through and soften, 10 minutes. While this is cooking, finely chop the parsley.

5. Season the soup to taste with salt and pepper. Remove the pan from the heat and add the parsley. Serve the Parmesan on the side.

SECOND TIME AROUND

Add some water to the soup to thin it. Then bring it to a simmer over low heat, and stir in pesto or an herb purée (see pages 224 and 225) to taste.

Lemon Chicken Soup with Rice

MAKES: *4 servings*
TIME: *30 minutes*

This soup has a refreshing zing and fabulous texture. The green beans remain as crisp as the pieces of raw red pepper, and the color remains vibrant too if you serve the soup immediately. Eventually, though, the acidity of the lemon juice transforms the cilantro and the green beans from a bright shade of green to a dull one. Happily, the flavor won't suffer.

2 cups chicken broth
4 cups water
¾ cup long-grain rice
Salt
1 to 1¼ pounds skinless, boneless chicken
    (breasts or thighs)
12 scallions
1 large red bell pepper,
    stemmed and seeded
¼ cup (packed) fresh
    cilantro leaves
1 or 2 lemons
1 package
    (10 ounces) frozen
    chopped green beans, thawed
Freshly ground black pepper

1. Place the broth, water, rice, and 1 teaspoon salt in a large saucepan and bring to a boil over high heat. Cover and simmer over medium heat until the rice is almost tender, 10 minutes.

2. Meanwhile, cut the chicken into 1 × ¼-inch strips. Trim and thinly slice the scallions (white and green parts), cut the bell pepper into ½-inch dice, and finely chop the cilantro. Grate ½ teaspoon lemon zest, and squeeze the lemons to have ⅓ cup juice.

3. Add the lemon zest, juice, and chicken to the soup and bring the liquid back to a simmer, uncovered, over medium heat until the chicken is just cooked through, 3 to 5 minutes.

4. Add the green beans and simmer until cooked through but still crisp, 2 minutes longer. Season the soup to taste with salt and pepper, and stir in the cilantro, bell pepper, and scallions. Serve immediately.

VARIATION

In step 4, omit the green beans. Instead, beat 4 eggs. When the chicken is cooked through, slowly beat 2 cupfuls of the hot broth into the eggs, whisking them constantly so they don't curdle. Return the warmed eggs to the soup and stir constantly over low heat until the soup thickens. Immediately remove the saucepan from the heat. Then stir in the cilantro, bell pepper, and scallions. Don't boil the soup or the eggs will curdle. If the eggs do scramble, however, don't worry—serve it as a lemon chicken soup with egg ribbons!

Spiced Chili Chicken Soup

MAKES: *4 servings*
TIME: *45 minutes*

The taste of packaged tortillas improves immeasurably with a brief stay on a hot griddle or in an ungreased cast-iron skillet. Or, if you'd rather not have to watch them, wrap the tortillas in aluminum foil and, in the last 10 minutes of cooking the soup, bake them in a 300°F oven to heat through; or wrap them in plastic wrap and heat them in the microwave for a couple of minutes.

2 cups chicken broth
2½ cups water
2 teaspoons chili powder
3 cloves garlic, minced
3 ripe tomatoes, cored and chopped
 into ¼-inch dice
1 to 1¼ pounds skinless, boneless
 chicken (breasts or thighs)
1 lime
Salt and freshly ground black pepper
½ cup (packed) fresh cilantro leaves
Hot sauce (optional)
8 flour or corn tortillas, toasted
 lightly or baked

1. Place the broth, water, chili powder, garlic, and tomatoes in a large saucepan and bring to a boil over medium-high heat. Cover, and simmer over low heat for 10 minutes.

2. While this is cooking, cut the chicken into 2 × ¼ × ½-inch strips and set them aside in a bowl. Juice half the lime over the chicken strips, and season lightly with salt and pepper. Chop the cilantro.

3. Add the chicken strips to the broth and bring to a simmer, uncovered, over medium-high heat. Simmer to just cook the chicken through, 1 to 2 minutes. Juice the remaining lime half into the soup, and add the cilantro. Season with 1 teaspoon salt and pepper to taste. If you like, add hot sauce to taste. Serve with the toasted tortillas.

TOASTED TORTILLAS

To toast flour tortillas, heat an ungreased cast-iron skillet or griddle over high heat; toast the tortillas on each side until they take on some color and smell good, 45 to 60 seconds. If you are using corn tortillas, first dip them in cold water, so they won't crack and dry out, and then toast them in the skillet.

VARIATIONS

- Add ½ teaspoon cumin when you add the chili powder.

- Right before serving, scatter sliced raw mushrooms over the soup.

Three Times Fennel Chicken Soup

MAKES: *4 servings*
TIME: *35 to 40 minutes*

This soup is a licorice-lover's dream: the fresh fennel taste is intensified by flavoring the broth with dried fennel seeds and is echoed a third time by adding Pernod, a licorice-flavored liqueur, at the end.

2 tablespoons butter
¼ cup finely chopped onion
1 Granny Smith apple, cored, peeled,
    and finely diced
1 large bulb fennel (fronds reserved),
    cored and thinly sliced (2 cups)
½ teaspoon fennel seeds
2 cups water
2 cups chicken or vegetable
    broth
Salt
¼ cup long-grain rice
1 to 1¼ pounds skinless,
    boneless chicken (breasts
    or thighs)
Freshly ground black pepper
1 to 2 tablespoons Pernod
    (optional)

1. Melt the butter in a large saucepan over medium heat. Add the onion, apple, sliced fennel, and fennel seeds, and sauté for about 1 minute. Add 2 tablespoons of the water, cover, and cook until the ingredients are somewhat softened, about 5 minutes.

2. Add the remaining water and the broth, 1 teaspoon salt, and the rice. Bring the liquid to a boil, cover, and simmer over medium-low heat until the rice is soft, 15 minutes.

3. Meanwhile, cut the chicken into ½-inch cubes and chop some of the reserved fennel fronds for garnish.

4. Add the chicken to the broth and simmer, uncovered, over low heat for 5 minutes or until cooked through. Season to taste with salt and pepper. Stir in the Pernod if you wish. Ladle out the soup, and garnish each portion with the feathery fronds.

ESPECIALLY GOOD FOR COMPANY

Creamed Fennel Chicken Soup: In step 2, after the rice is cooked, strain the solids from the liquid. Return the liquid to the saucepan and cook the cubes of chicken in it. In a blender or food processor, purée the solids with ½ cup heavy cream. Season the purée to taste with salt and pepper, and return it to the saucepan. Mix the purée into the liquid and bring to a simmer. Adjust the seasoning, and serve garnished with fennel fronds.

Re-Curried Chicken Soup

MAKES: *4 servings*
TIME: *30 to 35 minutes*

You can make this soup with leftover Thai or Indian chicken curry—both work well with the flavors in this recipe. If they are not already heavy on tomato flavor, combine the leftovers with tomato juice rather than with chicken broth.

3 cups leftover Indian or Thai chicken
  curry (rice can be part of the
  leftovers; see Note)
1 cup "light" or regular coconut milk
  (see Note)
2 cups thawed frozen vegetables, such as
  carrots and peas
2 cups chicken broth or tomato juice
Juice of 1 lemon (optional)
¼ chopped fresh mint or cilantro
  leaves
Salt and freshly ground black pepper

1. Combine the leftovers, coconut milk, vegetables, and broth in a saucepan over medium-low heat. Bring the mixture to a simmer and cook until hot, about 5 minutes.

2. If you are not using tomato juice, then add a nice zingy flavor by stirring in the lemon juice at the last minute. Remove the saucepan from the heat and stir in the mint. Season to taste with salt and pepper; serve hot.

Note: Tandoori chicken works well in this dish, as do any of the common chicken curries. If your leftovers already contain coconut milk, reduce the coconut milk to ½ cup and mix with ½ cup of water.

Summer Green Gazpacho with Chicken

MAKES: 4 servings
TIME: 20 to 25 minutes

How much cooked chicken you need for this recipe depends simply on how much you have in the house. The chicken should be skinless, unsauced, with all fat removed so that it does not interfere with the fresh flavor and texture of the soup. Use a low-fat or "ready-to-eat" broth because you don't want congealed bits of chicken fat floating in your lovely cold soup. The longer you chill the soup before serving, the better it will taste.

2 cups canned chicken or vegetable broth
1 cup water
1 large green bell pepper, stemmed,
  seeded, and coarsely chopped
4 Kirby or 2 medium cucumbers, peeled
  and coarsely chopped
2 cloves garlic
1 scallion, trimmed and coarsely chopped
  (white and green parts)
½ cup (packed) fresh mint leaves
1 cup plain yogurt
Salt
¾ to 1 pound cooked chicken, preferably
  roasted or grilled
2 ripe Hass avocados
Tabasco sauce, to taste

SECOND-TIME-AROUND CHICKEN SOUPS

These soups are great when you have just enough leftover plainly roasted, grilled, or poached chicken for two people.

Speedy, Speedy Chicken Soup: Bring 2 cups each of chicken broth and water to a boil in a large saucepan. Stir in ¼ to ½ cup of an herb purée (see pages 224 and 225), along with 2 cups bite-size chunks of skinned cooked chicken and 2 cups shredded lettuce leaves. Simmer until the chicken is heated through and the lettuce has wilted, 3 minutes. Season to taste with salt and pepper. Makes 2 servings.

Spinach Chicken Soup: Combine 2 cups each of chicken broth and water, 1 teaspoon Dijon mustard, 2 cups bite-size chunks of skinless cooked chicken, and 1 minced clove garlic in a large saucepan, and bring to a simmer over high heat. As this is coming to a boil, trim and rinse 8 ounces of fresh spinach; then tear the leaves into 2-inch pieces. Lightly toast 4 slices of French or Italian bread. When the soup is at a simmer, stir in the spinach leaves and cook for a few seconds, just until the leaves wilt. Place 2 slices of toast in each soup bowl. Season the soup to taste with salt and pepper, and ladle it over the bread. Makes 2 servings.

Herbed Vegetable and Scallion Chicken Soup: Combine 2 cups each of chicken broth and water and 1 package (10 ounces) frozen lima beans, thawed, in a large saucepan. Bring to a boil over high heat. Cover the saucepan, and simmer over medium-low heat until the lima beans are tender, 10 minutes. While the lima beans are cooking, thinly slice 2 scallions (white and green parts) and mince ½ cup (packed) parsley leaves. When the lima beans are tender, add 2 cups bite-size chunks of skinless cooked chicken, and simmer for a couple of minutes, just to warm the chicken through. Stir in the parsley and scallions, and season to taste with salt and pepper. Makes 2 servings.

Mushroom and Pastina Chicken Soup: Bring 2 cups each of chicken broth and water, 2 teaspoons Asian sesame oil, and 1 tablespoon soy sauce to a boil in a large saucepan over high heat. Add 10 ounces thinly sliced fresh mushrooms, along with ¼ cup couscous or pastina. Simmer until the pasta is tender, 3 to 5 minutes. Add 2 cups bite-size chunks of skinless cooked chicken, 2 thinly sliced scallions, and ¼ teaspoon crushed red pepper flakes. Simmer until the chicken is warmed through, 2 to 3 minutes. Season with salt. Makes 2 servings.

1. In two or three batches, combine the broth, water, bell pepper, cucumbers, garlic, scallion, mint, ½ cup of the yogurt, and 1 teaspoon salt in a blender and purée until smooth. Pour into a serving bowl, cover, and chill in the refrigerator while you cut up the chicken.

2. Remove all fat from the chicken, and finely chop or shred the meat. Add the chicken to the soup, cover, and chill until serving time.

3. Right before serving, peel, pit, and cut the avocados into small dice; stir into the soup. Adjust the seasoning for salt, and add a dash of Tabasco sauce if you wish. Garnish each portion with an additional 2 tablespoons of yogurt, and serve immediately.

VARIATION

To turn this into a more authentic-looking gazpacho, substitute 2 cups tomato juice for the broth, and add 1 chopped, seeded fresh tomato to the avocado.

Coconut and Cilantro Soup

MAKES: *4 servings*
TIME: *25 minutes*

The coconut milk gives this soup a velvety finish, in exquisite contrast to the tang of the lime juice and the grassy freshness of the cilantro. Don't cut back on the volume of cilantro—it is the generous quantity that gives the soup its special character. When you sauté the ground poultry before adding the liquids, be sure to stir continuously to thoroughly break it up into small crumbled pieces. This way you won't end up with unattractive clumps of meat.

> 2 tablespoons vegetable oil
> 1 to 1¼ pounds ground chicken or
>   turkey
> 2 small cloves garlic, minced
> 1 quarter-size slice fresh ginger, minced
> 2 cups water
> 4 cups chicken or vegetable broth
> Salt
> ¼ pound vermicelli, capellini, or very
>   fine egg noodles, broken into 2-inch
>   lengths
> 2 limes
> 2 scallions
> ½ cup (packed) fresh cilantro leaves
> 7 to 8 ounces unsweetened coconut milk
> ½ teaspoon dried red pepper flakes

USING COCONUT MILK

Coconut milk usually comes in 14- to 15-ounce cans, so you'll have more than you need for this recipe. Store what you don't use in a covered jar in the fridge, where it will keep for a week. Or transfer it to a plastic container and stick it in the freezer, where it will keep for a few months. Here are a few ideas on how to use up leftover unsweetened coconut milk:

- Use some as part of the liquid in which to simmer rice.
- Add some to a vinaigrette for a fabulous dressing over Napa cabbage with red bell pepper and chopped peanuts.
- Sweeten it with some brown sugar and spoon it over a fruit salad made of oranges or mangoes and bananas.
- Mix it with lime juice, honey, seltzer, and ice for a refreshing drink.
- Add a teaspoonful of it to your cereal milk.

1. Heat the oil in a medium-size saucepan over medium heat. Add the ground chicken and sauté, mashing and stirring constantly until the chicken is crumbled and partially cooked, 3 minutes. Add the garlic and ginger and cook until the moisture evaporates and the chicken begins to dry out, about 1 minute.

2. Add the water and broth and bring the liquid to a boil. Add 1 teaspoon salt and the vermicelli. Cover the pan and cook over medium-low heat until the noodles are tender, about 5 minutes.

3. While this is cooking, juice the limes, trim the scallions (white and green parts) and slice them into ¼-inch rounds, and coarsely chop the cilantro. When the vermicelli is tender, remove the saucepan from the heat, stir in the lime juice and coconut milk, and season to taste with salt and red pepper flakes. Ladle the soup into deep soup bowls and serve sprinkled with the scallions and cilantro.

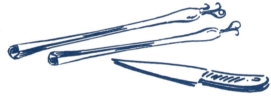

Chicken Corn Chowder

MAKES: *4 servings*
TIME: *40 minutes*

This unfussy trio of potatoes, vegetables, and chicken is a meal unto itself as well as a pattern recipe that invites variations. Chicken bits swim in a well-flavored broth and are combined with a starch, a vegetable, and an abundance of chopped fresh herbs.

2 tablespoons butter
1 onion, finely chopped
2 boiling or all-purpose
    potatoes (1 pound)
2 cups chicken broth
4 cups water
1 to 1¼ pounds skinless, boneless
    chicken or turkey breast
1 package (10 ounces) frozen corn
    kernels, thawed
Salt
2 cups (packed) stemmed fresh herbs,
    such as parsley, cilantro, or dill
Freshly ground black pepper
Tabasco or other hot sauce (optional)

1. Melt the butter in a large saucepan over low heat. Add the onion, cover, and cook until tender and translucent, about 5 minutes. While the onion softens, peel the potatoes and cut them into ½-inch cubes.

2. Add the broth, water, and potatoes to the pan and bring the liquid to a simmer over high heat. Cover and cook until the potatoes are tender, 10 minutes. While this is cooking, remove all fat from the chicken and cut it into ½-inch cubes.

3. Add the corn and 1 teaspoon salt to the soup and simmer for another 5 minutes. Then add the chicken and simmer until it is cooked through, about 5 minutes. While this is cooking, chop the fresh herbs.

4. Remove the pan from the heat, stir in the herbs, and season to taste with salt and pepper. Add the Tabasco to each portion, if you wish.

VARIATIONS

Chicken Chowder with Rice: In step 2, instead of the potatoes add ½ cup long-grain rice or orzo.

Tomato Chicken Chowder: In step 2, instead of the water add 4 cups tomato juice.

Spiced Chicken Chowder: In step 3, add ½ to 1 teaspoon of ground cumin, caraway, or fennel seeds when you add the corn.

Chicken Chowder with Greens: In step 3, when you add the chicken, add 3 cups finely shredded fresh spinach or kale, or chopped watercress or arugula leaves.

Velvet Chicken Chowder: In step 4, right before adding the herbs, stir in 2 ounces grated Swiss cheese and ¼ cup heavy or sour cream.

Cheddar Chicken Chowder

MAKES: *4 servings*
TIME: *35 minutes*

I call this "chowder" rather than soup because I can't resist the alliteration, but it is not a real chowder because it doesn't contain potatoes. Be sure to add all of the Cheddar to give the soup its smooth finish, which is a lovely contrast to the crisp bell pepper garnish.

2 tablespoons butter
½ small onion, finely chopped
2 cups chicken or vegetable broth
½ cup beer or dry white wine
1¼ cups water
1 teaspoon Dijon mustard
2 tablespoons all-purpose flour
Salt
2 whole skinless, boneless chicken breasts
    (about 1½ pounds total)
6 ounces sharp Cheddar cheese
2 red bell peppers (8 ounces each),
    stemmed and seeded
2 tablespoons chopped green canned
    chiles, or 1 tablespoon pickled
    jalapeño peppers, finely diced
Freshly ground black pepper

1. Melt the butter in a medium-size saucepan over medium heat. Add the onion, cover, and cook until tender and translucent, about 5 minutes. While this is cooking, combine the broth, beer, and water in a 4-cup measuring cup.

2. Whisk the mustard and flour into the onion and cook over low heat, stirring constantly so the flour doesn't burn, 2 minutes. Whisking vigorously, add the broth mixture ¼ cup at a time, until a smooth, thick paste forms. Continue to gradually add the remaining liquid, stirring, until all has been incorporated. Then add ½ teaspoon salt.

3. Bring the liquid to a boil, then reduce to a simmer over low heat, and cook, partially covered, for 15 minutes. Meanwhile, remove all fat from the chicken and cut it into ½-inch dice. Grate the cheese or cut it into wafer-thin slices, and cut the bell peppers into ½-inch pieces.

4. Add the chicken, bring the liquid back to a simmer, and cook gently, uncovered, until it is just cooked through, 5 minutes.

5. Add the chiles and the cheese, and simmer over low heat, stirring constantly so that the cheese dissolves in the soup without scorching, for 1 minute. Season to taste with salt and pepper. Divide the bell peppers among 4 soup bowls, and ladle the hot soup over them.

VARIATIONS

▪ Instead of bell pepper, add 1 cup thawed frozen "petite" peas in step 4, after the chicken is cooked and before you add the cheese.

▪ This soup is a great vehicle for using up odds and ends of leftover cheese. Some cheeses, such as Brie and blue, can't be grated, so you'll have to dice or crumble them, and stir them into the soup at step 5.

ESPECIALLY GOOD FOR CHILDREN

Plain chicken and Cheddar is what kids love. So when making Cheddar Chicken Chowder, omit the mustard, chiles, and red bell pepper.

SECOND TIME AROUND

Because cheese sinks to the bottom of the saucepan and might burn, reheat leftovers in a double boiler or by the portion in a microwave oven.

Creamy New England Chicken Chowder

MAKES: *4 servings*
TIME: *30 minutes*

This is a bit skimpy for dinner, so make a salad to serve after the soup and be sure to serve lots of bread on the side. If you have leftover boiled potatoes, chunk them and add them to the soup, making it heartier—and more of an official chowder. On special occasions, substitute 1 cup chicken broth and 1 cup heavy cream for the evaporated milk.

4 slices bacon, chopped
6 scallions, trimmed and thinly sliced (white and green parts)
1 package (10 ounces) frozen corn kernels, thawed
½ teaspoon dried thyme
2 cups chicken broth
1 pound skinless, boneless chicken (breasts or thighs)
1 can (12 ounces) evaporated skim or low-fat milk
Salt
Scant ¼ teaspoon dried red pepper flakes
¼ cup chopped fresh parsley
Soda or oyster crackers, for garnish

1. Cook the bacon in a large saucepan over medium heat. When the bacon bits are crisp, add the scallions and sauté just until they begin to wilt, 1 minute.

2. Add the corn, thyme, and broth and bring the liquid to a simmer. Cook, covered, for 10 minutes. Meanwhile, cut the chicken into ½-inch pieces.

3. Add the chicken to the broth mixture, cover, and simmer to cook through, 3 to 5 minutes. Add the evaporated milk and simmer, uncovered, for 1 minute to heat through. Do not boil. Season with salt to taste and the red pepper flakes. Remove the soup from the heat and stir in the parsley. Ladle the soup into soup bowls, and crumble the crackers over the top.

Red Chicken Chowder

MAKES: *4 servings*
TIME: *30 minutes*

Here, again, I use the word "chowder" loosely to describe a soup full of chunks of ingredients, rather than a soup that includes potatoes (which would make it a more authentic chowder). The lavish use of tomatoes colors this soup red.

> 2 cloves garlic
> 2 cups canned plum tomatoes with their juices
> 2 cups chicken or vegetable broth
> 2 cups water
> ½ cup long-grain rice
> 1 to 1¼ pounds skinless, boneless chicken (breasts or thighs)
> 1 cup (packed) fresh parsley or basil leaves
> 1 package (10 ounces) frozen corn kernels, thawed
> Salt and freshly ground black pepper
> ½ cup sour cream or plain yogurt (optional)

1. Press the garlic cloves through a garlic press and into a medium-size saucepan. Add the tomatoes and their juices, chicken broth, and water. Cover the saucepan and bring the liquid to a boil over high heat, mashing the tomatoes against the sides of the pan.

2. Add the rice, cover, and simmer over medium heat until the rice is almost completely soft, about 15 minutes. While this is cooking, cut the chicken into 2 × ¼ × ½-inch strips. Finely chop the parsley.

3. Add the chicken and corn to the rice, and continue to simmer until the chicken is just cooked through, 3 to 5 minutes. Season to taste with salt and pepper. Remove the soup from the heat and stir in the parsley. Garnish each portion with 2 tablespoons sour cream, if you wish.

White Beans and Escarole Chicken Soup

MAKES: *4 servings*
TIME: *25 minutes*

There are a variety of poultry sausages on the market; some are terrific, others quite mediocre. My favorite poultry sausage manufacturer is Aidells, a San Francisco company, and among my favorites of their selection is the Smoked Turkey and Chicken Pesto variety, which I recommend in this recipe. A terrific accompaniment to this soup would be slices of Italian or French bread, cut on the diagonal, toasted, and rubbed with garlic while still warm.

1 head (8 to 10 ounces) escarole,
    romaine lettuce, or broccoli rabe
2 tablespoons olive oil
6 smoked chicken sausages (about 1
    pound), cut into ½-inch-thick rounds
2 cans (15 ounces each) white beans
    (cannellini), rinsed and drained
Salt
2 cups chicken broth
2¼ cups water
1 teaspoon ground dried sage
4 slices Italian bread, toasted
Freshly ground black pepper
1 cup freshly grated Parmesan
    cheese

1. Cut the escarole into pieces about 2 to 3 inches square.

2. Heat the oil in a large saucepan over medium heat. Add the sausage slices and cook them until slightly stiffened and brown, about 2 to 3 minutes per side. Using a slotted spoon, remove the sausage slices to a bowl.

3. Add the escarole to the same saucepan, cover, and simmer over medium heat until it has wilted but is still bright green, 2 to 3 minutes. Transfer the escarole to the bowl with the sausages.

4. Add half the beans to the same saucepan, and using a potato masher or a spoon, purée them (if the beans are not fully puréed, that's fine).

5. Add the remaining beans, leaving them whole, along with 1 teaspoon salt and the broth, water, and sage. Bring the liquid to a simmer, and cook over medium heat until the beans are hot, 5 minutes. Return the sausage rounds and escarole to the soup, and simmer, uncovered, until heated through, 2 to 3 minutes.

6. Set a slice of toast in each of 4 soup bowls. Season the soup to taste with salt and pepper, and remove it from the heat. Ladle the soup into the bowls and top each portion with ¼ cup of the Parmesan cheese. Serve immediately.

VARIATION

Add a spoonful of Basil and Garlic Purée or other herb purée (see page 224) in step 5, when you return the sausage and escarole to the soup.

Winter Cabbage Chicken Soup

MAKES: *4 servings*
TIME: *40 minutes*

Use real sour cream, not a low-fat variety, in this soup—its smooth richness balances the tang of the sauerkraut and the smokiness of the sausage. Because the potatoes take a while to soften, this soup takes somewhat longer to simmer than others, but it's still easy to prepare and does not require extra effort.

2 tablespoons butter
1 onion (4 to 6 ounces), sliced into
*   thin half-moons*
1 can (14½ ounces) stewed tomatoes,
*   chopped, juices reserved*
3 cups water
1 teaspoon sugar
1 teaspoon paprika
1 pound new potatoes (2 large), peeled
*   and cut into ½-inch dice*
6 cooked smoked chicken or turkey
*   sausages (about 1*
*   pound)*
6 ounces cabbage
¼ cup (packed) dill
*   leaves*
8 ounces sauerkraut
*   (½ package)*
Salt and freshly ground black pepper
1 cup sour cream

1. Melt the butter in a large saucepan over medium heat. Add the onion, cover, and cook until it begins to stick to the pan and turn golden, 2 to 3 minutes.

2. Add the stewed tomatoes and their juices, along with the water, sugar, paprika, and potatoes. Bring to a boil over high heat. Reduce the heat to a simmer and cook, covered, until the potatoes are almost tender, 10 minutes.

3. While the potatoes are cooking, thinly slice the sausages, finely shred the cabbage (to make 2 cups), and mince the dill. Rinse the sauerkraut and squeeze out the excess moisture.

4. Add the sauerkraut and cabbage to the saucepan, cover, and cook over medium heat until the cabbage has wilted and is tender but still somewhat crisp, 10 minutes.

5. Add the sausages and simmer, covered, until hot, 5 minutes. Season to taste with salt and pepper. Remove the pan from the heat and ladle the soup into bowls. Garnish each portion with ¼ cup of the sour cream, and sprinkle with the chopped dill.

WHAT TO DO WITH THE OTHER
HALF OF THE SAUERKRAUT

Sauté 1 minced clove garlic and 1 peeled, cored, finely sliced Granny Smith apple in 2 tablespoons melted butter until tender, 5 minutes. Stir in 8 ounces sauerkraut and ½ teaspoon caraway seeds, and simmer for 5 minutes or until hot. Season to taste with salt and pepper. Remove from the heat and stir in ½ cup sour cream. Serve with pork chops or roasted chicken and mashed potatoes.

Pretty Fast Chicken Gumbo

MAKES: *4 servings*
TIME: *40 minutes*

Gumbo seesaws between being a stew and a soup. What you call it matters little, because either way it's delicious. A classic gumbo is simmered with whole chicken parts and thickened with a dark roux, and filé powder or okra. It always sports a mild smoky flavor and is served over rice. While the real McCoy is an inspired dish, it takes too long to prepare for a weeknight meal. I've made judicious cuts and changes in the classic dish to approximate the flavor and still make dinner in a reasonable amount of time. Instead of cooking whole chicken parts, I cook smoked chicken sausage to impart the requisite smoky taste, and I cook okra and rice right in the broth to help thicken the soup without having to cook a dark roux.

> ¼ cup vegetable oil
> 6 medium (about 1 pound) spicy
>   chicken or turkey sausages, cut
>   into ½-inch rounds
> 1 small onion, finely chopped
> 1 red bell pepper, cut into ¼-inch pieces
> 2 cloves garlic, minced
> 4 cups chicken or vegetable broth
> 2 cups canned plum tomatoes with their
>   juices
> ½ cup long-grain rice
> 1 teaspoon dried thyme
> 1 package (10 ounces) frozen okra,
>   thawed, cut into ½-inch slices
> Salt
> Cayenne pepper, or Tabasco or another
>   hot sauce, to taste

1. Heat the vegetable oil in a large saucepan over medium heat. In a couple of batches, brown the sausage slices for about 2 minutes per side. Remove them with a slotted spoon and set aside. Add the onion, bell pepper, and garlic to the pan. Cover and simmer over medium heat, stirring occasionally, until they are tender, 5 minutes.

2. Add the broth, tomatoes with their juices, rice, and thyme and bring the liquid to a

simmer. Return the sausage slices to the liquid, cover the pan, and simmer until the rice is tender and the seasonings come together, 15 minutes.

3. Add the okra and simmer just to heat through, 2 minutes only (don't simmer longer or it turns slimy). Season to taste with salt and cayenne pepper or Tabasco sauce.

A FEW STEWS

Chicken Braised with Fresh Tomatoes

MAKES: *4 servings*
TIME: *1 hour*

I adore this recipe for its full fresh and simple flavor. Now that vine-ripened tomatoes are available for the better part of the year, I pull it from my files more often than just at the end of the summer. To keep the flesh as moist as possible, I cook the chicken with the skin on and discard it later.

¼ *cup olive oil*
1 *chicken, quartered or cut into 8*
　pieces (3½ to 4 pounds total)
1 *onion, thinly sliced*
6 *medium (2 pounds) vine-ripened*
　fresh tomatoes
4 *cloves garlic, minced*
1 *strip (1 × ¼-inch)*
　orange zest
½ *teaspoon dried oregano, thyme, or*
　rosemary
Salt and freshly ground black pepper

1. Heat the oil in a deep 6-quart flameproof casserole over medium-high heat. Sauté the chicken, just to stiffen the skin, turning the pieces once, about 8 to 10 minutes.

2. Remove the chicken to a plate and add the onion to the casserole. Cover and cook over low heat until tender, 3 to 5 minutes. If the onion begins to stick, add a tablespoon-ful of water and continue to cook until tender.

3. Meanwhile, core and cut the tomatoes into quarters; then halve the tomato quarters. When the onion is tender, add the tomatoes, garlic, orange zest, and oregano and cook, uncovered, until the tomatoes begin to give off their juices, 1 minute. Return the dark meat to the casserole, cover, and simmer over low heat for 10 minutes. Add the white meat, cover, and simmer until the chicken is just done, 20 minutes more.

4. Place the chicken on a plate and let it rest until it is cool enough to handle, 10 minutes.

While the chicken is resting, mash the tomatoes a bit with a wooden spoon to integrate them into the sauce. Season to taste with salt and pepper and bring the juices back to a simmer. Remove and discard the chicken skin and the fat underneath the skin. Return the chicken to the sauce and simmer over low heat just to reheat, 2 to 3 minutes.

VARIATION

While the chicken is cooking in step 3, wash 1 pound of young slim zucchini. Remove the stem ends and cut the zucchini into ½-inch-thick rounds. In step 4, after you remove the chicken to a plate to cool and after mashing the tomatoes, add the zucchini to the casserole, cover, and simmer until it is cooked but still crisp, 3 to 5 minutes.

ESPECIALLY GOOD FOR CHILDREN

In general kids don't like tomato skins and lumpy sauces. So what I do for my daughter (who even as a teenager won't eat sauce with bits of "stuff" in it) is to remove some of the sauce and pass it through a sieve. For little kids you can also remove the chicken from the bone, cut it into small pieces, and return the pieces to the strained sauce. Then they will love it served as is or over rice, noodles, or potatoes.

SECOND TIME AROUND

This dish gives off more juice than you will need for dinner. Use it for the beginning of a pasta sauce. Or add some chicken broth to the leftover juices and cook some vegetables and rice in it for a hearty, speedy soup.

Fiery Asian Chicken Braised with Mushrooms

MAKES: *4 servings*
TIME: *1 hour*

This dish has an exotically appealing flavor because of the cinnamon stick, lime zest, and generous dose of cilantro. If you want less fierce heat in your dinner, then reduce the dried pepper flakes to ¼ teaspoon.

2 tablespoons vegetable oil
2 tablespoons Asian sesame oil
1 chicken, quartered or cut into
    8 pieces (3½ to 4 pounds total)
2 cloves garlic, thinly sliced
10 ounces mushrooms, thinly sliced
¼ cup rice vinegar
2 tablespoons soy sauce
1 cinnamon stick (1 inch long)
1 strip lime zest (1 inch long)
½ teaspoon dried red pepper flakes
1 cup (loosely packed) cilantro leaves
Salt

1. Heat the vegetable and sesame oils in a deep 6-quart flameproof casserole over medium-high heat. Sauté the chicken, just to stiffen the skin, turning the pieces once, 8 to 10 minutes. Remove the chicken to a plate and set aside.

2. Add the garlic, mushrooms, rice vinegar, soy sauce, cinnamon, lime zest, and red pepper flakes. Sauté, stirring, until the mushrooms begin to wilt, for a couple of minutes.

3. Return only the dark meat to the casserole, cover, and simmer over low heat for 10 minutes. Add the white meat, cover and simmer until the chicken is just done, 20 minutes longer.

4. Remove the cooked chicken to a plate and let it rest for 10 minutes or until cool enough to remove and discard the skin and fat underneath the skin. While the chicken is resting, strain the juices from the casserole into a bowl or degreasing cup and reserve the mushrooms. Discard the cinnamon stick and lime strip. Remove all of the surface fat. Return the degreased juices to the pan and bring them back to a simmer.

5. Coarsely chop the cilantro and add it to the sauce. Simmer for 30 seconds or until barely wilted. Season to taste with salt. Return the skinned chicken to the sauce and simmer over low heat to reheat, 2 to 3 minutes.

Greek-Style Chicken and Bean Stew

MAKES: *4 servings*
TIME: *25 to 30 minutes*

This fragrant, comforting, luscious mixture is lovely in the summer, served with a wedge of Tuscan or other type of Italian bread. In my neighborhood it can be hard finding plum tomatoes in any can smaller than 28 ounces, and so I often find myself with a half-full opened can of tomatoes in the fridge. If this happens to you, take a look at the box for a suggestion on how to use them up.

¼ cup olive oil
2 large cloves garlic, minced
1¼ pounds ground chicken or turkey
½ teaspoon dried mint
½ teaspoon dried oregano
1½ cups whole plum tomatoes, with their juices
1 can (15.5 ounces) pinto beans, drained and rinsed
1 lemon
½ cup pitted Kalamata olives
2 zucchini or yellow squash (1 pound total)
Salt and freshly ground black pepper

WHAT TO DO WITH LEFTOVER CANNED TOMATOES

Drain the tomatoes, and remove and discard the seeds. Cut the tomatoes into lengthwise strips and put them in a mixing bowl. Add 1 tablespoon olive oil, and season with salt and freshly ground pepper. Marinate for 20 minutes. Set the marinated strips on some pita bread or flour tortillas. Top the tomatoes with grated or diced mozzarella cheese, and bake on a baking sheet in a 400° F oven until the cheese melts. It makes a great snack or light lunch.

1. Heat the olive oil in a large saucepan over medium-high heat. Add the garlic and ground chicken and sauté, mashing and stirring the chicken constantly, until the chicken is crumbled and no longer pink, about 5 minutes.

2. Add the mint, oregano, and tomatoes with their juices. Break up the tomatoes with the side of a wooden spoon. Then add the beans, cover, and simmer over low heat until the ingredients are heated through, 10 minutes.

3. While the chicken is simmering, grate the zest and juice the lemon (don't worry about how much zest and juice you have; whatever you get is fine). Quarter the olives. Scrub the zucchini, cut them in half lengthwise, remove the seeds with a spoon, and cut the remaining pulp into ¼-inch dice.

4. Add the zucchini to the saucepan, cover, and simmer over low heat until it is just tender, about 5 minutes. Remove the saucepan from the heat and stir in the lemon zest, juice, and olives. Season to taste with salt and pepper, and serve immediately.

Orange-Braised Chicken with Almond Sauce

MAKES: *4 servings*
TIME: *15 minutes preparation*
1 hour no-work cooking time

Try serving polenta with this for a delicious side dish. It makes a perfect companion for the luscious almond sauce.

¼ cup olive oil
1 onion, finely chopped
2 cloves garlic, minced
¼ teaspoon ground allspice
4 whole skinless chicken legs, or
  8 skinless chicken thighs or
  drumsticks (1½ to 2 pounds total)
½ cup chicken broth
Salt
1-inch cube fresh ginger
2 fresh jalapeño peppers
6 navel oranges
4 ounces blanched almonds
1 teaspoon sugar

1. Heat the olive oil in a 4-quart nonreactive saucepan over medium-high heat. Add the onion and sauté until it begins to brown, 5 minutes.

2. Add the garlic, allspice, and chicken, and cook until the meat stiffens, about 2 minutes on each side.

3. Add the broth and bring to a simmer. Season with about 1 teaspoon salt. Cover and cook over very low heat until the chicken is cooked through, 45 minutes.

4. Meanwhile, peel the ginger and chop it coarsely. Remove almost all the seeds from the jalapeños (leave some in to give the sauce a good, albeit bearable, bite), and grate 1 teaspoon orange zest. Add these to a food processor along with the almonds, sugar, and ½ teaspoon salt. Process until the mixture resembles almond paste. Transfer it to a bowl and set aside.

5. With a sharp knife, pare away all the remaining peel and white pith from the oranges. Cut in between the membranes to release the orange segments, and reserve them for later.

6. Remove the chicken to a plate. Add the almond purée to the liquid in the pan, and whisk to combine. Remove the pan from the heat, add the orange segments, season with salt to taste, and spoon over the chicken.

VARIATIONS

Coconut-Orange Braised Chicken: In step 6, after you add the almond purée, add ½ cup unsweetened coconut milk and proceed with the recipe.

Cilantro-Orange Braised Chicken: In step 4, chop 2 cups cilantro leaves. In step 6, when you add the orange segments, add the cilantro as well.

SECOND TIME AROUND

Serve leftovers as a soup by thinning them with chicken broth and fresh orange juice.

Game Hen Stew for Two

MAKES: *2 servings*
TIME: *35 minutes*

This recipe tastes spectacular because I have kept the ingredients simple and few in number and haven't camouflaged their distinctive character by adding too many seasonings. Be sure to serve the stew in deep bowls to catch all the rich juices.

1 Rock Cornish hen (about 1½ pounds)
1 tablespoon olive oil
1 tablespoon butter
1 medium onion
4 carrots
½ cup chicken broth
½ teaspoon dried
   rosemary
1 package (10
   ounces) frozen lima
   beans, thawed
1 lemon
½ cup (packed) fresh dill
Salt and freshly ground black pepper

1. Remove the giblets from the interior of the game hen. With heavy-duty kitchen shears, cut along either side of the backbone and remove it. Cut off and remove the first two joints of the wings, so only the fleshy joint is left on the breast. Also cut off and remove any excess neck skin. Cut each half in half again, separating the breast and wing piece from the thigh and drumstick. Pat the skin dry with paper towels.

2. Heat the oil and butter in a medium-size saucepan over medium heat. Add the game hen pieces, skin side down, and cook, uncovered, for 5 minutes. Meanwhile, thinly slice the onion.

3. Add the onion to the pan, turn the game hen over, and continue to cook, uncovered, 5 minutes more. During this time, thinly slice the carrots.

4. Add the carrots, broth, and rosemary to the pan and cook, covered, over low heat for 10 minutes. Add the lima beans, cover, and cook until the lima beans are tender and the game hen is cooked through, 10 minutes more. During this time, juice the lemon (you need 2 tablespoons) and finely chop the dill.

5. Stir in the lemon juice and dill, and immediately remove the pan from the heat. Season to taste with salt and pepper.

Dinner Salads

Think "salad" as a dinner solution throughout the entire year. After all, where is it written that dinner must always be served hot? At our house, on all but the coldest of winter days, we're perfectly content with a delicious main course salad for supper because we believe that if it's filling and delicious, it's dinner.

Chicken salads offer clever versatile options for the hurried workweek because poultry pairs so happily with a variety of textures and tastes. To make a good chicken salad fast, start out with store-bought cooked chicken: basic barbecued or roasted chicken is available everywhere today, from giant suburban supermarkets to tiny city specialty stores, and short of that, at the very least, baked or smoked turkey is offered at the deli counter in every market. With the cooked chicken in hand, dinner's almost done; the only remaining work is to chop up a few companionable vegetables, combine them with the chicken, and toss it all with a tasty dressing.

THE BEST CHICKEN FOR SALAD

The best-tasting chicken salads are served at room temperature and are fashioned out of freshly cooked poultry rather than chilled leftovers. Slightly warm just-cooked chicken is the juiciest and most flavorful. Before you cut into it, though, be sure the poultry has cooled long enough for the juices to retreat back into the fibers of the meat. If you cut into the chicken while it's still hot, the juices will run over your cutting board and release moisture in the salad bowl.

If you like a mix of white and dark meat in your chicken salad, then start out with the flesh of a whole cooked bird. The dark meat yields a moister bite, but if you want the leanest, densest meat possible, then make the salad with boneless chicken breasts. And if it's sophistication you're looking for, try a dice of smoked poultry (my favorite, as you will notice in the recipes).

If you want to use those remains of your Sunday roasted chicken for salad, be sure that before you store the leftover chicken, you discard all skin and fat and cut the meat from the bone. To keep the flesh as moist as possible and infuse it with some flavor, tear the chicken into bite-size pieces and coat them lightly with a bit of dressing before chilling.

HOW MUCH CHICKEN FOR SALAD

How much poultry do you need for a salad? By the time you're done with removing the meat, fat, and skin from a whole cooked bird, you're left with only 1 cup of diced meat per pound of chicken on the bone.

A whole boneless chicken breast weighs 8 to 12 ounces on average. After cooking, it will yield 1½ to 2 cups of diced cooked meat, just enough for a main course salad for 2.

When cooking bone-in chicken breasts, you'll need 1 pound for 2 people. For chicken salads made with smoked poultry, which has such a powerful flavor, 3 to 4 ounces per person will do.

BEST GREENS AND VEGETABLES FOR SALADS

I used to forgo main course chicken salads mixed with lettuce because I hated the time it took to wash and dry a mix of greens. With the wide availability of bagged mixed greens, serving salads is once again do-able during the hectic week. What is this boon to the Monday-to-Friday cook? They are bagged mixes of a variety of lettuces, from romaine and baby spinach to strong-flavored greens such as escarole and radicchio, torn into manageable bite-size pieces. The mix isn't gritty and is easy to rinse and dry quickly.

BEST-DRESSED CHICKEN SALAD

Cold deadens flavor a bit, so add a generous amount of salt and pepper to your chicken salads to compensate. The type of dressing depends on what else is in the mix. When the salad is made with dark meat, I like a vinaigrette with a high proportion of vinegar or lemon juice, whereas in salads made with the white breast meat or where there is a greater quantity of vegetables than chicken, I find creamy dressings to be more satisfying.

STORING AND SERVING CHICKEN SALADS

Leftover chicken salad, even one composed of the remains of your Sunday dinner, is terrific as a sandwich stuffer. If you want to serve the leftovers as a salad the second time around, moisten it with more dressing and freshen up the color and texture with a couple of new vegetable additions.

Chicken Salad Formula

2 servings

Cooked Chicken	2 cups	
Crunchy ingredients such as celery, apples, or nuts	1 cup	
Vegetables and legumes, such as tomatoes, corn, potatoes, peas, black beans, or chickpeas	1 cup	
Dressing	¼ to ½ cup	
Soft salad greens torn into bite-size pieces	4 cups (loosely packed)	

SALAD SKETCHES

Here are a few examples of how the preceding formula plays out.

■ Barbecued chicken + water chestnuts + vinaigrette made with Asian sesame oil mixed with chili paste and garlic and served over spinach leaves.

■ Smoked turkey + diced apples + chickpeas + creamy dressing mixed with blue cheese and served over mesclun.

■ Roasted chicken + chopped walnuts + vinaigrette mixed with barbecue sauce and served over red-leaf lettuce.

■ Poached chicken + sliced fennel + cooked potatoes + vinaigrette mixed with chopped black olives and served over arugula.

■ Grilled chicken + cooked corn + black beans + vinaigrette mixed with store-bought salsa and served over escarole.

Poached Chicken Breasts for Salads

MAKES: *4 servings*
TIME: *30 minutes*

Many of my recipes for salads and sandwiches call for cooked chicken. If you have no cooked chicken on hand but do have boneless chicken breasts, here's a speedy way to poach them so you can proceed with the other recipe. While this doesn't rate as the most exciting recipe in the book, top the plain poached chicken with a salsa and end up with a chicken dish that tastes darned good. If you are in need of an even quicker way to get your chicken poached, see the box on this page.

*2 pounds (2 to 3 whole) skinless,
   boneless chicken breasts
Salt and freshly ground black pepper
Water or chicken broth for poaching
1 tablespoon pickling spices, or
   1 teaspoon peppercorns and
   1 to 2 bay leaves
2 tablespoons dry white wine or
   white wine vinegar*

1. Cut each chicken breast in half and remove the tenderloins. Season the chicken lightly with salt and pepper. Set the tenderloins in one small skillet and the breast halves in another.

2. Add enough water to cover the chicken by ½ inch. Add half the pickling spices and wine to each skillet. Bring the liquid to a simmer, cover, and cook over low heat until the chicken is cooked through; the tenderloins will take about 5 minutes and the larger pieces 7 to 8 minutes.

3. If you have the time, let the chicken cool in the liquid for half an hour so it remains moist.

JIFFY-COOK CHICKEN

If you don't have cooked poultry on hand, here's the quickest way I know to cook some up fast. This microwave method is quicker and less messy than simple Poached Chicken Breasts.

Place 1¼ to 1½ pounds of skinless, boneless chicken or turkey breasts, thicker sides facing outward, on a 12-inch round microwave-safe dish. Season with the juice of 1 lemon and some salt and pepper. Cover loosely and microwave on High for 5 minutes. Turn the chicken pieces over, and cook, uncovered, for 5 minutes longer. Remove the chicken from the oven and let it stand for 1 to 2 minutes. Cut into one of the breasts at the thickest point, to make sure it is cooked through; if not, return the uncooked parts to the microwave oven and cook them until done, checking at 1-minute intervals. Let the chicken cool to room temperature, pat it dry, and cut into bite-size pieces for salad.

Pure Pantry
Chicken Salad

MAKES: *4 servings*
TIME: *15 to 20 minutes*

....

This salad tastes best if the beans, salsa, and black olives are cold. So if you can plan ahead, refrigerate them overnight before making the salad. If that isn't feasible, simply chill the assembled salad for as long as possible before serving. Sourdough bread makes a good accompaniment, as do warm corn or flour tortillas.

1 can (16 or 19 ounces) black beans, preferably chilled
1 package (10 ounces) frozen corn kernels, thawed and patted dry
1 whole boneless smoked chicken breast (12 ounces)
1 can (6 ounces drained weight) pitted jumbo black olives, preferably chilled
1 jar (about 12 ounces) mild or hot salsa, preferably chilled
⅓ cup regular or low-fat mayonnaise
2 tablespoons red or white wine vinegar
Salt

1. Rinse and drain the black beans and pat them dry. Transfer them to a mixing bowl, and add the corn.

2. Discard the skin and fat from the chicken, cut it into ½-inch dice, and add it to the bowl. Drain the olives and pat them dry. Slice them lengthwise or cut them into rounds, and add them to the chicken.

3. Combine the salsa, mayonnaise, and vinegar in a bowl, and season with 1¼ teaspoons salt. Mix this dressing into the beans and chicken, and toss well to combine. Adjust the seasoning, and if you have time, chill the salad before serving.

Potato
Chicken Salad
with Dill

MAKES: *4 servings*
TIME: *35 to 40 minutes*

....

Absolutely fantastic when served warm, this salad is also delicious chilled. The warmth of the chicken and potatoes gently wilts the watercress and both are uniquely satisfying against the cool crunch of the bell pepper. For a different though equally aromatic touch in the summer, substitute basil for the dill.

1 pound red new or all-purpose
   potatoes
2 whole skinless, boneless chicken
   breasts
½ cup regular or low-fat mayonnaise
2 tablespoons white wine vinegar
¼ cup (packed) chopped fresh dill
2 scallions, trimmed and thinly
   sliced (white and green parts)
Salt and freshly ground black pepper
2 bunches watercress
2 large red bell peppers

1. Peel the potatoes and cut them into ½-inch dice. Set them in a large saucepan and add water to cover. Bring the water to a boil over high heat, cover, and simmer over medium heat until the potatoes are almost done, about 10 minutes.

2. While the potatoes are cooking, cut the chicken breasts into halves and cut each half in half again, lengthwise, so you end up with 4 wide strips of chicken; set aside. Combine the mayonnaise, vinegar, dill, and scallions in a salad bowl. Mix well and season to taste with salt and pepper.

3. Rinse the watercress leaves, pat them dry, cut off the stems, and add the leaves to the dressing. Stem and seed the bell peppers, and cut them into ½-inch pieces; add them to the dressing.

PANTRY SALAD SKETCHES
4 servings

Rice, Chicken, and Corn with Blue Cheese Dressing: Cook 1 cup of long-grain rice. Drain the rice and spread it out on a baking sheet to cool quickly. Mix the rice with 2 to 3 cups diced cooked chicken or turkey, 1 package thawed frozen corn kernels, patted dry, a 4-ounce jar of roasted red peppers, cut into thin strips, and about ½ cup blue cheese dressing, store-bought or homemade (see page 74). Season to taste with salt and pepper.

Pasta, Turkey, and Peas with Mustard Vinaigrette: Cook 8 ounces elbow macaroni or other short-shaped pasta. Drain, rinse under cold water, and spread on a baking sheet to cool quickly. Dry the pasta with paper towels and mix with 2 cups diced smoked turkey, 1 package thawed frozen petite peas, patted dry, and ½ cup vinaigrette mixed with 2 teaspoons Dijon mustard and 1 teaspoon pressed fresh garlic or garlic paste. Season to taste with salt and dried red pepper flakes.

4. When the potatoes are almost tender, add the chicken to the saucepan and simmer, uncovered, over low heat until just done, 3 to 4 minutes. When it is cooked, remove the chicken to a plate to cool.

5. Drain the potatoes. Rinse them under cold water to cool, pat dry, and add to the salad bowl. Cut the cooked chicken diagonally into ½-inch pieces and add them to the bowl. Toss all the ingredients together, season with salt and lots of pepper, and serve immediately.

VARIATION

Instead of the bell peppers, use 2 unpeeled McIntosh apples, cut into ½-inch dice, and add ½ cup chopped walnuts.

Mediterranean Poached Chicken Salad

MAKES: *4 servings*
TIME: *35 minutes*

T he only type of green beans I like are skinny haricots verts (which means green beans in French), because they are sweeter and more tender than the ordinary supermarket variety. These beauties are sold in specialty grocery or fancy produce stores. If you can't find them, substitute 2 red bell peppers or 4 Kirby cucumbers. Serve this delicious salad with slices of lightly toasted Italian semolina bread or Tuscan bread, gently rubbed with garlic and drizzled with olive oil.

1 to 1¼ pounds whole skinless,
    boneless chicken breasts, halved
12 ounces haricots verts
4 medium tomatoes
⅓ cup olive oil
¼ cup red wine vinegar
1 can (2 ounces) flat
    anchovy fillets, drained
1 tablespoon Dijon mustard
Salt and freshly ground
    black pepper
½ cup (4 ounces) pitted
    Kalamata or Spanish green olives
8 Boston or romaine lettuce leaves

1. Place the chicken breasts in a 12-inch skillet and add enough water to just cover them. Bring the water to a simmer and gently poach the chicken over low heat, covered, until just cooked, 10 minutes.

2. While the chicken is cooking, snap the tips off the haricots verts; then cut them into 1-inch lengths.

3. Remove the cooked chicken to a plate to cool, but save the cooking water. Bring it back to a boil over high heat. Add the green beans and cook, uncovered, over high heat, until just tender but cooked through, 3 to 4 minutes. Drain them under cold water, pat dry, and put in a mixing bowl. Core the tomatoes, cut them into 1-inch chunks, and combine them with the green beans.

4. Purée the oil, vinegar, anchovies, and mustard in a blender or food processor; season to taste with salt and pepper. Combine

the dressing with the green beans and tomatoes. Quarter the olives lengthwise. When the chicken has cooled down somewhat, pat it dry and cut it into 2 × ¾-inch strips. Add the chicken and the olives to the green beans and tomatoes. Toss the ingredients together to combine, and adjust the seasoning.

5. Rinse and dry the lettuce leaves, tear them into large pieces, and arrange them in a wreath on a platter. With a slotted spoon, transfer the chicken mixture to the middle of the platter. Drizzle the dressing remaining in the bowl over the lettuce.

HARICOTS VERTS

Years ago, green beans had to be picked by hand because they were so thin and tender. Today they have been bred to be thick and tough enough to be machine picked. This new variety of green bean may be great for the growers, but it's not terrific for the eaters, which is why I prefer the more expensive haricots verts. And speaking of delicious green beans, make sure you cook them long enough so they taste really good. It takes from 3 to 4 minutes for the slender haricots verts to be cooked through, and 5 minutes at least for the tougher American variety.

Confetti Pasta Chicken Salad

MAKES: *4 servings*
TIME: *25 to 30 minutes*

This recipe is so adaptable that it becomes the perfect "blueprint" for pasta chicken salads in general. Blending the raw carrots into the dressing gives the salad a marvelously subtle orange hue.

Salt
8 ounces (3 cups) fusilli or corkscrew pasta
2 whole skinless, boneless chicken breasts, halved (1 to 1¼ pounds)
2 carrots
½ cup olive oil
3 to 4 tablespoons white wine vinegar
2 teaspoons Dijon mustard
1 small red bell pepper
1 small green bell pepper
1 package (10 ounces) frozen corn (preferably white shoepeg corn), thawed
1 can (6 ounces drained weight) pitted jumbo black olives
Freshly ground black pepper

1. Bring a large pot of salted water to a boil over high heat. Add the pasta and cook until tender but still firm to the bite, 10 minutes. In

the last 4 minutes of cooking time, add the chicken breasts and simmer them gently, uncovered, over medium-low heat until cooked through.

2. While the water is coming to a boil and the pasta and chicken are cooking, prepare the rest of the salad. Coarsely chop the carrots, then purée them in a blender with the oil, vinegar, and mustard until they are minced and the dressing looks orange. Pour the dressing into a salad bowl.

3. Stem and seed the bell peppers, cut them into ½-inch dice, and add them to the carrot dressing. Pat the corn dry and add it to the peppers. Quarter the olives lengthwise, and add them to the corn. Toss these ingredients together, and season well with salt and pepper.

4. Remove the chicken from the pot and drain it on a plate. Drain the pasta separately, run it under cold water to stop the cooking process, and let it stand in a colander to drain while you cut the chicken.

5. Pat the chicken dry, and cut it into lengthwise strips about ½ inch wide. Then cut it into ½-inch cubes and add them to the salad bowl. Pat the pasta dry and add it to the salad bowl. Adjust the seasoning. Serve at room temperature, or if there is time, chill in the refrigerator before serving.

VARIATIONS

■ Instead of making a dressing of olive oil, vinegar, and mustard on the spot, use ¾ cup of the Basic Vinaigrette (page 64).
■ Instead of the mustard, add 2 to 4 tablespoons homemade basil purée, pesto, or any other herb purée (see pages 224 and 225).

Chicken Salad à la Caesar

MAKES: *4 servings*
TIME: *25 to 30 minutes*

Round up the usual Caesar Salad suspects—romaine lettuce, Parmesan cheese, and anchovies—hold the raw egg, add a dash of bell peppers and some slivers of cooked chicken, and you've got yourself one delicious dinner.

6 tablespoons extra-virgin olive oil

1½ pounds skinless, boneless chicken
  breasts, pounded thin

¼ cup vegetable oil

¼ cup white wine vinegar

2 cans (2 ounces each) flat
  anchovy fillets,
  drained

2 cloves garlic

Salt and freshly ground
  black pepper

4 scallions

2 red bell peppers, stemmed and
  seeded

8 to 12 leaves romaine lettuce,
  rinsed and dried

1 chunk (2 ounces) fresh Parmesan
  cheese

2 to 3 cups store-bought or homemade
  garlic croutons (see box)

1. Heat 2 tablespoons of the oil in a large skillet over medium-high heat. Sauté the chicken until cooked through, about 5 minutes per side. Remove it to a plate to cool for 10 minutes (or grill the chicken on a stovetop grill; see box, page 60).

2. While the chicken is cooking, combine the remaining 4 tablespoons olive oil with the vegetable oil, vinegar, anchovies, and garlic cloves in a blender and purée. Season to taste with salt and pepper, and transfer half of the dressing to a large mixing bowl.

3. Trim and thinly slice the scallions (white and green parts), and cut the bell peppers into

¾-inch dice; add them to the mixing bowl. Tear the lettuce into ¾-inch pieces and add them to the bowl. Toss the ingredients well to combine them with the dressing.

4. Cut the cooled chicken into 1-inch lengthwise strips, then across into ½-inch strips. Pour the remaining dressing over the chicken and let it stand for as long as possible so the chicken absorbs the flavor.

5. Right before serving, add the chicken to the mixing bowl and toss the ingredients together. Season to taste with salt and pepper. Let each person grate some Parmesan over their portion of salad, and garnish with croutons.

HOMEMADE GARLIC CROUTONS

Heat 2 tablespoons olive oil in a large skillet (preferably nonstick). Add 2 minced or pressed cloves garlic and sauté until you get a whiff of its aroma, about 10 seconds. Add 4 slices white bread, cut into ¾-inch cubes, and sauté over low heat, stirring frequently until the bread cubes have dried out and are somewhat crisp, 5 to 7 minutes. (The fresher and softer the bread, the more tender the croutons will be.) Season with salt and pepper. An alternative method, but one that takes more time, is to toss the bread cubes in the oil and garlic, then bake them in a 400°F oven until golden, 20 to 30 minutes.

Florida-Style Grilled Chicken Salad

MAKES: *4 servings*
TIME: *25 to 30 minutes*

This salad of grilled chicken set on a bed of avocado, mango, and cucumber is as stunning as it is delicious. If grilling is out of the question, then poach the chicken or substitute a roasted or barbecued chicken from the deli.

1¼ pounds skinless, boneless chicken
    (breasts or thighs)
Juice of 2 limes
1 teaspoon ground
    cumin
Salt
2 ripe mangoes
4 Kirby or 2 regular cucumbers
2 Hass avocados
Freshly ground black pepper
1 scallion, trimmed
⅓ cup vegetable oil
½ cup (packed) fresh cilantro leaves,
    rinsed
2 tablespoons white wine vinegar, or 4
    tablespoons Verjus (see page 16)

1. Trim the chicken of fat, and if the pieces are thicker than ½ inch, pound them between sheets of plastic wrap until they are more uniformly even. Combine half of the lime juice

OUTDOOR GRILLING INDOORS

While I have always been perfectly content with my urban lifestyle, one aspect of suburban summer living I always envied was my friends' access to an outdoor grill. My envy subsided with the advent of the stovetop grill pan. My favorite is probably the simplest one on the market: a heavy, wide cast-iron skillet with a ridged surface. You heat the pan on the stove, lightly brush the ingredients with oil, grill, and voilà—some of the flavor of outdoor living brought indoors.

with the cumin and 1 teaspoon salt, and rub this over the chicken.

2. Preheat the broiler or a stovetop grill over high heat.

3. While this is heating, peel the mangoes, cut them into ½-inch dice, and place them in a mixing bowl.

4. Broil or grill the chicken until cooked through, 4 to 6 minutes per side (depending upon the cut you are using). While the chicken is cooking, peel the cucumbers and cut them into thin slices (if you are using regular cucumbers, seed them before slicing) and add them to the mangoes.

5. Peel and pit the avocados, and cut into ½-inch dice; add them to the mangoes and cucumbers. Combine the remaining lime juice

with the mango mixture and season to taste with salt and pepper.

6. Remove the chicken to a cutting board to cool for 5 minutes. Cut the scallion (white and green parts) into chunks. Purée the oil, cilantro, scallion, and vinegar in a blender or food processor. Season well with salt and pepper. Cut the cooled chicken across the grain, on the diagonal, into thin slices.

7. To assemble, transfer some of the mango mixture to each plate, fan the chicken slices over it, and spoon the cilantro vinaigrette over the chicken. Serve at room temperature.

Asian Chicken Slaw

MAKES: *3 to 4 servings*
TIME: *25 to 30 minutes*

....

O ne night after work, I decided to create a no-cook salad out of ingredients that had been designated for a stir-fry. A spicy dressing emerged from the items intended for the sauce, and to that I added cabbage, carrot, and smoked chicken. The combination tasted too salty and needed something gentle to tame it. Luckily I had angel-hair pasta in the house, so I cooked some up,

tossed it with the other ingredients, and a delicious combination was born!

Salt
¼ cup vegetable oil
2 tablespoons Asian sesame oil
1 clove garlic, minced
¼ cup rice vinegar or white wine
    vinegar
1 teaspoon sugar
½ teaspoon dried red pepper flakes
2 tablespoons nuoc mam (bottled
    Asian fish sauce), or 1 tablespoon
    anchovy paste (optional)
¾ to 1 pound boneless smoked
    chicken or turkey breast
8 ounces angel-hair pasta or
    capellini
½ small head napa or Chinese
    cabbage, cored
2 carrots
½ cup (packed) basil leaves

1. Bring a large pot of salted water to a boil.

2. Meanwhile, combine the vegetable and sesame oils, garlic, vinegar, sugar, red pepper flakes, and nuoc mam in a mixing bowl. Remove the skin and fat from the chicken and cut the meat into thin lengthwise strips. Then cut the strips crosswise into thin shreds and add them to the bowl.

3. Add the pasta to the boiling water and cook until it is tender but

still firm to the bite, 3 to 4 minutes. Drain the pasta and rinse it under cold water to cool it completely. Drain the pasta again, pat it dry, and add it to the mixing bowl.

4. Finely shred the cabbage, and grate or finely chop the carrots. Roll the basil leaves up into tight cylinders, and cut across them to create fine shreds. Add the cabbage, carrots, and basil to the mixing bowl. Toss the salad and dressing, and adjust the seasoning if necessary.

VARIATION

If you don't have the time or desire to cook the pasta, then add twice as much cabbage. Or add 2 to 3 diced cucumbers and omit the nuoc mam. (If you don't make these adjustments, your salad will taste too salty.)

WHAT TO DO WITH THE OTHER HALF OF THE CABBAGE

If you are wondering what to do with the other half of that napa cabbage, substitute it for iceberg lettuce as taco topping or just use it up in salads throughout the week.

The Big Easy Chicken Salad

MAKES: *4 servings*
TIME: *20 to 25 minutes*

This chicken salad is described as the "big easy" not because of any New Orleans roots but because the flavors are big and yet it's incredibly easy to assemble. What makes it delicious is a complex flavor that emerges from the mingling of ingredients that, taken individually, are rather simple. What is crucial, however, is the quality of each ingredient. The tomatoes must be ripe, the asparagus at their peak season, the olive oil extra virgin, and the Parmesan cheese of the highest order.

> *1 pound fresh asparagus*
> *Salt*
> *2 whole boneless smoked chicken breasts (12 ounces each), or 4 cups bite-size pieces roasted or grilled chicken*
> *4 very ripe beefsteak tomatoes, cored*
> *Extra-virgin olive oil to taste*
> *Freshly ground black pepper*
> *Wedge of imported high-quality Parmesan cheese (preferably Parmigiano-Reggiano)*

1. Cut 1 inch off the bottoms of the asparagus and peel the stems. Bring an inch of salted water to a boil in a wide skillet. Add the asparagus and

cook them over medium heat until just cooked through, 4 to 5 minutes. Drain and rinse under cold water to stop the cooking process. Put the asparagus on a cloth towel to dry and cool to room temperature.

2. Remove the skin and fat from the chicken. Cutting on the diagonal, thinly slice the meat (the slices will come out unevenly shaped, but it doesn't matter). Slice the tomatoes into thin rounds.

3. To assemble the salad, set some of the asparagus on one side of each plate, and arrange a bed of sliced tomatoes next to the asparagus. Drizzle some oil over the asparagus and the tomatoes, and season them to taste with salt and pepper.

4. Using a vegetable peeler, shave thin slices of Parmesan over the tomatoes. Top them with slices of the chicken. Shave more Parmesan over the chicken, and drizzle more oil on top. Sprinkle with a generous grinding of pepper.

Bread and Chicken Salad

MAKES: *4 servings*
TIME: *30 minutes*

This salad is terrific for intolerably hot summer evenings because not a lick of cooking is required. This is inspired by *panzanella*, a clever Italian idea that turns dried-out bread into a delicious salad. This will be delicious *only* if you use a high-quality bread, such as a coarse-grain Italian-style country loaf or a great French bread. Also, the bread should be merely dried out—not stale, because stale taste can never be masked, no matter how flavorful the dressing.

> 8 ounces dried-out high-quality
>   whole-wheat country-style Italian
>   or French bread
> 1 whole (12 ounces) boneless smoked
>   chicken breast, or 2 cups bite-size
>   pieces of roasted or grilled chicken
> 2 Kirby cucumbers
> 2 scallions
> 4 tomatoes (about 1½ pounds)
> ½ cup (packed) fresh mint or parsley leaves
> 1 cup (4 ounces) walnut halves
> ½ cup Basic Vinaigrette (recipe follows)
> Salt and freshly ground black pepper

1. Cut the bread into 1-inch chunks and place them in a mixing bowl. Add cold water to cover, and let the bread soften while you work on the next steps.

2. Discard the skin and fat from the chicken, and cut the meat into ½-inch dice. Split the cucumbers in half lengthwise, remove the seeds, and cut into ½-inch dice. Trim and thinly slice the scallions (white and green parts). Quarter the tomatoes, remove the seeds with a spoon, and cut into ½-inch dice. Chop the mint and the walnuts. Prepare the dressing.

3. Thoroughly squeeze the bread to rid it of excess water, tear it into ½-inch pieces, and combine them with the other ingredients and the vinaigrette. Season to taste with 1 teaspoon salt and lots of pepper. Serve immediately, or chill for 30 minutes to blend the flavors.

VARIATIONS

- This bread salad combines well with diced Black Forest ham or smoked mozzarella cheese, as alternatives to the chicken.
- Omit the cucumbers and substitute 2 more tomatoes, seeded and diced.
- To add the right note of crunch without the fat, substitute 1 cup finely chopped fresh fennel or celery for the walnuts.

SECOND TIME AROUND

Roll up leftovers in Boston lettuce leaves and enjoy them as a snack. Or add lots of fresh arugula leaves to the leftover salad to wake up the taste.

Basic Vinaigrette

MAKES: *1 quart*
TIME: *15 minutes*

I can't understand why anyone would waste their money on bottled dressings when, in just a few minutes, a far superior one can be made at home. It's useful to make this basic dressing in a large batch because it stores indefinitely and you can remove a small amount and change its character daily by adding fresh herbs, spices, or grated cheeses. I prefer white to red wine vinegar because the color stays neutral and looks better on greens.

2 cups vegetable oil
1 cup extra-virgin olive oil
1 cup white wine vinegar
2 cloves garlic, lightly crushed
4 teaspoons Dijon mustard
Salt and freshly ground black pepper

1. Combine the vegetable and olive oils, the vinegar, garlic, and mustard in a mixing bowl. Whisk well to blend and season with 2 teaspoons of salt and freshly ground pepper to taste.

2. Transfer the mixture to a clean glass bottle with a lid. Cover and store in the refrigerator. Shake well before using.

VARIATIONS

- To each ¼ cup of Basic Vinaigrette, add 1 or more of the following:
1 tablespoon chopped fresh herbs or chives
½ teaspoon dried herbs or ¼ teaspoon dried spices
1 tablespoon crumbled or grated cheese
1 tablespoon chopped capers, pimientos, or black olives
1 to 2 teaspoons Homemade Exotic Pantry Ingredient, such as Dried Chili Paste, Tandoori Paste, Basil and Garlic Purée, or Olivada (beginning on page 222)
- To turn Basic Vinaigrette into a sauce: Warm 1 cup diced, seeded tomatoes with 1 cup Basic Vinaigrette in a nonreactive saucepan over low heat. Remove and season with salt and pepper. Serve with poultry burgers or plainly roasted, grilled or sautéed chicken.

Smoked Chicken Salad with Pears

MAKES: *4 servings*
TIME: *20 to 25 minutes*

....

This is a superb example of how the judicious choice of ingredients, and the way they are combined, results in the creation of an exquisite dish. The sweet pears, moist endive, and buttery walnuts temper the assertive smoked chicken.

1 small head Boston lettuce, leaves separated
⅓ cup walnut or hazelnut oil
⅓ cup vegetable oil
¼ cup olive oil
3 to 4 tablespoons white wine vinegar
Salt and freshly ground black pepper
2 smoked boneless chicken breasts (12 ounces each)
1 cup walnut halves
2 medium Belgian endives
4 Comice pears

1. Rinse the lettuce, shake off the excess moisture, and place the leaves on a clean cloth towel. Set another clean cloth towel over the leaves and roll up tightly. The cloths will absorb the moisture while you prepare the rest of the salad.

2. Combine the walnut and vegetable oils with the vinegar in a mixing bowl, and season well with salt and pepper.

3. Discard the skin of the chicken, and cut the meat into ½-inch cubes. Add it to the mixing bowl. Chop the walnuts and slice the endives into ½-inch rounds, and add them to the mixing bowl. Toss the ingredients together and season

to taste with salt and pepper. If the salad tastes flat, sprinkle it with more drops of vinegar.

4. Right before serving, peel, core, and cut the pears into ½-inch cubes. Tear the lettuce leaves into bite-size pieces. Add the pears and lettuce to the mixing bowl. Toss the ingredients together and adjust the seasoning. Serve the salad immediately.

VARIATION

When Comice pears are not in season, substitute 6 plums or 4 slightly underripe nectarines. If you can't find nut oils, purée 8 ounces walnuts or toasted hazelnuts with ⅔ cup vegetable oil in a blender; strain out the nuts and blend the oil with the vinegar in step 2.

SECOND TIME AROUND

Leftovers will appear a bit unsightly because of the wilted greens and endive. No matter—they'll taste delicious hidden in pita pockets.

"DRESSING UP" CHICKEN

If you have leftover cooked chicken, before storing it in the refrigerator, remove all fat and skin and toss it with enough Basic Vinaigrette to moisten. This will flavor the leftovers and help preserve them a little while longer.

Chopped Vegetable Chicken Salad

MAKES: *4 servings*
TIME: *35 minutes*

This salad is a good example of a recipe where the sum is grander than its parts. The ingredients are simple, but the blend is a satisfying mix of clean flavors and rich textures. I love to serve a coarse multigrain bread with this salad, and follow it with a chocolate dessert.

½ cup regular or low-fat mayonnaise
¼ cup regular or low-fat sour cream
3 tablespoons white wine vinegar
Salt and freshly ground black pepper
2 or 3 small carrots, grated
2 ribs celery, grated
2 or 3 radishes, grated
3 to 4 cups diced cooked chicken
2 tomatoes, cored
2 Kirby cucumbers
1 yellow or green bell pepper
1 small head Boston lettuce, leaves separated
2 tablespoons salad dressing of choice (optional)
¼ cup finely chopped pickled jalapeño peppers (optional)

1. Combine the mayonnaise with the sour cream and vinegar in a mixing bowl, and season with salt and pepper. (Add as much as

1½ teaspoons salt, or the salad will taste flat and the distinctive flavors won't emerge.)

2. Add the carrots, celery, radishes, and chicken to the mayonnaise, and adjust the seasoning.

3. Cut the tomatoes in half, remove the seeds with a spoon, and cut into ¼-inch dice. Cut the cucumbers in half lengthwise, remove the seeds with a spoon, and cut into ¼-inch dice. Stem and seed the bell pepper and cut it into ¼-inch dice. Combine the tomatoes, cucumbers, and bell pepper in a bowl, season lightly with salt and pepper, and reserve until later.

4. Rinse the lettuce and dry it well; tear the leaves into pieces and toss them with dressing, if you wish. To assemble the salad, set a bed of lettuce on each dinner plate, and top with a portion of chicken salad. Garnish the chicken with the tomato-cucumber-pepper mixture, and if you like your food fiery hot, garnish with the jalapeños.

Chinese Chicken Salad

MAKES: *4 servings*
TIME: *20 minutes*

Try this hot and spicy mixture on a sultry summer evening, when you have enough energy to chop a few ingredients but not to cook. Roasted, barbecued, or plain grilled chicken works best in this salad.

6 tablespoons vegetable oil
2 tablespoons Asian sesame oil
1 large clove garlic, coarsely chopped
⅓ cup rice vinegar or white wine vinegar
½ teaspoon sugar
⅓ cup peanut butter or unsalted roasted peanuts
½ to 1 teaspoon dried red pepper flakes
3 to 4 cups diced (¾ inch) cooked chicken
3 medium Kirby cucumbers
3 medium carrots
Salt
12 to 16 leaves Boston or romaine lettuce, rinsed and dried

1. Combine the vegetable and sesame oils, garlic, vinegar, sugar, peanut butter, and red pepper flakes in a blender or food processor and purée. Transfer the mixture to a mixing bowl and add the chicken.

2. Thinly slice the cucumbers and grate the carrots, and toss them with the chicken. Season to taste with salt.

3. Tear the lettuce leaves into large pieces and arrange them in a wreath on a platter. Center the chicken salad in the middle. Toss the lettuce and salad together before serving.

VARIATIONS

■ Substitute 1 cup bean sprouts for one of the cucumbers.

■ For a more Southeast Asian flavor, add ¼ cup unsweetened coconut milk to the dressing, along with ½ cup (packed) fresh cilantro leaves. Substitute lime or lemon juice for the vinegar.

DRYING THE LETTUCE

When I find it too much of a bother to get my salad spinner down from the top cabinet, I dry lettuce in the following way: I set the washed leaves on a cloth towel, lay another towel on top, and roll the towels up and press out the moisture. The leaves emerge nice and dry and ready to absorb the dressing.

Crunchy Chicken Salad

MAKES: *3 to 4 servings*
TIME: *20 to 25 minutes*

Crunchy water chestnuts and Asian pears give this salad lots of texture and a subtle sweetness that is surprising against the chili-flavored dressing. While I did not design this to be a low-fat salad, it turned out that way, making it attractive for reasons other than its super taste.

> 2 tablespoons Asian sesame oil or
>   hazelnut oil
> ¼ cup rice vinegar or mirin, or more
>   to taste
> 2 to 3 teaspoons chili paste with garlic
> 4 cups cooked chicken in bite-size
>   pieces
> 2 medium Asian (or Comice) pears,
>   peeled and cut into small dice
> 1 can (8 ounces) sliced water chestnuts,
>   chilled, drained, and patted dry
> 1 teaspoon salt
> 3 bunches watercress

1. Combine the oil with the vinegar and chili paste in a mixing bowl. Add the chicken, pears, and water chestnuts, and toss to combine well. Season with the salt. Taste and adjust the seasoning, adding more chili paste or vinegar, if you wish.

2. Discard the watercress stems; then rinse the leaves and pat dry.

3. To serve the salad, arrange a wreath of watercress leaves on each plate and pile the salad in the center—or mix the watercress right into the chicken salad.

Chili Chicken Waldorf Salad

MAKES: *4 servings*
TIME: *30 minutes*

I had always thought that Waldorf Salad included chicken. Not so. The original salad, created in the late nineteenth century at the Waldorf-Astoria Hotel in New York City, was made of celery, apples, and walnuts. I can see how chicken snuck into this combination, because its soft texture and neutral flavor marry happily with the crunch and sweetness of the other ingredients. My contributions of chili powder and sharp Cheddar cheese finish the salad rather nicely.

½ cup regular or low-fat mayonnaise
3 tablespoons white wine vinegar or
  rice vinegar
1 teaspoon chili powder
½ teaspoon minced garlic
Salt and freshly ground black pepper
3 to 4 cups cooked chicken or turkey
  breast, cut into bite-size chunks
1 cup finely diced peeled apples
1 cup finely chopped celery
½ cup coarsely chopped walnuts
12 romaine lettuce leaves, rinsed,
  dried, and torn into pieces
½ cup (1 ounce) grated sharp Cheddar
  cheese

1. Combine the mayonnaise, vinegar, chili powder, garlic, 1 teaspoon salt, and pepper to taste in a mixing bowl. Stir well.

2. Add the chicken, apples, celery, and walnuts and toss the ingredients together to combine. Adjust the seasoning.

3. Set some lettuce leaves on each dinner plate and top with the salad; garnish with the grated cheese.

Chicken Salad with Jicama and Grapefruit

MAKES: *4 servings*
TIME: *30 minutes*

The interplay of flavors and textures here—between the chicken, jicama, grapefruit, and walnut oil—is intriguing and unexpected. If you think this light salad, perfect for small appetites, won't be filling enough, then augment it with a dice of 2 ripe Hass avocados.

2 medium red or pink grapefruit
8 cups (loosely packed) field or
    red-leaf lettuce
4 cups diced skinless chicken or turkey
    (roasted, grilled, or smoked),
    cut into bite-size pieces
1 pound jicama, peeled and cut into
    ¼-inch dice, or 2 cans
    (8 ounces each) sliced water
    chestnuts, drained and chilled
⅓ cup thinly sliced red onion
¼ cup walnut or hazelnut oil
¼ cup balsamic vinegar
½ cup (packed) fresh mint leaves
Salt and freshly ground black pepper

1. With a sharp knife, peel the grapefruit, removing all the skin and white pith. Holding the grapefruit over a bowl to catch the juices, cut between the membranes to loosen the segments, and drop them into the bowl. Remove any seeds from the grapefruit segments. Squeeze the remaining juice into the bowl.

2. Rinse and dry the lettuce, and tear the leaves into pieces.

3. Add the chicken, jicama, and red onion to the grapefruit and toss with the oil and vinegar. Roll up the mint leaves into tight little logs. With scissors, cut across the mint "logs" to form thin shreds and add them to the bowl. Season with 1 teaspoon salt (at least) and lots of freshly ground pepper. Toss the ingredients together to thoroughly combine them, and adjust the seasoning.

4. Set a wreath of lettuce on each dinner plate and pile the chicken salad in the middle.

JICAMA

Nutty-tasting jicama can range in size from a reasonable 8-ounce tuber to a giant as heavy as 5 or 6 pounds. If you are stuck with an oversize beauty and have lots left over after you've used some in this salad, here are a couple of ideas on how to make use of the remains: Jicama's raw flesh adds an equally lovely crunch to fruit salads; try thin strips or small dice with orange segments, sweetened with honey and drizzled with lime juice. It is also fabulous as a substitute for water chestnuts in sautés and stir-fries.

Warm Rice and Chicken Salad

MAKES: *4 servings*
TIME: *30 to 35 minutes*

This rice and chicken combo is so basic that any dressing will do, but dressings that include chopped fresh basil or grated Parmesan cheese are especially delicious with it. The tomatoes serve a dual purpose—to add flavor and to moisten the rice—so if you substitute another vegetable, add a tad more dressing.

1¾ cups water
1 cup long-grain rice
Salt
2 lemons
⅓ cup olive oil
1 teaspoon dried oregano, or chopped fresh oregano to taste
24 pitted Spanish green or Kalamata olives
4 small ripe tomatoes
4 cups diced cooked chicken or turkey
Freshly ground black pepper
6 cups torn rinsed red-leaf lettuce

1. Combine the water, rice, and ½ teaspoon salt in a medium-size saucepan. Bring to a boil over medium heat, cover, and simmer over low heat until the rice is tender, 16 to 18 minutes.

2. While the rice is cooking, grate the zest of 1 lemon; then juice it and juice the second lemon. Combine the zest and juice with the oil, oregano, and olives.

3. Core the tomatoes and cut them into ½-inch dice. Combine the chicken and tomatoes in a salad bowl. Add half of the dressing and season with 1 teaspoon salt (or more) and freshly ground black pepper to taste. Toss the ingredients to mix.

4. Drain the rice, toss it with the remaining dressing, and spread it out on a baking sheet to cool quickly. After 5 minutes, when the rice has cooled slightly, stir it into the chicken and tomatoes and adjust the seasoning. Serve the salad at room temperature, on top of the lettuce.

VARIATION

Using Uncooked Chicken: If you don't have cooked chicken on hand, you can make this salad by cooking some raw chicken in an unorthodox way. Cook the rice in a larger saucepan, and after it has cooked for 10 minutes, top it with 1¼ pounds of skinless, boneless chicken breasts cut into ¾-inch chunks. Cover the pot and continue to cook the rice and chicken together until they are both cooked through, 10 minutes more. Drain the chicken and rice, and spread them out on a baking sheet to cool quickly.

Tonnato Chicken Salad

MAKES: *4 servings*
TIME: *30 to 35 minutes*

This is obviously inspired by *vitello tonnato,* an Italian dish of cold veal slices spread with a dressing made of tuna, mayonnaise, capers, and anchovies. The dish is heavenly—and I find it equally delicious when prepared with chicken.

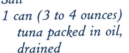
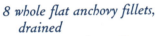

1¾ cups water
1 cup long-grain rice,
    preferably converted
Salt
1 can (3 to 4 ounces)
    tuna packed in oil,
    drained
8 whole flat anchovy fillets,
    drained
2 tablespoons drained capers
⅓ cup lemon juice, or more to taste
½ cup low-fat or regular mayonnaise
Dried red pepper flakes
3 cups diced cooked chicken or turkey
½ cup chopped fresh parsley
2 red or green bell peppers, stemmed,
    seeded, and cut into ½-inch dice

1. Place the water, rice, and ½ teaspoon salt in a medium-size saucepan. Bring to a boil over medium heat, cover and simmer over low heat until the rice is tender, 16 to 18 minutes.

2. Meanwhile, purée the tuna, anchovies, capers, lemon juice, and mayonnaise in a food processor or blender. Season to taste with salt and red pepper flakes, and add more lemon juice if needed.

3. Transfer half of the dressing to a bowl, and fold in the chicken and parsley.

4. Drain the rice and spread it on a baking sheet to cool to room temperature. Toss the rice with the remaining dressing. Toss with the bell peppers, and season to taste with salt and pepper. Serve the two salads side by side, or mix them together if you wish.

Greek-Style Chicken Salad

MAKES: *4 servings*
TIME: *30 to 35 minutes*

Kalamata olives and feta cheese capture the essence of Greek cuisine; however, for this salad to be as delicious as it should be, these ingredients must be of the highest quality. When in season, tomato wedges can be added to the mix. A coarse multigrain bread is delicious alongside; better yet, serve a room-temperature rice salad seasoned with slivers of roasted red peppers.

¾ cup Basic Vinaigrette (page 64)
1 teaspoon grated lemon zest
2 scallions, trimmed and thinly sliced
    (green and white parts)
4 cucumbers, preferably Kirby,
    seeded and sliced
24 pitted Kalamata
    olives, sliced
3 to 4 cups diced cooked chicken
    or turkey
Salt and freshly ground black pepper
1 head field or Boston lettuce, leaves
    separated
8 ounces feta cheese, crumbled

1. Place ½ cup of the salad dressing in a mixing bowl and stir in the lemon zest, scallions, cucumbers, olives, and chicken. Toss well to

combine, and season to taste with salt and freshly ground black pepper.

2. Rinse the lettuce leaves, pat them dry, and tear them into large pieces. In a separate mixing bowl, combine the lettuce with the remaining ¼ cup salad dressing.

3. Serve the chicken salad over the lettuce, and garnish with the feta cheese.

SECOND TIME AROUND

Leftovers are great as sandwich stuffers—especially delicious in pita bread pockets or wrapped in warm tortillas.

Turkey, Pecan, and Grape Salad

MAKES: *4 servings*
TIME: *20 to 25 minutes*

Sweet grapes and moist cucumbers provide a lovely contrast to the earthy turkey here. Whenever I use smoked poultry, I like to cut it fine so it's distributed throughout the salad.

½ cup regular or low-fat mayonnaise
¼ cup lime or lemon juice
Salt and freshly ground black pepper
1 small bunch fresh chives, or 1 scallion finely sliced (white and green parts)
1 to 1¼ pounds smoked turkey, in 1 piece, or 2 whole smoked or grilled chicken breasts, skinned
2 cups seedless green or red grapes
1 cup pecan halves, blanched almonds, or walnut halves
4 Kirby cucumbers
1 head Boston lettuce, leaves separated, rinsed, and dried

1. Combine the mayonnaise and lime juice in a mixing bowl. Season with ½ teaspoon salt and freshly ground black pepper to taste. With scissors, snip the chives into ⅛-inch pieces (you should have about ⅓ cup), and stir into the mayonnaise.

2. Cut the turkey into ½-inch dice and add to the mayonnaise. Rinse and dry the grapes, finely chop the nuts, and peel, seed, and dice the cucumbers. Add to the mixing bowl. Toss the ingredients together and adjust the seasoning.

3. Tear the lettuce into large pieces and serve the turkey salad over the lettuce.

ESPECIALLY GOOD FOR DIETERS

Substitute low-fat yogurt for the mayonnaise, and omit the nuts. This variation of the salad is so satisfying, you may prefer it to the original.

French Turkey Salad

MAKES: *4 servings*
TIME: *25 minutes*

....

This tastes most "French" when prepared with fresh tarragon, and is of course delightful served with a terrific loaf of French bread.

⅔ cup regular or low-fat
    mayonnaise
2 teaspoons Dijon mustard
2 tablespoons chopped fresh
    tarragon, or 2 teaspoons dried
¼ cup chopped cornichons or kosher
    dill pickles
¼ cup lemon juice, or more to taste
¼ cup finely diced red onion
Salt and freshly ground black pepper
2 cups finely diced fresh fennel,
    finely diced celery, or grated carrot
4 cups bite-size chunks of cooked
    turkey or chicken
8 cups mesclun

1. Combine the mayonnaise, mustard, tarragon, cornichons, lemon juice, and red onion in a large mixing bowl. Mix well and season to taste with salt and pepper. Add the fennel and the turkey or chicken, and toss to mix; adjust the seasoning.

2. Rinse and thoroughly dry the mesclun, and serve alongside or as a bed for the turkey salad.

VARIATION

To make this Italian in style, substitute basil for the tarragon and sliced pitted black olives for the pickles.

ESPECIALLY GOOD FOR CHILDREN

For the kids, make a dressing of ⅓ cup mayonnaise and ⅓ cup ketchup; combine it with half of the turkey and celery (not fennel).

Blue Cheese Dressing

MAKES: *About ½ cup*
TIME: *5 minutes*

....

Keep this recipe in mind when you have some leftover blue cheese in your refrigerator. This dressing is marvelous spooned over mild-flavored salads and vegetables, such as steamed broccoli.

⅓ cup regular or low-fat plain yogurt
¼ cup crumbled blue cheese, or more
    to taste
2 tablespoons mayonnaise

Place the yogurt, blue cheese, and mayonnaise in a small bowl. Gently stir to combine. Serve immediately or refrigerate, covered, until ready to use.

Sandwich Suppers

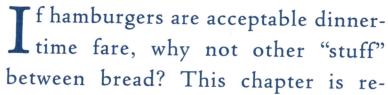

If hamburgers are acceptable dinner-time fare, why not other "stuff" between bread? This chapter is remarkably large because I love sandwiches—any time of the day, for any occasion, any time of the year—and had to restrain myself from adding even more recipes!

Sandwich suppers are perfect for nights when you have even less energy than usual to prepare dinner, and for times when your appetite is not enormous. Most of the recipes in this chapter are for 2 people only, because working couples and single people often have a large lunch and are more apt to be content with sandwiches and salad for dinner than are families with small children. If you need to serve more people, double the recipe—it will add only 5 to 10 minutes more to the preparation time.

My definition of a sandwich supper is broad and all-encompassing. It can consist of a towering double-decker club sandwich, an Italian loaf that is stuffed, baked, and served hot, or a creamy chicken and vegetable mélange spooned inside puff pastry shells. These sandwich confections come hot and cold, which means that there are delicious choices for winter as well as summer. An accompanying salad or vegetable is all it takes to turn the sandwich into a more than satisfying supper.

THE BIRD
BETWEEN THE BREAD

Any form of cooked chicken or turkey will do for sandwiches. Per person you need about 3 ounces of poultry—Sunday's roast chicken, slices of smoked turkey from the deli, chunks of warm grilled chicken, or rounds of spicy poultry sausage.

THE BREAD
AROUND THE BIRD

The bread part of the sandwich is what interests me the most. My husband introduced me to the essential pleasure of having bread on the table at every meal. Because it is such an integral part of our meals, I have come to rely on keeping a stash of various types of bread on hand, and their subtle differences introduce variety to our menu planning.

My definition of bread is a liberal one. As far as I am concerned, anything doughy—pizza crusts, corn tortillas, puff pastry cases—counts as bread. Using the same filling, a sandwich made with Italian semolina tastes different from one made with toasted rye. Often the bread itself inspires the flavor of the filling—pumpernickel makes me think of Eastern European and German flavors, whereas sliced white bread brings to mind the irresistible American chicken salad sandwich.

THE DRESSINGS AND
TOPPINGS

A sandwich changes from drab to delicious when you stash something special between the bread: a smear of eggplant caponata, a dash of roasted peppers, or an elaborate confection of mayonnaise blended with minced herbs and chopped pickles, to moisten the sandwich as it gives it character.

THE SALAD WITH
THE SANDWICH

Even though a chunky hero sandwich is dinner enough for me, I prefer to round out the meal by serving an accompanying salad. Sure, greens tossed with vinaigrette are always companionable, but don't get stuck on that idea. The salads that accompany the sandwiches in these recipes were developed to enhance the flavor of the chicken and dressing, and so the two, when eaten with each other, become an integral taste treat.

Chicken Po' Boys

MAKES: *2 to 3 servings*
TIME: *35 minutes*

This heavenly combo was inspired by a New Orleans sandwich of fried cornmeal-coated oysters, slathered with tartar sauce and wedged between pieces of crusty bread. In this

leaner but equally delicious version, mustard- and garlic-seasoned chicken replaces the oysters, but the tartar sauce remains. This is deliciously messy, so tie a large napkin around your neck before digging in.

> 8 to 10 ounces skinless, boneless
>   chicken breasts or chicken "tenders"
> 1 tablespoon Dijon mustard
> ½ teaspoon minced garlic or garlic paste
> Salt and freshly ground black pepper
> ¼ cup dried bread crumbs
> 1 loaf (8 to 12 ounces) Italian bread
> 2 to 3 tablespoons butter, melted
> 1 cup (2 ounces) iceberg lettuce or
>   1 small bunch arugula
> ¼ cup tartar sauce (store-bought or
>   homemade; recipe follows)
> 2 tomatoes, cored

1. Preheat the oven to 350°F.

2. Cut the chicken into ½-inch chunks. Combine the mustard and garlic in a mixing bowl; season to taste with salt and pepper. Toss the chicken with this mixture, and then dredge the pieces in the bread crumbs. Arrange the chicken on a nonstick baking sheet (or on one coated with vegetable spray). Bake until cooked through and crisp, 20 minutes.

3. While the chicken is cooking, slice the bread in half horizontally with a serrated knife. Pull out the soft crumbs from both top and bottom halves (reserve to make bread crumbs if you wish; see box, page 78). Spread the melted butter over the hollowed-out halves

and set them, cut side up, on a baking sheet. Bake for 15 minutes.

4. While the chicken and bread bake, rinse and shred the lettuce or rinse the arugula, and pat the leaves dry (you should have 1 cup of greens). Thinly slice the tomatoes, and start preparing the tartar sauce if you are making it from scratch.

5. To assemble the sandwiches, spread the top and bottom halves of the baked bread with the tartar sauce. Nestle the baked chicken in the bottom half, and top with lettuce and tomatoes. Cover with the remaining bread. Cut the sandwich in quarters, and if you care anything about neatness, eat them with a knife and fork.

ESPECIALLY GOOD FOR CHILDREN

For a milder version that children will enjoy, dip the chicken in ketchup or barbecue sauce rather than in mustard.

WHAT TO DO WITH THE INSIDE OF THE BREAD

While the oven is still on, bake the inner white bread crumbs at 350°F for 10 minutes, or until browned and dried. Pulverize in a food processor or blender, and keep as dried bread crumbs. Keep the crumbs in a loosely covered jar; don't store them airtight or they will turn moldy.

Homemade Tartar Sauce

*1 scallion, trimmed and cut into
    chunks (white and green parts)
1 small (2 ounces) sour dill pickle
¼ cup (packed) fresh parsley leaves
½ cup regular or low-fat mayonnaise
1 teaspoon Creole or Dijon mustard
Salt
⅛ teaspoon cayenne pepper*

Mince the scallion, pickle, and parsley in a food processor or blender. Combine with the mayonnaise and mustard, and season with salt and the cayenne pepper.

Pita Stuffed with Sesame Chicken

MAKES: *4 servings*
TIME: *30 minutes*

The grand flavors of tahini, garlic, lemon juice, and herbs can't help but make chicken taste great. I cook the chicken in an iron skillet that's just brushed with a bit of oil to give it a subtle charred taste. (You could also grill the chicken on an indoor grill if you have one.)

1 teaspoon vegetable oil
4 skinless, boneless chicken breast
    halves, "tenders" removed
2 tomatoes (8 ounces each)
4 Kirby cucumbers (3 ounces each)
1 cup plain yogurt
Salt
Cayenne pepper
4 tablespoons water
2 tablespoons tahini
    (see box, page 80)
2 tablespoons lemon
    juice
¼ teaspoon dried oregano
½ cup (packed) fresh flat-leaf parsley
    or cilantro leaves
1 teaspoon minced garlic
4 pita pockets (6-inch size)
2 cups (loosely packed) alfalfa, radish,
    or mustard sprouts

1. Preheat the oven to 300°F.

2. Wrap the pitas in aluminum foil and set
them in the oven to warm while you prepare
the filling.

3. Brush a 10-inch cast-iron skillet with the oil
and set it over medium heat. Add the chicken
breast halves and the tenders, and cook without moving for 5 minutes. A bit of smoke will
rise from the pan, but don't worry. Turn the
tenders and breast halves. Cook the tenders
until just cooked through, for 3 minutes more,
and the breast halves for 5 minutes more.

4. During this time, core the tomatoes and
cut them into ½-inch dice. Peel and halve the

cucumbers; if they are large, cut them in half
again lengthwise. Then cut them into thin
slices. In a bowl, combine the tomatoes and
cucumbers with the yogurt, and season to taste
with salt and cayenne pepper. In another
bowl, stir 2 tablespoons of the water into the
tahini, and combine it with the lemon juice
and oregano. Coarsely chop the parsley and
stir into the tahini; season to taste with salt and
cayenne pepper.

5. When the chicken is done, remove it to a
plate and remove the skillet from the heat. Add
the garlic and the remaining 2 tablespoons
water to the skillet (the pan will steam up), and
with a wooden spoon scrape up any drippings
from the pan. Add the contents of the skillet to
the tahini mixture. Cut the warm chicken into
½-inch chunks, and combine them with the
tahini sauce. Adjust the seasoning.

6. Remove the pitas from the oven, open
them up, and stuff with the chicken and
sprouts. Serve the stuffed pitas with the
tomato and cucumber salad alongside.

TAHINI TIPS

Tahini is a paste made of raw sesame seeds. It has the consistency of peanut butter and is used in the Middle East kitchen. Tahini has a wonderful flavor and is a boon to the Monday-to-Friday pantry because just a little can inject great flavor into a simple dish. It is available in specialty food stores and comes packaged in cans or jars. Once opened, it should be refrigerated so that is does not turn rancid. Given that tahini is sold in large quantities yet most recipes don't require a lot, here are a few ideas on ways to use it in everyday cooking. Tahini doesn't do well when subjected to heat, so use it in room-temperature or cold preparations only. Thinning it with water first prevents it from clumping up when you add other seasonings and flavorings.

■ Thin ¼ cup tahini with ¼ cup water, and flavor to taste with grated lemon zest and juice and lots of chopped scallions and parsley. This is a great dipping sauce for steamed vegetables.

■ Make a paste of tahini thinned with an equal amount of water. Flavor it with chopped fresh parsley, mint, chives, and cilantro. Add plain yogurt to taste, and add to warm boiled potatoes for a special dressing.

■ Thin 1 tablespoon tahini with 1 tablespoon water, and blend with 1 tablespoon balsamic vinegar. Season with pressed garlic and Dijon mustard for a salad dressing that's great with hearty greens such as escarole, frisée, or radicchio.

■ Make a paste of equal parts tahini and water, add minced garlic and lemon juice, and mix with cooled cooked spinach or broccoli di rabe. Season with dried red pepper flakes.

Creamed Chicken in Puff Pastry

MAKES: *4 servings*
TIME: *30 minutes*

O ne of my all-time favorite culinary memories from my childhood in Belgium is of puff pastry stuffed with creamed mushrooms. These elegant rounds were served as an appetizer in many a simple restaurant in Antwerp, where I grew up. Even then an appetizer portion was never enough. Here I've stretched the appetizer into a main course by amplifying the mushrooms with diced cooked chicken and peas. With frozen patty shells readily available, this comforting yet sophisticated dish becomes feasible even during the week.

8 frozen puff pastry shells
8 ounces mushrooms
2 tablespoons butter
2 tablespoons vegetable oil
1 large clove garlic, minced or
*   put through a garlic press*
3 tablespoons all-purpose flour
½ cup milk
1 cup chicken broth
2 tablespoons Madeira
10 to 12 ounces skinless grilled
*   or roasted chicken*
1 cup frozen "petite" peas, thawed
Salt
Pinch of cayenne pepper

1. Preheat the oven and bake the puff pastry shells according to the package instructions.

2. While the shells bake, trim ¼ inch off the bottom of the mushroom stems. Wipe the mushrooms clean with a damp paper towel, and cut into ¼-inch-thick slices. Heat the butter and oil in a large saucepan over medium heat. Add the garlic and sauté for a few seconds, until the aroma wafts up. Add the mushrooms and cook over medium-high heat, stirring frequently, until they begin to release their juices, about 3 minutes.

3. Add the flour and stir with a wooden spoon for about 1 minute, or until the mushrooms look dry and begin to stick to the bottom of the pan. Add the milk and whisk vigorously. When the mixture is thick, add the broth and Madeira. Simmer, uncovered, over low heat for about 5 minutes.

4. While the sauce mixture is cooking, cut the chicken into ½-inch dice (you should have about 3 cups), and add it to the sauce along with the peas. Simmer until the puff pastry shells are done, about 5 minutes more. Season carefully with salt and a pinch of cayenne.

5. Remove the puff pastry shells from the oven and set aside for 1 minute to cool. Remove the tops of the pastry shells. Place 2 shells on each of the serving plates. Spoon some filling in and

around each shell and place the pastry tops back onto each shell. Serve immediately.

VARIATIONS

- To intensify the mushroom flavor, substitute shiitake mushrooms for the cultivated ones, and the liquid from soaking porcini mushrooms (see page 235) for the chicken broth.
- A simpler way of serving this dish would be to spoon the mixture over toast rather than into pastry shells.
- If you add 1 cup each of milk and chicken broth, you will transform the filling into a rich cream soup.

Italian-Style Grilled Cheese and Chicken

MAKES: *2 servings*
TIME: *20 to 25 minutes*

This delicious recipe is my Italian version of the French *croque monsieur*, a ham and Swiss cheese sandwich that is dipped in egg and fried. I substitute chicken or turkey for the ham and mozzarella for the Swiss cheese, and I spread either eggplant purée or chopped sun-dried tomatoes on the meat to give it an Italian flair. The lush richness of the sandwich is balanced with a simple salad of steamed fresh fennel mingled with peppery watercress and tossed with an olive and lemon dressing.

> 1 large bulb (about 1½ pounds)
>   fresh fennel
> 2 tablespoons green or black olive paste
> 2 tablespoons lemon juice
> 1 bunch watercress
> Salt and freshly ground black pepper
> 4 slices egg bread or challah
> 4 ounces skinless roasted chicken or
>   turkey, sliced or diced
> 4 ounces fresh mozzarella cheese,
>   diced or thinly sliced
> 2 to 3 tablespoons eggplant purée
>   (caponata) or minced sun-dried
>   tomatoes packed in oil, drained
> 1 tablespoon olive or vegetable oil
> 1 egg
> 2 teaspoons water

1. Bring some water to a boil in a vegetable steamer. While the water is heating, cut away the feathery fronds and ribs of the fennel until you are left with just the bulb. Trim away any brownish parts. Cut out and discard the triangular core, and then cut the fennel lengthwise into ½-inch-wide strips. Rinse in cold water and place in the steamer. Cover, reduce the heat, and cook over sim-

mering water for 2 to 3 minutes to tenderize the fennel a bit. This softens the texture and tames the flavor.

2. While the fennel is steaming, combine the olive paste and lemon juice in a mixing bowl. Hold the bunch of watercress by the stems and rinse the leaves under running water. Pat the leaves dry and cut them away from the stems. (You can keep the stems for stir-fries.) When the fennel is done, remove it from the steamer, pat it dry, and toss it with the olive paste, lemon juice, and watercress. Toss again, and season to taste with salt and pepper.

3. Make 2 sandwiches, layering them as follows: bread, chicken, cheese, eggplant purée, then chicken again, cheese, and bread. Trim the meat so that it does not escape the bread. With your hands, press down to compress the sandwiches.

4. Brush a medium-size skillet with olive oil and heat it over moderate heat. Blend the egg and water together in a shallow dish. Dip the sandwiches in the egg, coating both sides, and cook on each side until they are golden brown and the cheese has melted, about 2 minutes per side.

5. To serve, arrange the fennel salad in the middle of a dinner plate. Cut each sandwich into 4 triangles, and surround the salad with the sandwich triangles.

ESPECIALLY GOOD FOR CHILDREN

I have found that most children enjoy this sandwich if the eggplant or sun-dried tomatoes is omitted.

Hot Picnic Loaf

MAKES: *4 to 6 servings (2 to 3 per loaf)*
TIME: *25 to 30 minutes*

In my first Monday-to-Friday cookbook, I have a recipe for picnic loaf, a hollowed-out crusty round bread filled with layers of peppers, chick-peas, capers, and smoked mussels. This version is more unusual but equally delicious: rounds of bread are hollowed out, stuffed with smoked turkey and ricotta cheese, and then baked until the cheese filling is oozy and the crust crackling. During the time it takes to bake this loaf, you can make the side dish of escarole or broccoli rabe cooked in garlic and olive oil. The slightly bitter edge of the greens is perfect against the smoked turkey and warm ricotta cheese.

2 *round white or whole-wheat Italian*
loaves (6 to 7 inches in diameter;
they should have a crisp crust and
feel heavy for their size)
6 *to 8 ounces thinly sliced smoked,*
baked, or roasted turkey
½ *cup marinated artichoke hearts,*
drained
½ *cup bottled roasted red peppers,*
drained
½ *cup pitted Kalamata olives*
1 *pint whole milk or part-skim*
ricotta cheese
¼ *cup olive oil*
2 *heads (1 pound)*
escarole or
broccoli rabe
2 *cloves garlic*
Salt
Dried red pepper
flakes

1. Preheat the oven to 350°F.

2. Using a sharp serrated knife, cut out a circle in the top of the breads (this will be the cap). Set the caps aside and with your fingers, remove as much of the bread interior as possible without breaking through the crust. (Save the interior to make dried bread crumbs; see box, page 78.)

3. Line each of the bread cavities with overlapping turkey slices, so they radiate from the center of the loaves, covering the interior sides and hanging over the edge.

4. Chop the artichokes, red peppers, and olives, and combine them with the ricotta. Spoon half of the mixture into each loaf, pushing it toward the outside edges. Fold the ends of the turkey slices over the mixture to enclose it, and set the bread caps back in place. Set the loaves on a baking sheet and brush the outside crusts with a tablespoon or so of the olive oil. Bake for 15 to 20 minutes so the insides warm throughout.

5. While the loaves are baking, remove the outer leaves of the escarole, cut off the base, and rinse the leaves in lots of cold water. Drain the escarole but do not dry it, and tear the leaves into big pieces.

6. Remove the bread from the oven and let it cool while you cook the escarole. Heat the remaining olive oil in a large skillet. Peel the garlic and crush it through a press into the skillet. Cook for a few seconds, or until golden but not brown. Add the escarole and cook, uncovered, stirring occasionally, until just wilted, 2 to 3 minutes. Season to taste with salt and red pepper flakes.

7. Cut the loaves into wedges, and serve with the escarole on the side.

**ESPECIALLY
GOOD FOR
CHILDREN**

Stuff one of the loaves with just turkey and plain ricotta cheese.

Chicken Reuben Sandwich

MAKES: *2 dinner servings*
TIME: *15 to 20 minutes*

Here's a wonderful hot sandwich, bound to satisfy those who want something hot yet light for dinner. In the classic Reuben, Swiss cheese and sauerkraut are paired with corned beef, but I think smoked turkey or roasted chicken is a terrific substitute. Don't stint on the quantity of cheese because you need its velvety quality to offset the tang of the beets and sauerkraut. The combination of the salad and sandwich is remarkable in its balance of flavors.

1 Granny Smith apple
1 jar (16 ounces) sliced pickled beets
Salt and freshly ground black pepper
8 ounces sauerkraut
6 slices seedless rye bread
8 slices Swiss cheese
8 slices roasted chicken or smoked turkey
2 tablespoons butter

1. Core, peel, and cut the apple into ½-inch dice; place in a mixing bowl. Drain the beets, rinse them under cold water, drain them again, and pat them dry. Add the beets to the apples and toss to combine. Season with salt and pepper, cover, and refrigerate until ready to serve.

2. Drain and rinse the sauerkraut, and squeeze out the excess moisture. For each sandwich, spread 1 slice of rye bread with a quarter of the sauerkraut; then add 2 slices of the Swiss cheese and 2 slices of the chicken. Cover this layer with another slice of rye bread, and layers of sauerkraut, cheese, and chicken. Top with a slice of rye and press down.

3. Right before you are ready to eat, melt the butter over medium heat in a skillet large enough to comfortably hold the sandwiches. When the foaming subsides, add the sandwiches, set another heavy skillet on top to press them down, and cook over low heat until the bottom side is brown and crusty and the cheese is beginning to melt, about 2 minutes. Turn the sandwiches over, set the second skillet on top, and cook until the second side is brown and crusty and the cheese is completely melted, 2 minutes more. Remove the sandwiches from the heat, slice each one in half, and serve with the beet and apple salad.

ESPECIALLY GOOD FOR CHILDREN

Substitute coleslaw for the sauerkraut and serve on whole-wheat or multigrain bread.

Quick Chicken Pizzas

MAKES: *1 large or 2 small servings*
TIME: *10 minutes to assemble*
10 minutes to bake

These chicken pizzas are fast to prepare because you start out with baked bready dough, such as tortillas, pita breads, or Boboli shells, which function as the crust. The topping is cooked chicken combined with bottled sauce, cheese, and a seasoning of choice. You'll have just a little bit of work in grating or crumbling the cheese or pitting some olives or snipping fresh herbs—but that's about it. Of course a couple of small pizzas does not a dinner make (for adults, that is), so precede them with a steamed vegetable or accompany them with a vegetable salad. The proportions are for 1 serving only; use the recipe as a blueprint to fashion as many pizzas as there are people and appetites.

THE DOUGH
1 or 2 pizza crusts, such as Boboli shells, regular or whole-wheat pita breads, or burrito-size tortillas

THE SAUCE
2 small ripe tomatoes, sliced, or ½ cup prepared tomato sauce

THE CHICKEN
1 cup finely diced or shredded cooked chicken or turkey

THE CHEESE
¼ to ½ cup crumbled or shredded mozzarella, goat's cheese, ricotta, or extra-sharp Cheddar

THE FLAVORINGS OR TOPPINGS
¼ teaspoon dried herb, such as oregano or rosemary, or 2 tablespoons chopped fresh basil or parsley, or 2 tablespoons sliced pitted black olives or chopped onion

1 to 2 teaspoons olive oil
Salt and freshly ground black pepper

1. Preheat the oven to 450°F.

2. Set the crust or crusts on a baking sheet. Scatter the tomatoes or sauce over the top, then dot with the chicken, cheese, and flavorings or toppings of choice.

3. Drizzle the toppings with the olive oil, and season to taste with salt and pepper. Bake until the cheese has melted, 10 minutes.

Chicken Pizza Pockets

MAKES: *2 adult or 4 children's servings*
TIME: *15 minutes preparation*
20 minutes no-work baking time

....

These pizza pockets stuffed with chicken and cheese are great for kids and are wonderful for nights when everyone's on the run. During the time it takes to bake them, prepare a side dish of tomatoes vinaigrette or steamed broccoli.

1 cup finely chopped grilled or roasted chicken
½ cup shredded mozzarella cheese
¼ cup grated Parmesan cheese
Salt and freshly ground black pepper
All-purpose flour
1 package (10 ounces) refrigerated pizza dough

1. Preheat the oven to 425°F. Lightly oil a baking sheet.

2. Combine the chicken with the cheeses in a mixing bowl, and season carefully with salt and pepper (if you don't, these pockets won't have much flavor).

3. Lightly flour a work surface and unroll the dough. Divide the dough into 4 equal pieces.

4. Spread the filling over the 4 pieces of dough, leaving a ½-inch border unfilled.

Brush the edges of one piece of dough with water, and fold the dough in half, stretching it over the filling to form a small rectangle. Using a spatula, transfer the pocket to the prepared baking sheet. Flatten the pocket with your hands, and seal the edges well with the tines of a fork. Repeat with the other 3 packages. Bake the pockets for 5 minutes.

5. Prick the tops with a fork and bake for another 10 minutes. Turn the pockets over and bake until they are golden brown, 10 minutes more. Cool for 5 minutes before serving.

VARIATIONS

■ Substitute ½ cup ricotta cheese for the mozzarella.
■ To the chicken and cheese, add either 2 to 3 tablespoons chopped fresh basil or olive paste, or ½ cup chopped drained marinated artichoke hearts, caponata, or slivered roasted peppers.

Chicken Club Sandwich

MAKES: *2 servings*
TIME: *20 minutes*

....

When I was a little girl, I thought a club sandwich was the height of elegance. I don't know what it was about the sandwich that appealed to me so—maybe the towering look of it—but eating it made me feel grown-up and special. Today, at the end of a busy day, every now and then I treat myself to a club sandwich because it brings back such pleasant childhood memories.

> 6 slices turkey bacon or regular bacon
> 6 to 8 leaves field, Boston, or romaine lettuce
> 3 tablespoons salad dressing of choice, such as Basic Vinaigrette (page 64)
> 1 beefsteak tomato, cored
> 6 ounces cooked chicken or turkey
> 6 slices white or whole-wheat bread
> 3 to 4 tablespoons low-fat or regular mayonnaise
> Salt and freshly ground black pepper

1. Cook the bacon slices in an iron skillet over low heat, turning them frequently, until crisp, about 10 minutes. (If you prefer, cook the bacon in your microwave oven following the manufacturer's directions.) Set the bacon aside on paper towels.

2. Rinse and dry the lettuce leaves, and tear them into pieces to make about 4 cups. Toss the lettuce with the dressing and set aside until later. Thinly slice the tomato, and tear the chicken into bite-size chunks.

3. Right before dinner, toast the bread lightly and spread the slices with the mayonnaise. To assemble a sandwich, cover 1 slice of toast with 3 strips of bacon and some slices of tomato.

Add a second slice of toast, mayonnaise side down. Top the toast with half of the chicken and more tomato slices, and season lightly with salt and pepper. Cover with the third slice of toast, mayonnaise side down, and cut the sandwich in half on the diagonal. Repeat for the second sandwich. Serve the sandwiches with the salad.

VARIATIONS

- *Instead of plain mayonnaise, spread the bread with mayonnaise mixed with chili powder or ground cumin.*
- *Mix the mayonnaise with Indian chutney to taste, and substitute slices of sharp Cheddar cheese for the bacon. (This works nicely with smoked and grilled poultry as well as regular cooked chicken or turkey.)*

Tearoom Sandwiches with Carrot and Apple Slaw

MAKES: *2 servings*
TIME: *20 minutes*

This sandwich is filled with a chicken paste so delicate and fine, it is reminiscent of the sandwiches served in England for high tea.

The curry powder lends a subtle flair, and the crunch of the apple and carrot slaw is lovely against the smooth filling.

>   4 carrots
>   1 McIntosh apple
>   2 tablespoons vegetable oil
>   4 tablespoons lemon juice
>   Salt and freshly ground black pepper
>   2 to 3 tablespoons regular or
>   low-fat mayonnaise
>   ⅛ teaspoon curry powder
>   ½ cup walnut halves or pieces
>   1 cup diced cooked chicken
>   4 slices white or whole-wheat bread

1. Slice the carrots wafer thin, or grate them with the shredding disk in a food processor. Peel and core the apple, and finely dice it or grate in the food processor. Combine the oil with 2 tablespoons of the lemon juice, and toss with the carrots and apple. Season to taste with salt and pepper, and set aside.

2. Combine the mayonnaise with the remaining 2 tablespoons lemon juice, the curry powder, and the walnuts in the food processor, and purée. When the mixture is finely puréed, add the chicken and pulse until finely chopped. Don't worry if the mixture turns a bit pasty; that's an appropriate texture for this type of sandwich. Season the chicken mixture with salt and pepper, and spread between the bread slices. Serve with the carrot and apple slaw.

ESPECIALLY GOOD FOR DIETERS

Substitute yogurt for the mayonnaise and omit the walnuts, adding a bit more carrot for crunch.

ESPECIALLY GOOD FOR COMPANY

These Tearoom Sandwiches are wonderful sandwiches to serve if you are entertaining at brunch or lunchtime. Add just a pinch of cayenne pepper to really liven things up.

California Pita Pockets

MAKES: *2 servings*
TIME: *25 minutes*

I named these "California" pockets because when I think of alfalfa sprouts and cilantro in a sandwich, I am always reminded of the style of eating in that state. The flavors are vibrant and tangy—a refreshing sandwich for a summer evening.

½ cup (packed) fresh cilantro leaves
¼ cup low-fat or regular mayonnaise
2 limes
2 cups finely chopped cooked chicken
Salt
Pinch of cayenne pepper
1 beefsteak tomato (12 ounces), cored
1 Hass avocado
2 pita pockets (6-inch size)
1 cup alfalfa sprouts

1. Rinse, dry, and finely chop the cilantro leaves. Combine the cilantro with the mayonnaise and the juice of 1 lime. Mix the chicken with the mayonnaise, and season to taste with salt and cayenne pepper.

2. Cut the tomato into ½-inch dice. Peel and pit the avocado, and cut into ½-inch dice. Combine the tomato and avocado in a bowl, and squeeze the juice of ½ lime over them. Taste, and add more lime juice if necessary. Season to taste with salt and cayenne pepper.

3. Right before eating, warm the pita breads for a few seconds on each side in an ungreased iron skillet set over medium heat. Remove the breads from the heat, open them up, and stuff them with the chicken salad and sprouts. Serve with the tomato and avocado salad.

VARIATION

Middle Eastern Style: Substitute ¼ cup (packed) fresh mint leaves for the cilantro, and ¼ cup plain yogurt for the mayonnaise; omit the lime juice. Toss the tomatoes with 2 diced peeled Kirby cucumbers instead of the avocado, and season with plain yogurt to taste, salt, and cayenne pepper.

Cheddar Chicken Rarebit

MAKES: *2 dinner servings*
TIME: *15 to 20 minutes*

Y ou won't find a quicker or more comforting and delicious meal than this amplified version of Welsh Rarebit. By piling chicken and tomatoes on the toast before spooning on the satiny cheese sauce, the traditional luncheon dish turns into a substantial supper. Crisp slices of bell pepper are all you need for a satisfying accompaniment.

4 ounces extra-sharp Cheddar cheese
3 tablespoons milk, chicken broth,
    dry white wine, or beer
1 teaspoon Dijon mustard
2 tablespoons butter
Salt and freshly ground black pepper
2 small ripe tomatoes, at room
    temperature
2 green bell peppers
4 slices pumpernickel
    bread
6 ounces shredded
    roasted or grilled
    skinless, boneless chicken or sliced
    smoked turkey

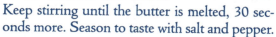

1. Grate the cheese into a small saucepan. Add the milk and melt the cheese over low heat, stirring continuously, until it is almost melted, about 30 seconds. Remove the pan from the heat and stir in the mustard and butter. Keep stirring until the butter is melted, 30 seconds more. Season to taste with salt and pepper.

2. Core and thinly slice the tomatoes. Stem and seed the bell peppers, and cut them into 1-inch strips.

3. Toast the bread and set the slices on dinner plates. Cover the toast with a layer of chicken and a layer of tomatoes. Reheat the sauce, and when it is bubbling, spoon it over the tomatoes. Garnish with the green bell pepper and serve immediately.

VARIATIONS

▪ In step 1, add ¼ cup chopped pimientos to the cheese right before stirring in the butter.
▪ For extra kick, add 2 tablespoons chopped pickled jalapeño peppers to the cheese after you have melted it in step 1.

ESPECIALLY GOOD FOR COMPANY

Toast the bread on a baking sheet at 375°F for 10 minutes. Set out the sliced chicken and tomatoes, and let everyone assemble their own open-faced sandwiches while you make the sauce.

Tex-Mex Chicken Burritos

MAKES: *4 servings*
TIME: *30 minutes*

Outrageously rich and delicious on any bread, the combination of chicken, avocado, and barbecue dressing works especially well with warm tortillas or lavash (very thin flatbread from Armenia). This tastes best when made with freshly grilled chicken, but, as with all of my Monday-to-Friday recipes, if you find it more convenient, you can substitute any type of cooked chicken you have on hand. If the avocados and tomatoes don't fit inside the tortillas, serve them on the side.

½ cup low-fat or regular mayonnaise
1 tablespoon bottled barbecue sauce
1 teaspoon ground cumin
Salt and freshly ground black pepper
2 limes
2 ripe tomatoes, cored
2 Hass avocados
1 cup (loosely packed) fresh cilantro leaves
2 fresh jalapeño peppers, seeded (optional)
2 scallions
¾ to 1 pound grilled or roasted chicken, at room temperature
10 to 12 flour tortillas (9-inch size) or lavash breads (8-inch size)

1. Preheat the oven to 300°F.

2. Wrap the tortillas in aluminum foil and heat them while you prepare the filling.

3. Combine the mayonnaise, barbecue sauce, and cumin in a small bowl. Season to taste with salt, pepper, and the juice of half a lime; set aside.

4. Cut the tomatoes into quarters, remove the seeds with a spoon, and cut them into ½-inch dice. Peel and pit the avocados, and cut them into ½-inch dice. In a bowl, toss the tomatoes and avocados with the juice of the remaining lime half. Coarsely chop the cilantro leaves, and mince the jalapeño peppers, if using. Trim and thinly slice the scallions, including the green tops, and cut the remaining lime into wedges. Slice the chicken into thin strips.

5. Place the chicken and all the accompaniments in individual bowls on the table so each family member can assemble his or her own burrito. Bring the tortillas to the table, still wrapped (each time you take one out of the package, rewrap the remainder).

6. To assemble, spread the barbecue mayonnaise over a tortilla. Scatter some chicken, tomato and avocado, scallions, cilantro, and jalapeños in the middle of each tortilla. Fold the bottom of the tortilla up toward the center, then fold the sides toward the middle, leaving only the top open, so the filling doesn't fall out.

VARIATIONS

California Style: Substitute 1 can (6 ounces) crushed pineapple, drained and rinsed, for the tomatoes. The sweetness of the pineapple is wonderful against the buttery avocado and fiery jalapeños.

With Cheese: Omit the mayonnaise and spread the tortillas with a bit of plain barbecue sauce. Scatter crumbled tangy goat's cheese over the chicken before you roll it up.

To Turn into Tostadas: Cook the tortillas in oil for a few seconds on each side, or bake them, turning once, in a 350°F oven for 6 minutes, to crisp up. Spoon the chicken and accompaniments in the middle, and eat the tostadas with a knife and fork.

Chinese Chicken Burritos

MAKES: *2 servings*
TIME: *20 minutes*

Coupling tortillas with Chinese ingredients may seem odd, but it isn't if you think of dishes like Mu-Shu Pork, which is served with flour pancakes. If you want a more substantial dinner, serve a bean sprout salad alongside or begin with the spinach broth described on the facing page.

6 flour tortillas (12-inch size)
1 tablespoon Asian sesame oil
1 tablespoon vegetable oil
1 teaspoon minced garlic
1 teaspoon minced fresh ginger
1 can (8 ounces) sliced bamboo
    shoots, drained
2 bunches watercress, rinsed,
    stems removed
2 scallions, trimmed and finely sliced
    (white and green parts)
2 cups finely sliced or diced cooked
    chicken
1 tablespoon rice vinegar
1 tablespoon water
2 tablespoons hoisin sauce
Salt
Dried red pepper flakes
½ cup chopped unsalted cashews or
    roasted peanuts (optional)
Light soy sauce for dipping (optional)

1. Preheat the oven to 350°F.

2. Wrap the tortillas in aluminum foil, and set them in the oven to warm while you prepare the filling.

3. Heat the sesame and vegetable oils in a large skillet over medium-high heat. Add the garlic and ginger and cook, stirring continuously, until you get their aroma, 10 seconds. Add the bamboo shoots, watercress, scallions, and chicken. Cook, stirring, until the watercress leaves just wilt, 1 or 2 minutes.

4. Add the vinegar, water, and hoisin sauce and mix well. Remove the skillet from the heat and season to taste with salt and red pepper flakes.

5. Remove the tortillas from the oven, spread the chicken mixture over them, and scatter some cashews, if using, on top. Fold the tortillas or roll them up like burritos, and serve with soy sauce for dipping, if you wish.

SPINACH BROTH

Combine 2 cups chicken broth, 2 cups water, 1 tablespoon soy sauce, and ½ teaspoon salt in a medium-size saucepan. Bring to a boil. Meanwhile, wash 4 cups fresh spinach leaves or thaw 1 package (10 ounces) frozen chopped spinach. When the broth is at a boil, add the spinach. When the spinach has wilted or is cooked through, remove the soup from the heat and serve it with the burritos.

Puffed Turkey Toasts

MAKES: *2 dinner servings*
TIME: *20 minutes*

....

When I was a little girl, my mom used to make fabulous hors d'oeuvres that consisted of melba toast spread with a mixture of mayonnaise, onion, and cheese. I liked them so much that I always thought I could make a meal of them—and so I have devised a way of doing so. I blanket open-face roasted turkey sandwiches with the mayonnaise and cheese mixture, broil them until puffy, and serve them with a bracing salad of tomatoes and arugula drizzled with balsamic vinegar.

2 tomatoes, cored
2 cups stemmed arugula
1 tablespoon balsamic vinegar
¼ cup regular or low-fat mayonnaise
1 tablespoon grated onion, or 2
    tablespoons minced scallions
½ cup (2 ounces) grated
    Parmesan or sharp white
    Cheddar cheese
Tabasco sauce, to taste
4 slices white bread
8 slices roasted turkey

1. Preheat the broiler.

2. Thinly slice the tomatoes. Swish the arugula leaves in a bowl of cold water, lift them out of the water, and discard the water. Rinse the bowl, add fresh water, swish the leaves again, then lift them out of the water and dry them well. Combine the arugula with the tomatoes in a salad bowl, and toss with the balsamic vinegar.

3. Combine the mayonnaise, onion, and cheese in a small bowl. Season with a drop or two of Tabasco sauce.

4. Broil the bread on both sides until lightly toasted. Divide the turkey among the slices of bread, and spread the mayonnaise mixture on top of the turkey. Broil for a few seconds until the mixture puffs up. Serve immediately, with the salad alongside.

Turkey Blue Cheese Sandwich with Grape Salad

MAKES: *2 servings*
TIME: *20 minutes*

....

This sandwich and salad combo provides a remarkable taste treat for the sophisticated palate. The powerful taste of the turkey and blue cheese is a match for the equally flavorful peppery watercress. The combination of these three is then softened and pulled together by the sweetness of the grapes and the richness of the buttery pecans. Be sure to get a bite of all flavors with each mouthful.

2 tablespoons vegetable oil
2 tablespoons sherry vinegar or
  balsamic vinegar
Salt and freshly ground black pepper
1 bunch (4 ounces) watercress
1½ cups seedless grapes, preferably red
½ cup pecan halves
4 slices whole-wheat bread
2 tablespoons butter
4 ounces blue cheese, crumbled
6 ounces sliced baked or smoked turkey

1. Combine the oil and vinegar in a small bowl, and season lightly with salt and pepper. Rinse the watercress and cut off the leaves, leaving about ½ inch of stem. Dry the watercress. Rinse the grapes, and if they are small, leave them whole; otherwise halve them. Coarsely chop the pecans, and combine them in a mixing bowl with the watercress, grapes, and half the dressing.

2. Right before serving, toast the bread lightly. Butter the toasted bread slices while still warm, and sprinkle them with the blue cheese. Drape the turkey slices over the blue cheese, and drizzle the remaining dressing over the turkey.

3. Serve the sandwiches open-face, with the grape and watercress salad alongside.

EASY WATERCRESS WASH-UP

An easy way to wash watercress (or bunches of herbs, such as parsley) is to leave the bunch fastened with its rubber band. Grab hold of the stems and rinse the leaves under cold running water. Shake off the excess water and dry the leaves. With a knife, separate the leaves from the stems right about where the bunch is gathered (if you leave a bit of stem on, that's okay; if there's too much, you can remove it later). Scatter the watercress on a cloth towel and cover with another cloth towel. Press gently but firmly on the top towel to extract the moisture without bruising the delicate leaves.

A Burger of Many Tastes

MAKES: *4 servings*
TIME: *20 minutes*

Chicken's neutral flavor makes it a gracious partner to any and all seasonings. To experiment, add the spices, herbs, or flavored paste to the raw ground chicken, and season the mixture with salt (use enough or it will taste flat). Sauté a bit of it (never eat raw chicken) to see what it tastes like cooked, and then make the appropriate adjustments. The texture of poultry burgers is more compact and pasty than the familiar beef hamburger.

FOR THE BURGER

1¼ pounds ground chicken or turkey
1 egg, lightly beaten
1 tablespoon dried bread crumbs
2 tablespoons vegetable oil
2 tablespoons barbecue sauce
2 scallions
Salt
Freshly ground black pepper or
*   Tabasco or other hot sauce to taste*

FOR THE GARNISH (CHOOSE 2 OR 3)

Ripe tomato, thinly sliced
Lettuce leaves or alfalfa sprouts,
*   rinsed and patted dry*
Red onion, thinly sliced
Ripe avocado, sliced
Ketchup, mustard, or mayonnaise (see Note)

4 hamburger rolls, lightly toasted

1. Combine the ground chicken, egg, bread crumbs, 1 tablespoon of the vegetable oil, and the barbecue sauce in a mixing bowl. Trim and thinly slice the green and white parts of the scallions and add them to the mix. Season well with salt and pepper.

(Cook some of the mixture at this point to see how it tastes, and adjust the seasoning accordingly.)

2. Shape the mixture into four ½-inch-thick patties. Heat the remaining 1 tablespoon vegetable oil in a nonstick skillet. Sauté the burgers over medium heat until cooked through, 5 to 7 minutes on each side.

3. While the burgers are cooking, prepare the garnishes and toast the hamburger rolls.

4. Serve the burgers on the rolls, with the garnishes on separate plates for everyone to help themselves.

Note: I love to top these burgers with a mixture consisting of equal amounts of ketchup, Dijon mustard, and mayonnaise.

VARIATIONS

Diet Dijon Burgers: In step 1, instead of the barbecue sauce and oil, mix in 1 tablespoon Dijon mustard, ½ cup (packed) fresh parsley leaves, chopped, 1 teaspoon grated lemon zest, and 1 tablespoon lemon juice.

Gooey Burgers: In step 1, omit the barbecue sauce and egg. In step 2, after shaping the chicken into patties, stuff a tablespoon-size nugget of blue cheese in the center of each one.

Pesto Burgers: In step 1, substitute ¼ cup pesto or one of the herb purées on pages 224 and 225 for the barbecue sauce, scallions, and oil.

Spiced-up Burgers: In step 1, substitute 1 teaspoon ground coriander, cumin, curry powder, or chili powder for the barbecue sauce.

GREAT RED COLESLAW SIDE

A light, tangy coleslaw makes a fabulous accompaniment to these chicken burgers. Combine 4 cups shredded red cabbage with 1 thinly sliced scallion (white and green parts) and 1 minced seeded fresh jalapeño pepper. Make a dressing of ⅓ cup plain yogurt, ⅓ cup mayonnaise, and 2 tablespoons cider vinegar. Season with salt and pepper and toss with the cabbage.

Dogless Chicken Dogs

MAKES: *4 servings*
TIME: *25 to 30 minutes*

This amusing sandwich was inspired by "chili dogs," which are hot dogs blanketed by spoonfuls of ground beef chili. In my sandwich, the hot dogs are gone and just a ground chicken chili remains. This simplest of meals is accompanied by a white bean, corn, and bell pepper salad. If you like the idea of bean salads in general, keep a can of beans in the fridge at all times so they are chilled when you are ready to prepare your meal.

1 package (10 ounces) frozen
   corn kernels, thawed
1 can (16 or 19 ounces) white or red
   kidney beans, rinsed and drained
⅓ to ½ cup salad dressing of choice
Salt and freshly ground black pepper
2 tablespoons vegetable oil
1 onion, finely chopped
1¼ pounds ground chicken or turkey
1 tablespoon chili powder
1½ teaspoons
   ground cumin
1 teaspoon sugar
⅓ cup water
1 cup bottled
   or homemade
   spaghetti sauce
2 small green or red bell peppers
4 hot dog buns

1. Combine the corn, beans, and dressing in a mixing bowl. Season to taste with salt and pepper and refrigerate, covered, until serving time.

2. Heat the oil in a large skillet over medium-high heat. Add the onion and sauté until tender and beginning to turn golden, 4 to 5 minutes.

3. Add the chicken and cook for about 5 minutes, mashing and crumbling the meat with the side of a wooden spoon as you sauté it. (If you don't do this, the ground chicken just clumps together.)

4. Add the chili powder, cumin, sugar, water, and spaghetti sauce. Cover and simmer over low heat until the flavors have come together, 10 minutes. (It will taste better, of course, the longer you cook it.) While the sauce is cooking, stem and seed the peppers. Cut them into ½-inch pieces and mix them into the beans and corn.

5. When you are ready to eat, toast the hot dog buns and spoon the chili sauce over them. Serve with the beans, corn, and pepper salad.

ESPECIALLY GOOD FOR CHILDREN

If you like this chicken dog idea for your kids but think it is too spicy, reduce the amount of chili powder to 1 teaspoon and add some dried red pepper flakes or chopped fresh jalapeños to the adults' portions.

Curried Chicken Livers over Rye Toast

MAKES: *2 servings*
TIME: *25 to 30 minutes*

I have always loved chicken livers prepared Grandmother's way: cooked with onions in lots of chicken fat. Her method may have been speedy, but it had little to recommend it to my arteries. This recipe is as easy, quick, and delicious as her version, with the added bonus that it is healthier as well. The richness of the livers is offset by the tang of fresh tomatoes and the bite of the curry powder. The little salad of cucumbers and mint makes a fine simple accompaniment.

12 ounces chicken livers
1 tablespoon butter
1 tablespoon vegetable oil
1 onion, thinly sliced
2 tomatoes, cored
1 teaspoon curry powder
4 Kirby cucumbers
1 tablespoon rice vinegar or white
    wine vinegar
¼ teaspoon sugar
¼ cup (loosely packed) fresh mint
    leaves
4 slices rye bread
Salt and freshly ground black pepper

1. Trim the chicken livers of any stringy parts, cut them in half, and pat them dry with paper towels.

2. Heat the butter and oil in a medium skillet over medium heat. When the butter turns golden brown, add the livers and cook them until brown on one side, about 2 minutes. (Be

careful—they splatter.) Turn them over and brown them on the other side, without stirring, for 2 minutes more.

3. Remove the chicken livers to a plate, and add the onion to the skillet. Cover and cook over medium-low heat, stirring every now and then, until tender, 3 to 4 minutes. While the onion is cooking, cut the tomatoes into ½-inch dice.

4. Add the tomatoes and the curry powder to the skillet, and stir to combine. Cover and simmer over low heat for about 5 minutes.

5. Meanwhile, peel the cucumbers and cut them into ⅛-inch-thick rounds. Toss them with the vinegar and sugar. Coarsely chop the mint, and add it to the cucumbers. Cut the chicken livers in half again. Lightly toast the rye bread and put 2 slices on each plate.

6. Return the livers to the skillet, and reheat them gently with the onion and tomatoes (don't overcook; you want the livers slightly pink inside). Season to taste with salt and pepper, and spoon the mixture over the toast. Serve the cucumber salad on the side.

Chicken Sausage Heros

MAKES: *2 servings*
TIME: *20 minutes*

My husband finds Italian sausage heros the most irresistible of street-fair foods. He always indulges his craving and invariably has indigestion afterward. At home I give in to his lust for sausage heros by making a chicken version that is a tad lighter, equally flavorful, and easier on his stomach. This lovely sandwich consists of a mere toss of spicy chicken sausage rounds, mushrooms, and bell peppers spooned inside soft Italian bread. Topped off with sauerkraut and scallions, it is absolutely delicious as well as incredibly speedy to prepare. Of course what makes these so wonderful is the quality of the sausage. Aidells gets my vote for their superb and varied mixtures—the smoked chicken and pesto sausage being my favorite.

2 tablespoons olive oil
2 green or red bell peppers, stemmed, seeded, and thinly sliced
2 cups mushrooms
8 ounces spicy chicken or turkey sausages
1 cup sauerkraut
2 scallions
1 loaf (8 ounces) Italian bread

1. Heat the oil in a large skillet over medium heat. Add the peppers, cover, and cook until tender, 5 minutes.

2. While the peppers are cooking, trim ¼ inch off the end of the mushroom stems. Wipe the mushrooms clean with a damp paper towel, and cut into ¼-inch-thick slices.

3. Add the mushrooms to the skillet and cook, stirring occasionally, until they are tender, about 5 minutes. While the mushrooms are cooking, cut the sausages into ½-inch-thick rounds.

4. Preheat the oven to 350°F.

5. Add the sausages to the skillet, cover, and cook over medium heat until cooked through, 5 minutes. While the sausages are cooking, rinse the sauerkraut and squeeze it dry. Trim and thinly slice the scallions (white and green parts) and stir them into the sauerkraut. Heat the bread in the oven for 2 to 3 minutes just to warm it through.

6. Remove the bread from the oven and cut it in half so you have 2 smaller loaves. Split each half lengthwise and remove some of the soft interior crumb. Spoon the sauerkraut and scallions on one half, top with the peppers, mushrooms, and sausages, and cover with the other bread half. Cut each sandwich in half again, tie a napkin around your neck, and dig in.

In the Skillet and on the Grill

In this huge chapter, I have gathered some of my favorite chicken-in-a-skillet dishes. There are lots of recipes here, because skillet cooking is so speedy and efficient that, during the week, you'll want to make use of it as often as possible.

The chapter is divided into three sections, beginning with dishes that I consider lighter ones. Light Meals match chicken with a vegetable or two, but without an accompanying starch. These recipes are perfect for times when appetites are small (you've had a big lunch or it's hot outside) or you're eating late. Of course, if your partner had to skip lunch or you're feeding a ravenous teenager, a good crusty bread or starch can go along with any of these recipes, time and appetite permitting.

On nights when you want a heartier meal, turn to the Complete Meals section (page 133). In these recipes, the chicken and vegetables are cooked in the skillet, while the rice or pasta or potatoes or polenta cook alongside. The time given for the recipe includes the time necessary to cook the starch.

The third section includes great chicken dishes prepared On the Grill (page 164). These are designed, time-wise, for stovetop grill pans, but if you're lucky enough to have an outdoor model, by all means fire it up. Accompanied by a salad or bread, these recipes make delicious weekday meals.

LIGHT MEALS

Jicama and Chicken California Sauté

MAKES: *4 servings*
TIME: *30 to 35 minutes*

....

When it is beastly hot, I prefer to spend as much time as possible out of the kitchen, away from the heat. This recipe fits the bill because it takes some preparation time but involves little cooking. The recipe is marvelously flavorful, and you're at the stove for a mere 5 to 6 minutes.

> 2 tablespoons Asian sesame oil
> 1 tablespoon finely chopped garlic
> 1 tablespoon finely chopped peeled fresh ginger
> 8 ounces broccoli stems, peeled and cut into ¼-inch rounds (2 cups)
> 8 ounces jicama, peeled and cut into 1 × ¼-inch strips (2 cups)
> 2 whole skinless, boneless chicken breasts, cut into ½-inch dice (1 to 1¼ pounds total)
> ⅓ cup lime juice
> Salt
> 1 teaspoon cornstarch
> ½ cup (loosely packed) cilantro leaves, chopped
> Dried red pepper flakes

1. Heat the sesame oil in a 12-inch skillet or in a wok over medium heat. Add the garlic, ginger, and broccoli stems and cook, stirring continuously with tongs or a slotted spoon, until the broccoli begins to cook, 1 minute.

2. Add the jicama and cook, stirring continuously, for 1 minute. Then add the chicken, half the lime juice, and 1 teaspoon salt. Cover and simmer until the chicken is almost completely cooked, 2 minutes.

3. Stir the cornstarch into the remaining lime juice and add it to the chicken. Continue to cook, stirring, uncovered, until the chicken is

cooked through and the juices cling to the vegetables and chicken, about 1 minute longer. Remove the skillet from the heat, add the cilantro, and season to taste with salt and red pepper flakes.

VARIATIONS

- Off the heat, stir into the cooked chicken 2 Hass avocados, peeled, pitted, and cut into ¾-inch chunks.
- Or, off the heat, stir in ½ cup unsalted roasted peanuts.

Chicken and Vegetables

A BLUEPRINT RECIPE

MAKES: *4 servings*
TIME: *25 to 30 minutes*

This recipe is so flexible, easy, and appropriate any time of the year, I guarantee it will become a standard in your household. Use it as a blueprint—once you get the hang of the technique, you'll figure out how to substitute one vegetable or seasoning for another. This yields yummy juices, so serve something starchy along with the meal to sop them up.

> 2 whole skinless, boneless chicken breasts or chicken "tenders" (about 1¼ pounds)
> 6 carrots (12 to 16 ounces)
> 2 tablespoons olive oil
> 1 tablespoon white wine vinegar, or 2 tablespoons Verjus (page 16)
> 1 tablespoon water
> 6 tablespoons olive paste (olivada), commercial or homemade (page 231)
> Salt and freshly ground black pepper

1. Cut the chicken into ½-inch dice. Cut the carrots, on a slight diagonal, into ¼-inch-thick ovals.

2. Heat the oil over medium-high heat in a large skillet. Add the carrots and chicken and sauté, stirring continuously, until the chicken turns opaque, about 2 minutes. Add the vinegar and water, cover, and simmer over low heat until the chicken is cooked through, 5 minutes.

3. Remove the chicken from the heat and stir in the olivada. Mix until the ingredients are thoroughly combined. Season to taste with salt and pepper, and serve at once.

VARIATIONS

Chicken, Carrots, and Caponata: In step 3, substitute 1 cup (7- or 8-ounce jar or can) commercially prepared or homemade caponata for the olivada. Serve over egg noodles or with bread.

Chicken, Corn, and Salsa: In step 2, instead of the carrots, add 1 package (10 ounces) thawed frozen corn kernels. In step 3, substitute ⅓ to ½ cup salsa for the olivada. Serve over rice or with tortillas.

Chicken, Peas, and Pesto: In step 2, substitute 1 package (10 ounces) thawed frozen "petite" peas for the carrots. In step 3, instead of the olivada, add ⅓ cup pesto or ⅓ cup basil or Mint Purée (page 225). Serve with rice or polenta.

Chicken and Broccoli Asian-Style: In step 2, sauté the chicken in 2 tablespoons Asian sesame oil until opaque, 2 minutes. Add 1 package (10 ounces) thawed frozen chopped broccoli and sauté until the chicken is cooked through and the broccoli is hot, 2 to 3 minutes. Add 1 tablespoon rice vinegar and evaporate over high heat. In step 3, instead of the olivada, add ¼ cup Cilantro Purée (page 225) and a sprinkling of dried red pepper flakes. Serve over vermicelli noodles or with an aromatic rice such as Texmati.

Lemon Chicken

A BLUEPRINT RECIPE

MAKES: *4 servings*
TIME: *20 minutes*

Here's another blueprint recipe that's quick, easy, and has plenty of variations. The quantity of lemon zest is what gives this chicken its full citrus flavor. I sprinkle the scallions over the chicken at the end, rather than integrate them into the sauce, because the acid of the lemon juice turns them a dull, darkish color.

> 2 whole skinless, boneless chicken breasts,
>   halved (about 1½ pounds total)
> Salt
> 2 tablespoons olive oil
> 2 lemons
> 2 teaspoons cornstarch
> ½ cup chicken broth
> 1 small scallion, trimmed
> 2 tablespoons chilled butter (optional)
> Freshly ground black pepper

1. Separate the tenderloins from the breast halves. Place the breast halves between sheets of plastic wrap and pound the thicker side to make the breasts more even in thickness. Season lightly with salt.

2. Heat the oil in a large skillet over medium heat. Add the chicken breasts and tenderloins. Cook the chicken, without disturbing

the pieces, for 4 to 5 minutes. When the top looks opaque, turn the chicken over and cook undisturbed again, until cooked through, 4 to 5 minutes (the tenderloins may take only 2 to 3 minutes per side).

3. Meanwhile, grate enough zest from the lemons to make 1 teaspoon. Juice the lemons to get ¼ cup of juice. Mix the cornstarch into the broth, and add the lemon zest and juice. Thinly slice the scallion (both white and green parts).

4. Remove the chicken to a plate and discard the fat from the skillet. Give the cornstarch mixture a stir and add it to the skillet. Whisk in any accumulated juices from the chicken into the liquid, bring it to a simmer, and cook until the sauce looks thick and glossy, about 2 minutes. Remove the skillet from the heat, and whisk in the butter, if you wish. Season to taste with salt and pepper, and spoon the sauce over the chicken. Sprinkle the scallions on top.

VARIATIONS

Chinese-Style Sauce: In step 2, substitute Asian sesame oil for the olive oil.

In step 3, omit the lemons and cornstarch. Mince 1 clove garlic and measure out 1 teaspoon Chinese five-spice powder. Whisk 1 tablespoon hoisin sauce and 2 tablespoons soy sauce into the chicken broth.

In step 4, after you transfer the chicken to a plate, leave 1 tablespoon fat in the skillet. Add the garlic and five-spice powder, and sauté for 10 seconds. Stir in the broth mixture and boil down until ¼ cup remains and the sauce is syrupy. Remove the skillet from the heat, stir in the butter, and spoon the sauce over the chicken. Garnish with the scallion.

Southwest-Style Sauce: In step 3, omit the lemons, cornstarch, and scallion. Mince 1 clove garlic and measure out 1 teaspoon each of ground cumin and chili powder. Whisk 1 tablespoon tomato paste and ½ cup chopped green chiles (or a mild green salsa) into the chicken broth. Coarsely chop 1 cup (packed) fresh cilantro leaves.

In step 4, after you remove the chicken to a plate, leave 1 tablespoon fat in the skillet. Add the garlic and spices to the skillet, and sauté for 10 seconds. Stir in the broth mixture and simmer until about ¾ cup remains or until the sauce is thick. Season to taste with salt, remove the skillet from the heat, and stir in the butter and the cilantro. Spoon the sauce over the chicken.

Curried Sauce: In step 3, omit the lemons, cornstarch, and scallion. Mince 1 clove garlic and measure out 1 teaspoon each of ground cumin and curry powder. Whisk 1 tablespoon tomato paste into the chicken broth. Coarsely chop 1 cup (packed) fresh cilantro leaves.

In step 4, after you remove the chicken to a plate, leave 1 tablespoon fat in the skillet.

Add the garlic, cumin, and curry powder, and sauté for 10 seconds. Whisk in the broth mixture and simmer for about a minute or until the sauce has thickened. Season to taste with salt and pepper. (Omit the butter.) Remove the skillet from the heat, add 2 tablespoons yogurt, and whisk until smooth. Add the cilantro and spoon the sauce over the chicken.

Citrus Chicken Steamed with Snow Peas

MAKES: *4 servings*
TIME: *20 minutes*

What's fabulous about this recipe is that it is utterly simple and fast, yet the flavor can be as intense as you wish. This recipe is especially good for dieters, and family members not on a diet will be especially grateful for the caloric touches I suggest they add to their portion.

2 whole skinless, boneless chicken breasts, halved (about 1½ pounds total)
2 tablespoons lemon, lime, or orange juice, or any of the herb purées (pages 224 and 225), or vinaigrette or salad dressing of choice
8 ounces snow peas or sugar snap peas
½ cup water
Salt
3 quarter-size pieces of fresh ginger
1 large scallion
¼ cup (packed) fresh parsley or cilantro leaves (optional)
1 lemon, quartered
Dried red pepper flakes

1. Cut the chicken into strips about 3 inches long and ½ inch wide. Marinate them in the citrus juice while you trim the snow peas.

2. In a 12-inch skillet bring the water to a boil with ½ teaspoon salt and the slices of ginger over high heat. Add the chicken, lower the heat to medium, cover, and simmer for 5 minutes. During this time, trim the scallion and slice it fine (white and green parts). Chop the parsley.

3. Place the snow peas on top of the chicken in the skillet, cover again, and simmer over medium heat until the snow peas are cooked but still crunchy, 2 minutes.

4. Spoon the chicken, snow peas, and skillet juices into shallow bowls. Garnish each portion with scallion and chopped parsley. Serve with lemon wedges and red pepper flakes to taste.

VARIATIONS

In step 3, instead of the snow peas, add 1 package (10 ounces) thawed frozen "petite" peas, 4 carrots, grated, 3 cups bean sprouts, 3 cups shredded romaine lettuce, or 2 zucchini cut into ¼-inch slices. Cook until the vegetable is tender but still crisp.

ESPECIALLY GOOD FOR NONDIETERS

At the table, each person can stir 1 tablespoon coconut milk or 1 teaspoon sesame or walnut oil into his or her portion.

Anise-Poached Chicken with Carrots and Snow Peas

MAKES: *4 servings*
TIME: *25 minutes*

The consistency of this dish lies somewhere between a soup and a stew; it is a mix of chicken slices, carrots, and snow peas, simmered in an anise-infused broth that flavors the chicken as it moistens it. Because this is so lean, it won't hurt your diet if you serve this over a starch (soba or rice noodles are delicious).

2 whole skinless, boneless chicken breasts, halved (about 1½ pounds total)
1 orange
1 pound carrots
½ cup chicken broth
1 small clove garlic
⅛ teaspoon Chinese five-spice powder
Salt
⅛ teaspoon dried red pepper flakes
2 cups fresh snow peas, trimmed

1. Cut the chicken into strips about 2 inches long and ¼ inch wide. Juice the orange and marinate the chicken in the juice. Peel and cut the carrots into ¼-inch-thick rounds.

2. Combine the broth, garlic, five-spice powder, and ½ teaspoon salt in a medium-size saucepan and bring to a boil over high heat. Add the carrots, cover, and simmer until almost tender, 3 minutes.

3. Add the chicken along with the orange juice. Cover and simmer over low heat until the chicken is almost done, 3 minutes more. Add the red pepper flakes and snow peas, cover, and cook until the snow peas are tender but still crisp, 2 to 3 minutes.

4. Remove and discard the garlic clove, and adjust the seasoning. Serve immediately in deep bowls, before the acidity of the orange juice has a chance to turn the snow peas an unappetizingly dull green.

VARIATIONS

In step 3, instead of the snow peas, add 1 package (10 ounces) thawed frozen "petite" peas, 3 cups bean sprouts, 3 cups shredded romaine lettuce, or 2 zucchini cut into ¼-inch slices. Cook until the vegetable is tender but still crisp.

ESPECIALLY GOOD FOR NONDIETERS

Before serving the Anise-Poached Chicken, drizzle some Asian sesame oil over each portion.

PANTRY-QUICK EGGPLANT CHICKEN

Dip skinless, boneless chicken breast halves in a commercial eggplant caponata or eggplant ratatouille, then dip in dried bread crumbs. Set them on a rack placed on a baking sheet and bake at 400°F until cooked through, 30 minutes. Serve with olive bread from an Italian bakery and a mesclun salad.

Chicken Breasts with Sun-Dried Tomatoes

MAKES: *4 servings*
TIME: *25 to 30 minutes*

This is an excellent example of how a pantry stocked with richly flavored keepers, such as sun-dried tomatoes, capers, and olives, can transform ho-hum chicken into a spectacular dish.

> 2 whole skinless, boneless chicken breasts (about 1½ pounds total)
> 2 tablespoons olive oil
> 12 sun-dried tomatoes, packed in oil
> 12 pitted green or black olives, packed in oil
> 2 cloves garlic
> 2 teaspoons cornstarch
> ¾ cup chicken broth
> ¼ cup dry white wine or Verjus (page 16)
> 2 tablespoons drained capers
> Salt and freshly ground black pepper

1. Separate the tenderloins from the breast meat. Cut the chicken breasts into halves along the breastbone line. Cut each half in half again, vertically, so you end up with 8 slender strips.

2. Heat the oil in a large skillet over medium-high heat. Add the chicken strips and tenderloins and reduce the heat to medium. Cook

the chicken, undisturbed, for about 5 minutes. When the top looks opaque, turn the chicken over and cook until cooked through, 6 to 8 minutes longer. (The tenderloins take less time to cook, so remove them from the pan sooner.)

3. While the chicken is cooking, slice the sun-dried tomatoes into ⅛-inch slivers, cut each olive into quarters, and mince the garlic. Stir the cornstarch into the chicken broth.

4. When the chicken is cooked through, remove it to a plate. Discard the oil in the skillet and return the skillet to medium-high heat.

5. Add the garlic and wine, and boil it down until 2 tablespoons remain. Stir in the sun-dried tomatoes, capers, and olives and heat for 30 seconds. Using a fork, give the cornstarch mixture a stir and add it to the skillet. Bring the liquid to a boil and simmer until slightly thickened and glossy, 1 minute. Season to taste with salt and pepper. Spoon the sauce over the chicken and serve immediately.

Pecan-Breaded Chicken Breasts

MAKES: *4 servings*
TIME: *35 minutes*

In 1979, David Liederman and I wrote *Cooking the Nouvelle Cuisine in America.* In that book we offered a recipe for Pecan-Breaded Chicken Breasts, a dish subsequently made famous by one of David's restaurants. David and I then found our original recipe in many other cookbooks and were flattered that it was delicious enough to have inspired so many variations and imitations. However, by today's standards, the original recipe included too much butter—and the pecans kept falling off the chicken anyway. In this version I use less butter, dip the chicken in egg so the pecans stick to it better, and deglaze the pan with an acidic ingredient to balance the richness of the sauce. Overall, I think this is a lovely updated version of the original.

> *2 whole skinless, boneless chicken breasts,*
> *halved (about 1½ pounds total)*
> *Salt and freshly ground black pepper*
> *4 tablespoons Dijon mustard*
> *1½ cups pecan halves*
> *1 large egg, lightly beaten*
> *2 teaspoons water*
> *2 tablespoons butter*
> *2 tablespoons vegetable oil*
> *½ cup sour cream*
> *¼ cup chopped fresh chives or scallions*
> *¼ cup white wine or Verjus (page 16)*
> *½ cup chicken broth*

1. Place the chicken breasts between sheets of plastic wrap and lightly flatten them with a meat pounder or a heavy skillet. Season them lightly with salt and pepper.

2. Rub 2 tablespoons of the mustard into the chicken breasts and set them aside. Finely

grind the pecans in a food processor and transfer them to a shallow bowl. In another shallow bowl, beat the egg and water together. Dip the chicken pieces in the egg and then coat them with the pecans.

3. Heat the butter and oil in a large skillet over medium heat. Add the chicken and cook, without disturbing, until the edges are beginning to turn opaque, 5 minutes. Turn the chicken over, reduce the heat to low and cook, without disturbing, until cooked through, 10 minutes longer. Meanwhile, combine the remaining 2 tablespoons mustard with the sour cream and chives.

4. Remove the chicken to a plate, and pour the fat from the skillet through a sieve to catch the bits of pecans. Spoon the strained pecans over the chicken. Return the skillet to medium-high heat.

5. Add the wine and boil for 1 minute. Add the broth and boil until almost entirely evaporated, 2 minutes longer. Remove the skillet from the heat and whisk in the sour cream mixture. When the sauce is smooth, season to taste with salt and pepper and spoon it over the chicken.

ESPECIALLY GOOD FOR CHILDREN

In step 1, cut the kids' portions into bite-size pieces. Cook as described but omit the sauce.

Sesame-Crusted Chicken over Green Pea Purée

MAKES: *4 servings*
TIME: *35 to 40 minutes*

The emerald pea purée adds the right touch of sweetness to the exotically flavored chicken, and it is as pretty to look at as it is good to eat. The extra steps in this recipe are worth the effort because the flavor of the dish is so delicious.

2 whole skinless, boneless chicken breasts,
    halved (about 1½ pounds total)
Salt and freshly ground black pepper
1 large egg
1 tablespoon soy sauce
3 tablespoons Asian sesame oil
⅓ cup sesame seeds
½ cup dried bread crumbs
2 tablespoons vegetable oil
¼ cup chicken broth
½ cup unsweetened coconut milk
¼ cup chopped fresh chives or scallions
¼ cup (packed) fresh cilantro leaves
¼ cup (packed) fresh mint leaves
2 packages (10 ounces each) frozen
    "petite" peas, thawed
¼ cup water
4 tablespoons (½ stick) butter,
    at room temperature
2 tablespoons rice vinegar

1. Place the chicken breasts between two sheets of plastic wrap and lightly flatten them with a meat pounder or heavy cast-iron skillet. Season lightly with salt and pepper.

2. In a shallow bowl, combine the egg with the soy sauce and 1 tablespoon of the sesame oil. In another shallow bowl, combine the sesame seeds with the bread crumbs. Dip the chicken in the egg mixture and then in the sesame seed mixture.

3. Heat the remaining 2 tablespoons sesame oil and the vegetable oil in a 12-inch skillet over medium heat. Add the chicken and cook over low heat until cooked through, 8 to 10 minutes per side. Meanwhile, combine the broth, coconut milk, chives, cilantro, and mint in a blender and purée until smooth. Season to taste with salt and pepper. Set aside.

4. Heat the thawed peas with the water for 5 minutes in a microwave oven or in a covered saucepan over medium heat. Purée the heated peas and cooking water with the butter in a food processor, and season to taste with salt and pepper. Remove to a platter and keep warm.

5. When the chicken is cooked through, remove it to a plate and discard the fat from the skillet. Return the skillet to medium-high heat and add the vinegar. Boil down for a few seconds or until almost evaporated. Add the coconut purée and boil down until slightly thickened, 2 minutes. Season with salt and pepper.

6. Place a portion of pea purée on each dinner plate, arrange a chicken breast on top, and spoon some sauce over the chicken. Serve immediately.

Tarragon Creamed Chicken

MAKES: *4 servings*
TIME: *25 minutes*

Be sure to include a side dish that will soak up this remarkably flavorful sauce. Mashed potatoes are especially delicious, but in a pinch, a slice of warm crusty French bread will do.

2 whole skinless, boneless chicken breasts
    (about 1½ pounds total)
2 tablespoons butter
½ cup chicken broth
1 teaspoon cornstarch
½ cup heavy (or whipping) cream
1 tablespoon Dijon mustard
2 teaspoons dried tarragon
¼ cup snipped fresh chives
¼ cup dry white wine or Verjus
    (page 16)
Salt and freshly ground black pepper

1. Separate the tenderloins from the breast meat. Cut the chicken breasts into halves along the breastbone line. Cut each breast half in half again, lengthwise, so you end up with 8 long pieces. Pound them and the tenderloins lightly between pieces of plastic wrap with a meat pounder or heavy skillet.

2. Melt the butter in a large skillet over medium-high heat. Add the chicken and reduce the heat to medium. Cook for 5 minutes. When the top looks opaque, turn the chicken over and cook until cooked through, 6 to 8 minutes longer. (The tenderloins take less time to cook, so remove them from the pan sooner.)

3. While the chicken is cooking, combine the broth with the cornstarch in a medium-size bowl. Stir in the cream and the mustard, tarragon, and chives; set aside.

4. Remove the chicken to a plate. Discard the butter in the skillet and return the skillet to medium heat. Add the wine and boil down until 2 tablespoons remain.

5. Give the cornstarch mixture a stir and add it to the skillet. Bring the liquid to a boil, and simmer until thickened, about 1 minute. Add any juices that have accumulated under the chicken on the plate, and add the cream mixture. Simmer until the sauce is thick enough to coat a spoon, 1 minute longer. Season to taste with salt and pepper. Spoon the sauce over the chicken and serve immediately.

Chicken with Tomatoes and Basil

MAKES: *4 servings*
TIME: *20 to 25 minutes*

Make this superbly flavored dish in late summer or early fall when the tomatoes are ripe and the basil is abundant. The chicken is seared lightly in olive oil, then simmered in a pool of chopped tomatoes, garlic, and basil. The tomatoes give off so much juice that you must serve this in deep soup bowls. Be sure to accompany the dish with lots of crusty bread to pick up the fragrant juices.

2 tablespoons extra-virgin olive oil
2 whole skinless, boneless chicken
*   breasts, halved, "tenders" separated*
*   (1½ pounds total)*
2 pounds fresh vine-ripened tomatoes
½ cup (packed) fresh basil leaves
2 cloves garlic
Salt and freshly ground black
*   pepper*
1 tablespoon wine vingar,
*   preferably balsamic*

1. Heat 1 tablespoon of the olive oil in a 12-inch skillet over medium heat. Add the chicken breasts and "tenders" and cook them, uncovered, until partially cooked, about 3 minutes per side.

2. While the chicken is cooking, cut each tomato into 8 wedges, then cut the wedges in half so you have nice big chunks. Rinse and sliver the basil. Mince the garlic.

3. Remove the chicken to a plate. Add the garlic to the skillet and cook for a few seconds to release the aroma. Add the tomatoes and basil and bring to a simmer; season to taste with salt and pepper. Place the chicken over the tomatoes, drizzle the remaining 1 tablespoon olive oil and the vinegar over the chicken, and season with salt and pepper.

4. Cover and cook until the chicken is just cooked through, 5 minutes. Transfer the chicken to deep bowls and spoon the tomatoes and juices on top. Serve immediately.

SECOND TIME AROUND

It's a natural to turn any juicy leftovers into a soup or pasta sauce. Separate the chicken from the tomatoes and dice it. Bring the tomatoes and juices to a simmer, add the chicken, and simmer gently until reheated. Serve as a soup, or boil down until thick enough to become a sauce. Grate fresh Parmesan cheese over the top before serving.

Deviled Chicken and Artichokes

MAKES: *4 servings*
TIME: *25 to 30 minutes*

....

This speedy delicious dish can be adapted for stovetop grilling: instead of sautéing the chicken, simply cook it on the grill. If you want to grill it, substitute boneless, skinless chicken thighs for the chicken breasts—they won't dry out on the grill.

2 cans (13¾ ounces each) artichoke
    hearts, drained
1 package (10 ounces) frozen
    corn kernels, thawed
1 jar (6 ounces) marinated
    artichoke hearts
2 tablespoons olive oil
2 whole skinless, boneless
    chicken breasts, halved,
    "tenders" separated
    (about 1½ pounds total)
2 scallions
2 cups (loosely packed) fresh
    parsley leaves
2 tablespoon Creole or spicy
    brown mustard
Salt and freshly ground black pepper

1. Cut the canned artichokes into ⅛-inch-thick slices and combine them with the corn and the marinated artichoke hearts and their

marinade in a nonreactive 10-inch skillet. Cover and bring to a simmer over very low heat.

2. While this is coming to a simmer, heat the olive oil in a large saucepan over medium heat. Add the chicken breasts and "tenders," and sauté until just cooked through, 4 to 5 minutes per side. (The "tenders" will be cooked sooner, so remove them from the pan when they are done.)

3. Trim and thinly slice the scallions (white and green parts). Rinse and dry the parsley and finely chop it. Stir the scallions, parsley, and 1 tablespoon of the mustard into the artichokes and corn. Cover the skillet and simmer until the flavors come together, 5 minutes. Season to taste with salt and pepper.

4. When the chicken is done, remove it to a plate and add the remaining 1 tablespoon mustard to the skillet. Scrape up the juices and spoon them over the chicken. Serve the artichokes and corn on the side.

Green Chile Chicken

MAKES: *4 servings*
TIME: *30 minutes*

T his delicious supper combines creamy and spicy at the same time. A fresh accompaniment, lovely in its contrasting

crunchy quality, is a salad of greens tossed with strips of raw red bell pepper and loads of chopped fresh cilantro. I like to serve this with bread that has as deep a flavor as the chiles: rye, pumpernickel, and multigrain breads are good, and of course grilled corn tortillas are always welcome.

> 2 tablespoons butter
> 1 onion, finely chopped
> 2 cloves garlic, minced
> ½ teaspoon dried oregano
> 1 teaspoon ground cumin
> 2 tablespoons all-purpose flour
> 2 cups milk
> Salt
> 1 package (10 ounces) frozen corn
>   kernels, thawed
> 2 cans (4 ounces each)
>   chopped green chiles,
>   drained
> 2 whole skinless, boneless chicken
>   breasts (about 1½ pounds total)
> 2 ounces Monterey Jack or sharp
>   Cheddar cheese
> Freshly ground black pepper

1. Melt the butter in a large saucepan over medium heat. Add the onion, cover, and simmer over low heat until it is translucent and tender, about 5 minutes. Add the garlic and sauté for a few seconds just to release its aroma.

2. Add the oregano, cumin, and flour and cook, stirring with a wooden spoon, for 1 minute. Gradually whisk in the milk, stirring continu-

Peppered Stir-Fry

MAKES: *4 servings*
TIME: *20 minutes*

Bell pepper makes a double appearance in this recipe: first as fresh red peppers, then as paprika—which is nothing more than the dried and pulverized form of a type of bell pepper.

> ¼ cup olive oil
> 2 medium red bell peppers (1 pound),
>   stemmed, seeded, and cut into
>   ¼-inch-wide strips
> 2 whole skinless, boneless chicken
>   breasts (about 1½ pounds total)
> 2 cloves garlic
> 1 package (10 ounces) frozen corn
>   kernels, thawed
> 1 tablespoon paprika
> Salt
> Cayenne pepper
> ¼ cup plain yogurt

ously, to create a smooth sauce. When all of the milk is incorporated, bring the liquid to a simmer over medium heat, and simmer to thicken, 2 minutes. Season to taste with salt.

3. Add the corn and chiles and simmer, uncovered, while you prepare the chicken and cheese.

4. Cut the chicken into 1 × ½-inch strips, and grate the cheese or cut it into ¼-inch dice.

5. Add the chicken to the sauce, bring to a simmer over low heat, and cook, uncovered, until the chicken is just cooked through, 5 minutes. Remove the saucepan from the heat, add the cheese, and stir until the cheese is just melted. Season to taste with salt and pepper, and serve in deep bowls.

ESPECIALLY GOOD FOR CHILDREN

Omit the oregano and the green chiles. In step 5, after the chicken is cooked, remove half of the mixture and serve it to the kids with some cheese sprinkled on top. For the adults, add 1 can chopped green chiles, ¼ teaspoon oregano, and some dried red pepper flakes to the remaining portion in the saucepan. Then stir in the cheese.

1. Heat the oil in a large skillet over medium heat. Add the bell peppers and cook them, stirring, just to release their flavor, about 2 minutes. Cover the skillet and cook over low heat, until the peppers are completely soft, for 8 to 10 minutes.

2. While the peppers are cooking, cut the chicken into strips about 2 inches long and ¼ inch wide. Mince the garlic and measure out all of the remaining ingredients.

3. Push the peppers to the side of the skillet and add the chicken. Sauté, stirring, over medium-high heat, until the chicken is almost completely opaque, about 2 minutes.

4. Add the garlic, corn, and paprika, cover, and simmer over low heat to heat the corn and cook the chicken through, 2 minutes. Remove the lid, cook over high heat to evaporate any liquid, about 30 seconds. Season to taste with salt and cayenne pepper.

5. Remove the skillet from the heat, add the yogurt, and stir until it is evenly distributed.

SECOND TIME AROUND

Recycle leftovers by moistening them with an additional spoonful or so of yogurt to which you have added a generous pinch of ground cumin. Serve in pita bread with shredded lettuce or sliced cucumbers.

Pimiento Comfort Chicken

MAKES: *4 servings*
TIME: *25 minutes*

This uncomplicated recipe is refreshing in its direct, clean simplicity. It was inspired by a retro 1950s recipe for creamed chicken, but has been updated to be lighter, fresher, and of course quicker. While I like this chicken

over toast, I adore it spooned over biscuits or cornbread. A tangy fruit dessert would contrast nicely with the rich, silky chicken.

> 2 tablespoons vegetable oil
> 2 tablespoons butter
> 1 small onion, finely chopped
> ¼ cup all-purpose flour
> 2 cups milk
> 2 cups plum or stewed tomatoes, chopped, with their juices
> Salt and freshly ground black pepper
> 1 jar (3 to 4 ounces) pimientos or roasted red peppers
> 2 whole skinless, boneless chicken breasts (about 1½ pounds total)
> 1 package (10 ounces) frozen "petite" peas, thawed
> Toast, biscuits, or cornbread, for serving

1. Heat the vegetable oil and butter in a large saucepan over medium heat. Add the onion, cover, and simmer over low heat until it is translucent and tender, about 5 minutes.

2. Add the flour and stir to cook out the raw taste, about 1 minute. Gradually whisk in 1 cup of the milk and stir vigorously until the

it to a simmer. Add the pimientos and diced chicken, and simmer just until the chicken is cooked through.

sauce is thick, about 5 minutes. Then add the tomatoes with their juices and bring the liquid to a simmer. Stir the sauce occasionally to make sure it doesn't scorch. Season with 1 teaspoon salt and pepper to taste. Simmer, uncovered, to thicken it slightly, about 5 minutes.

3. While the sauce is simmering, drain and finely dice the pimientos, and cut the chicken into ½-inch dice. Add them to the sauce along with the peas. Simmer over medium-low heat, stirring occasionally, until the chicken is cooked through, 8 to 10 minutes. Season to taste with salt and pepper, and serve immediately over toast, biscuits, or cornbread.

VARIATION

To save even more time, instead of creating white sauce from scratch, begin the recipe with a cream-of-something soup: Omit steps 1 and 2. Bring a can (12 ounces) of cream of mushroom, Cheddar cheese, or cream of tomato soup to a simmer. Add enough milk to thin the soup to a consistency you like, and bring

Sweet and Fiery Chicken Slivers

MAKES: *4 servings*
TIME: *25 to 30 minutes*

What I love about this recipe is the delightfully fresh counterpoint of the slightly bitter lettuce against the sweetness of the honey and the heat of the spices.

1 large head (1 pound) romaine
  lettuce or escarole
2 large navel oranges
2 whole skinless, boneless chicken
  breasts (about 1½ pounds total)
2 tablespoons honey
1 tablespoon light soy sauce
2 cloves garlic
2 tablespoons Asian sesame oil
½ teaspoon ground ginger
2 cans (8 ounces each) sliced water
  chestnuts, drained
Salt
Dried red pepper flakes

1. Separate the romaine into leaves, and tear each leaf into 4 or 5 pieces. Rinse well, shake off the excess water, and set aside.

2. Grate enough orange zest to give ½ teaspoon. Cut away the peel and white pith from both oranges. Then cut each orange into 8 wedges, and cut the wedges in half. Combine them with the grated zest and set aside.

3. Cut the chicken into 1 × ¼-inch strips. Combine the honey and soy sauce in a small bowl. Mince the garlic.

4. Heat 1 tablespoon of the sesame oil in a 12-inch skillet or wok over medium-high heat. Add the garlic and chicken, and stir continuously until partially cooked, 1 minute. Add the ginger and water chestnuts, and sauté for another minute to warm up. Then add the soy sauce mixture and cook, uncovered, until the chicken is completely cooked, 2 to 3 minutes more.

5. While the chicken is cooking, heat the remaining 1 tablespoon sesame oil in a large skillet over medium-high heat. Add the romaine leaves, and stir them around for just a minute or until almost wilted; season to taste with salt and red pepper flakes, and immediately remove the skillet from the heat.

6. Add the orange zest and oranges to the chicken, and stir for about 30 seconds just to warm the fruit. Immediately remove the skillet from the heat and adjust the seasoning. Arrange a bed of romaine on each dinner plate, and spoon the chicken, oranges, and water chestnuts in the center.

ESPECIALLY GOOD FOR CHILDREN

Omit the romaine or escarole, and serve the chicken and oranges over rice instead. In step 5, omit the red pepper flakes.

Fennel-Smothered Chicken

MAKES: *4 servings*
TIME: *30 to 35 minutes*

The juices from the fennel and tomatoes flavor the chicken as they help cook it, making this dish intensely delicious. The touches of olive paste, freshly grated lemon zest, and golden raisins are inspired by the cooking of Sicily.

> ⅓ cup extra-virgin olive oil
> 4 skinless chicken legs, thighs and
>   drumsticks separated, fat removed
>   (about 2 pounds total)
> 2 medium to large fennel bulbs
> 4 ripe tomatoes (2 pounds), cored
> 4 large cloves garlic
> Salt and freshly ground black pepper
> 1 to 2 lemons
> 1 tablespoon black or green olive paste

1. Heat the olive oil in a deep 12-inch skillet over medium heat. Sauté the

chicken thighs just to begin cooking them, about 2 minutes on each side.

2. While the chicken is cooking, split the fennel bulbs in half vertically and remove the triangular core. Cut the bulbs crosswise into ½-inch-thick slices. Place the fennel on top of the chicken, cover, and continue to cook over medium heat for 5 minutes, or for however long it takes to chop the tomatoes and garlic.

3. Cut the tomatoes into 1-inch chunks and add them on top of the fennel. Coarsely chop the garlic, and add it to the skillet. Season with 1½ teaspoons salt, stir the ingredients together, cover, and continue to cook until the chicken is just cooked through, 20 minutes longer.

4. While the chicken is cooking, grate enough lemon zest to make 1 teaspoon. When the chicken is done, add the olive paste and lemon zest and season to taste with pepper. Serve in deep bowls.

VARIATION

Substitute celery for the fennel: In step 2, cut into 1-inch lengths enough celery ribs to yield about 4 cups.

Chicken and Carrots in Dill Yogurt Sauce

MAKES: *4 servings*
TIME: *30 minutes*

The trick in this recipe is to sauté the chicken thighs long enough so the skin becomes crusty; it will remain crisp even after you cover the skillet to cook the chicken through. I happen to like carrots crisp rather than limp, so I don't cook them for longer than 3 minutes. If you prefer a softer texture, cook them a few minutes more. Serve this chicken dish with pita, focaccia, or Lebanon flatbread.

> 2 tablespoons butter
> 6 to 8 chicken thighs (2 pounds total)
> 1 tablespoon Dijon mustard
> 4 large carrots (1 pound)
> 1 cup (loosely packed) fresh dill or
>   mint leaves
> 1 cup plain yogurt, preferably
>   whole-milk
> Salt and freshly ground black pepper

1. Melt the butter in a large skillet over medium heat. Add the chicken, skin side down, and sauté until the skin is crisp, about 10 minutes. Be sure to turn the chicken several times so it crisps and browns evenly.

2. Using the back of a spoon or a spatula, spread the mustard on both sides of the chicken. Cover the skillet and reduce heat to

low and cook, turning the chicken every now and then, until just cooked through, about 15 minutes.

3. While the chicken is cooking, grate the carrots in a food processor. Remove them to a mixing bowl, and wipe out the bowl of the processor. Rinse and stem the dill, pat it dry, and add it to the processor along with the yogurt. Purée until smooth, and set aside.

4. Remove the chicken to a plate. Add the grated carrots to the skillet along with 1 teaspoon salt, and sauté, stirring continuously, over medium heat until the carrots begin to wilt and are warmed through but still crisp, 3 to 4 minutes.

5. Add the yogurt mixture to the skillet and stir gently over low heat, uncovered, until warmed through, about 1 minute. Take care not to boil the yogurt or it will curdle. Season to taste with salt and pepper. Spoon carrots onto a serving platter and top with the chicken.

Chicken with Lemon Eggplant

MAKES: *4 servings*
TIME: *35 minutes*

The kicker in this Mediterranean-style stew is the lemon zest and juice, which are added right before serving. I prefer to cook this with the juicier dark meat of the chicken, but substitute white meat if you like it better. If you do, cook it for only 4 to 5 minutes or it will be dry. If you don't have a large enough skillet, cook the eggplant in batches in step 1 and transfer it to a 4-quart saucepan. In step 2, add the zucchini to the saucepan and proceed with the recipe.

> *¼ cup olive oil*
> *1 large eggplant (1½ pounds), cut into 1-inch cubes*
> *2 zucchini (1 pound)*
> *3 large cloves garlic*
> *½ teaspoon thyme*
> *2 cups canned plum tomatoes with their juices*
> *Salt*
> *2 pounds skinless, boneless chicken thighs*
> *1 or 2 lemons*
> *½ cup (packed) fresh basil or flat-leaf parsley leaves*
> *Freshly ground black pepper*

1. Heat the olive oil in a 14-inch skillet over medium-high heat. Add the eggplant and sauté, stirring occasionally, until it begins to become tender and turns golden, about 5 minutes.

2. While the eggplant is cooking, slice the zucchini into ½-inch rounds or chunks (if they are thick, cut them in half lengthwise first). Add the zucchini to the eggplant and sauté for about 1 to 2 minutes or until it is well mixed with eggplant and beginning to soften. Add the whole

garlic cloves, thyme, and tomatoes with their juices. Season with 1 teaspoon salt. Bring the liquid to a simmer, cover, and cook over low heat until the vegetables are tender, 15 minutes.

3. While the vegetables are cooking, cut the chicken into 2-inch chunks. Grate the zest of the lemon (you should have ½ teaspoon) and juice the lemon (you should have 2 to 3 tablespoons at least).

4. Add the chicken to the eggplant stew, cover, and simmer until the chicken has just cooked through, for 6 to 7 minutes. While the chicken is cooking, snip the basil with scissors. When the chicken is done, remove the skillet from the heat and add the lemon zest, juice, and basil. Adjust the seasoning for salt and pepper, and serve in deep bowls.

VARIATION:

For a softer garlic flavor, remove the whole garlic cloves. For more garlic flavor, mash the garlic cloves with the back of a spoon and stir them into the stew before adding the lemon zest.

SECOND TIME AROUND

■ *To stretch leftovers into a second stew, cook some additional zucchini in 1 tablespoonful olive oil, add 1 cup diced ham and the leftovers, and simmer until hot. Serve over rice.*

■ *You can turn leftovers into a soup by combining them with chicken broth and 1 cup thawed frozen "petite" peas.*

Jumble of Stir-Fried Vegetables and Chicken

MAKES: *4 servings*
TIME: *30 to 35 minutes*

This wonderful toss of sliced vegetables and chicken is terrific on hot summer nights because you spend only 5 minutes at the stove. I've seasoned this dish in a subtly Chinese style, but it can be flavored any way you please.

2 medium bell peppers, preferably red
12 ounces fresh mushrooms (preferably portobellos)
6 scallions
1¾ pounds boneless chicken thighs
2 tablespoons vegetable oil
1 can (15 ounces) baby corn, drained
2 teaspoons chili paste with garlic
2 tablespoons hoisin sauce
½ cup salted peanuts
Salt

1. Stem and seed the bell peppers. Cut them into strips ¼ inch wide and 1 inch long. If you

are using portobello mushrooms, remove the tough stems; otherwise trim ¼ inch off the ends of the mushroom stems. Wipe the caps clean with a damp paper towel and cut the mushrooms into ¼-inch-thick slices. Trim off 2 inches of the green tops, and thinly slice the scallions (white and green parts).

2. Pull the skin off the chicken, and remove all visible fat. Cut the chicken into ¼-inch pieces.

3. In a wok or in a wide skillet (at least 12 inches in diameter), heat the vegetable oil over high heat. Add the peppers and stir continuously, until they begin to soften, for 1 minute. Add the chicken and stir continuously until it is almost cooked through, for 2 minutes. Add the mushrooms and stir continuously, until they begin to release their juices, for 1 minute. Add the baby corn and scallions and cook, stirring continuously, until the chicken is thoroughly cooked and the corn is heated through, about 2 minutes longer.

4. Remove the skillet from the heat and stir in the chili paste, hoisin sauce, and peanuts. Stir to thoroughly combine, and season to taste with salt.

VARIATIONS

■ In step 4, substitute ¼ cup Cilantro Purée (page 225) or Coconut Peanut Sauce (page 226) for the chili paste, hoisin sauce, and peanuts.

■ In step 4, substitute ½ cup "hot" salsa and ½ cup chopped fresh cilantro for the chili paste, hoisin sauce, and peanuts.
■ Omit the scallions, and in step 4 substitute ¼ cup pesto, ¼ cup olive paste, and ½ cup pine nuts for the chili paste, hoisin sauce, and peanuts.

Garlic Game Hens in a Skillet

MAKES: *4 servings*
TIME: *45 to 50 minutes*

Simple cooking with few ingredients is always a winning idea, as illustrated by this sophisticated recipe that is done in a minimum of preparation time. A good side dish to serve with these garlicky hens would be mashed potatoes or polenta.

*Rock Cornish hens
    (about 1½ pounds
    each)
3 tablespoons olive oil
4 cloves garlic, lightly
    smashed
¼ cup red wine vinegar
½ cup chicken broth
½ teaspoon dried thyme leaves
½ teaspoon dried rosemary
2 teaspoons Dijon mustard
Salt and freshly ground black pepper*

1. Remove the giblets from the interior of each game hen. With heavy-duty kitchen shears, cut along either side of the backbone and remove it. Cut off and remove the first two joints of the wings, so only the fleshy joint is left on the breast. Also cut off and remove any excess neck skin. Pat the skin dry with paper towels.

2. Heat the oil in a large skillet over medium heat until very hot, about 2 minutes. Add the game hens, skin side down, and cook until golden, 5 minutes. Using tongs, turn the hens over. Add the garlic and sauté for another 5 minutes.

3. Add the vinegar and broth (which will bubble up), then the thyme and rosemary. Cover and simmer over low heat until the juices run clear when a thigh is pricked with a fork, 25 to 30 minutes.

4. Transfer the hens to a plate. Stir the mustard into the juices in the skillet, scraping up the brown cooking bits into the sauce, and boil down furiously over high heat until ½ cup of liquid remains, 1 to 2 minutes. Season to taste with salt and pepper, spoon over the hens, and serve immediately.

Pecan Chicken Patties

MAKES: *2 servings*
TIME: *20 minutes*

This is a wonderful way to recycle any type of leftover chicken: it works with chicken mixed with other ingredients, seasonings, and even vegetables, and of course it works great with cooked plain chicken of any sort. I like these little patties on bread and eat them as I would a burger, but my husband and daughter prefer them with a side of pasta. They're delicious, too, with coleslaw or with a green salad tossed with a mustard vinaigrette.

1 tablespoon vegetable oil
½ cup chopped onion
½ Granny Smith apple, peeled, cored, and chopped
2 cups coarsely chopped cooked chicken
½ cup walnuts or pecans
1 large egg
1 tablespoon butter
Salt and freshly ground black pepper

1.   Heat the oil in small skillet, over low heat. Add onion and apple and cook, covered, until soft, about 3 minutes.

2.   Further chop the chicken in a food processor; then add the nuts and chop again. Add the cooked onion and apple and the egg, and process until the mixture is combined and comes together but is not pasty. Season with ½ teaspoon salt and pepper to taste. Divide and shape the mixture into 4 patties.

3.   Melt the butter in a 9-inch nonstick skillet over medium heat. Cook the patties until heated through and golden, 3 minutes on each side.

Warm Spiced Chicken Patties

MAKES: *4 servings*
TIME: *35 minutes*

Mayonnaise adds a lovely flavor to these chicken patties and prevents them from turning dry. Have the corn coleslaw ready before you begin cooking the patties so you don't miss out on the delightful contrast between the cool slaw and the warm patties. Cornbread or biscuits would be a satisfying way to round out this meal.

⅔ cup regular or low-fat mayonnaise
¼ cup chopped pimientos
2 tablespoons white wine vinegar or
    cider vinegar
2 teaspoons celery salt
4 cups (8 ounces) shredded cabbage
1 package (10 ounces) frozen corn
    kernels, thawed and patted dry
Salt and freshly ground black pepper
1 clove garlic, minced
½ teaspoon Tabasco or other hot
    sauce, to taste
1 egg, lightly beaten
1¼ pounds ground chicken or turkey
½ cup dried bread or cracker crumbs
4 tablespoons (½ stick) butter

1.   In a large mixing bowl, combine ⅓ cup of the mayonnaise with the pimientos, wine vinegar, and 1 teaspoon of the celery salt. Add the cabbage and corn. Mix well, season to taste with salt and pepper, and chill while the chicken patties cook.

2.   In another mixing bowl, thoroughly combine the remaining ⅓ cup mayonnaise and 1 teaspoon celery salt with the garlic, Tabasco, and egg. Add the chicken and mix well. Divide the mixture into 8 portions and pat to form patties. Coat the patties in the bread crumbs and set aside.

3.   Melt the butter in a large skillet over medium heat. When the foaming subsides, add the chicken patties and cook until cooked through, about 6 minutes per side.

4.   Remove the coleslaw from the refrigerator

and divide it among 4 dinner plates. Center 2 chicken patties over each portion and serve immediately.

RITZY CRUMBS

My favorite coating for these chicken patties is Ritz cracker crumbs, which I like because of their buttery saltiness. Pulverize 2 ounces of Ritz crackers in a food processor or in a sealable plastic bag with a rolling pin or heavy skillet to create the ½ cup of crumbs needed.

Fried Green Bananas with Spiced Ground Chicken

MAKES: *4 servings*
TIME: *30 minutes*

This is a wonderfully exotic dinner inspired by *picadillo*, a Latin American version of spiced ground beef. Ripe plantains would be delicious with this picadillo, and they are quick to cook, but I have substituted green bananas because plantains aren't common in most U.S. markets. The bananas must be very green and unripe so that they are starchy and not sweet.

Even after cooking, the green bananas taste more like potatoes than they do bananas. The yogurt moistens the dish and the cilantro brings in a note of freshness.

4 very green unripe medium
    bananas
2 tablespoons butter
2 tablespoons all-purpose flour
½ teaspoon ground cinnamon
Salt
2 tablespoons olive oil
2 cloves garlic, minced
½ teaspoon ground allspice
2 teaspoons chili powder
½ teaspoon dried oregano
1½ pounds ground chicken or turkey
2 tablespoons water
2 tablespoons tomato paste
¼ cup dried currants, or ½ cup
    golden raisins
½ cup pimiento-stuffed olives,
    coarsely chopped
¼ teaspoon cayenne pepper
1 cup plain yogurt or sour cream
Honey (optional)
1 cup (loosely packed) fresh mint or
    cilantro leaves, chopped

1. Peel the bananas with a paring knife (the peel doesn't come off easily when the bananas are unripe). Cut them in half lengthwise, then in half lengthwise again, so you have 4 long strips, each about ½ inch wide.

2. Melt the butter in a large nonstick skillet over medium heat. Using a fork, mix the flour, cinnamon, and ½ teaspoon salt together on a plate. Dip the bananas in the seasoned flour and set them, flat side down, in the skillet. Sauté over medium heat, for 3 minutes. Turn them over, cover, and cook until brown and crisp all over, 3 to 4 minutes longer.

3. While the bananas are cooking, heat the olive oil in a 12-inch skillet over medium heat. When the oil is hot, add the garlic, allspice, chili powder, and oregano and sauté until aromatic, 10 seconds.

4. Add the ground chicken and cook until almost cooked through, about 5 minutes. As you cook the chicken, keep mashing it with the side of a wooden spoon so that it crumbles evenly.

5. Stir the water into the tomato paste to dissolve it, and add it to the chicken along with the currants and olives. Simmer until cooked through, 2 to 3 minutes. Season to taste with salt and cayenne pepper.

6. Remove the skillet from the heat. Spoon the chicken in the center of each dinner plate and top with some yogurt. Surround the chicken with slices of banana. Drizzle a tiny bit of honey over the bananas if you wish. Garnish the chicken and bananas with the mint.

VARIATION

If you want to substitute plantains for the green bananas, pick ones that are black—they will be ripe and sweet. Ripe plantains are so sugary, in fact, that you should omit the honey in step 6. Three plantains should be ample here.

SECOND TIME AROUND

■ *Chop leftover cooked bananas and mix them with leftover cooked chicken. Stuff corn tortillas with the mixture and place the tortillas, seam side down, in a baking dish; top with tomato sauce. Bake until heated through, 15 minutes.*

■ *You could also just add spaghetti sauce to the leftovers and serve them over hamburger buns as you would Sloppy Joes.*

ESPECIALLY GOOD FOR CHILDREN

If you just omit the cayenne pepper, most kids will love this dish. My daughter did, much to her own amazement.

Pesto Chicken Meatballs

MAKES: *4 servings*
TIME: *40 minutes*

These delicious meatballs are easy enough to make during the week, and perfect to do in batches on a weekend. If you make extra, after browning, cook them, covered, without a sauce, for 5 minutes; then let them cool to room temperature. Freeze them, uncovered, in a single layer on a baking dish. When frozen solid, drop them into a plastic bag and store them in the freezer for a night when you yearn for a hearty meal but don't have much time to cook. Reheat the meatballs straight from the freezer in a tomato sauce. They make great hero sandwiches, but if there's time, do try them over spaghetti.

1¼ pounds ground chicken or turkey
¼ cup prepared pesto or Basil and Garlic Purée (page 224)
½ cup dried bread crumbs
1 egg, slightly beaten
Salt and freshly ground black pepper
½ cup all-purpose flour
3 tablespoons olive oil
2 cups prepared tomato sauce

1. Combine the chicken, pesto, bread crumbs, and egg in a mixing bowl. Using your hands, squeeze the ingredients together until they are evenly mixed, but don't overwork the mixture. Season to taste with salt and pepper.

2. Shape the mixture into small balls, using about a tablespoon per round. If you are having difficulty shaping them, chill the mixture for 10 minutes. When they are all shaped, dredge them in flour and shake off the excess.

3. Heat the oil in a 12-inch skillet over medium-high heat. Add the meatballs in a single layer and cook them, undisturbed, until one side is deep brown, 1½ to 2 minutes.

4. Using a slotted spoon, turn the meatballs and cook, undisturbed again, until the other side is deep brown, about 2 minutes. Loosen the meatballs from the bottom of the skillet with your slotted spoon to make sure they are not sticking.

5. Add the tomato sauce, cover, and simmer over medium heat until they are cooked through, 10 minutes.

VARIATIONS

■ In step 1, instead of the pesto, substitute ¼ cup minced fresh parsley, dill, or basil, and use only ⅓ cup dried bread crumbs.

■ In step 1, instead of the pesto, use 2 tablespoons black olive paste, tapenade, or any of the herb purées (see pages 224 and 225).

■ In step 1, substitute 2 small cloves minced garlic or ½ cup finely sliced scallions (white and green parts) for the pesto.

Chicken Curry, Michèle's Way

MAKES: *4 servings*
TIME: *30 minutes*

Т his is my Monday-to-Friday interpretation of a southern recipe called Country Captain, which is itself a loosely interpreted version of an Indian curry. I've turned it into a fabulously soupy mixture that is delicious spooned over toasted hamburger buns, pasta, or rice. The recipe gives you a choice of cooking the chicken with 1 or 2 cups of broth. Less broth means a thicker mixture, better to spoon over bread; more broth means a more fluid texture, better to spoon over rice or noodles.

1 onion
2 ribs celery
1 Granny Smith apple, peeled
    and cored
2 tablespoons vegetable oil
4 tablespoons (½ stick) butter
4 teaspoons curry powder
1 to 1¼ pounds ground chicken or turkey
1 tablespoon tomato paste
1 to 2 cups chicken broth
2 cups frozen "petite" peas, thawed
Salt
Cayenne pepper
¾ cup plain yogurt or sour cream

1. Finely chop the onion, celery, and apple in a food processor.

2. Heat the oil and butter in a large skillet over medium heat. Add the onion, celery, and apple, and cook, stirring occasionally, until the ingredients are tender, 6 to 7 minutes.

3. Add the curry powder and stir it into the mixture. Add the ground chicken and cook until it is crumbled and no longer pink, about 5 minutes. As you cook the chicken, keep mashing it with the side of a wooden spoon so that it crumbles evenly.

4. Add the tomato paste, broth, and peas. Bring the liquid to a simmer and cook over low heat until the peas are just heated through, 3 to 4 minutes.

5. Season to taste with salt and cayenne pepper, and remove the skillet from the heat. Stir in the yogurt and serve immediately.

VARIATIONS

▪ In step 1, substitute an unripe pear for the apple, and in step 4 add ½ cup raisins after you add the chicken broth. Garnish with 1 cup chopped unsalted roasted peanuts.

▪ In step 3, instead of curry powder, add 4 teaspoons of a mixture of spices, such as ground cumin, cardamom, cloves, cinnamon, coriander, and turmeric, to create a more authentic "Indian" curry.

Lemon Turkey and Creamy Chickpeas

MAKES: *4 servings*
TIME: *20 to 25 minutes*

I always overeat when I prepare this dish—that's how fabulous it is. The chickpeas are partially puréed to release their nutty flavor and provide a velvety texture without any heavy cream. The contrast of the vibrant lemon-perfumed turkey with this silky purée is just terrific. What also doesn't hurt is the fact that the meal can be on the table in 20 minutes!

2 cans (19 ounces each) chickpeas rinsed and drained
½ cup water
4 tablespoons olive oil
½ teaspoon dried oregano
2 large cloves garlic, minced
½ teaspoon ground cinnamon
1½ pounds ground turkey or chicken
2 lemons
½ cup (packed) fresh mint or cilantro leaves
½ cup (packed) fresh parsley leaves
Salt and freshly ground black pepper

1. Purée half the chickpeas with the water and 2 tablespoons of the oil in a blender or food processor. Transfer the purée to a small saucepan, and combine it with the remaining chickpeas and the oregano. Bring the purée to a simmer over very low heat, stirring every now and then so it doesn't scorch.

2. Meanwhile, heat the remaining 2 tablespoons oil in a large skillet over medium heat. Add the garlic and cinnamon and sauté for a few seconds, until the garlic releases its aroma. Add the turkey and cook, stirring and mashing the turkey with a wooden spoon against the sides of the pan to crumble it, about 5 minutes.

3. While the turkey is cooking, grate ½ tea-

spoon of lemon zest and juice the lemons (you should have close to ⅓ cup of juice). Finely chop the mint and parsley.

4. When the chickpea purée is hot and the turkey is cooked through, add the lemon zest and juice to the turkey and continue to cook until the turkey has absorbed most of the juice, about 1 minute. Season to taste with salt and pepper, and add the chopped mint and parsley.

5. To serve, make a wreath of turkey on each dinner plate and spoon the chickpea purée in the middle.

VARIATION

A lovely, more Italian-tasting version, is to make this dish with white cannellini beans rather than chickpeas. In step 1, purée half the white beans with the water and olive oil, season it with ½ teaspoon dried sage and ½ teaspoon dried marjoram instead of the oregano. Omit the cinnamon in step 2 and the mint in step 4.

SECOND TIME AROUND

Combine the leftovers with 2 cups chopped plum tomatoes and enough broth to turn it into a soup.

Smoked Chicken Sausage in Red Wine

MAKES: *4 servings*
TIME: *30 minutes*

*B*oeuf bourguignon, that hearty French stew of beef cubes braised in Burgundy wine and mushrooms, was the inspiration for this fabulous chicken stew. I've substituted a smoked spicy chicken sausage for the beef chunks, and given that I don't have the time to peel, parboil, and braise pearl onions, I use onions from a jar, which come already peeled and softened. A wide variety of poultry sausages is available in specialty food shops, and even at the butcher counters of large supermarket chains. I happen to like a spicy smoked sausage, but you could use an unsmoked one just as well.

2 tablespoons olive oil
6 smoked chicken sausages (1½ pounds)
10 ounces mushrooms
¼ cup (packed) fresh parsley leaves
1½ cups (15-ounce jar) whole pearl onions, drained
1 cup good-quality red wine
1 cup chicken broth
Salt and freshly ground black pepper
2 tablespoons butter (optional)

1. Heat the olive oil in a large skillet over medium heat. Prick the sausages with a fork, add them to the skillet, and sauté to stiffen the skin, about 2 minutes. Cover, and cook the sausages on one side over medium-high heat for 5 minutes.

2. While the sausages are cooking, trim ¼ inch off the mushroom stems. Clean the mushrooms with a damp paper towel, and cut them into ¼-inch-thick slices.

3. Turn the sausages over, prick them again, cover, and cook over medium heat for another 10 minutes. While they are cooking, mince the parsley.

4. Transfer the sausages to a plate. Add the mushrooms and onions to the remaining liquid in the skillet, and toss to combine. Add the wine and broth and bring to a boil. Cook over high heat, uncovered, until only half of the liquid remains, about 10 minutes. While the liquid is reducing, slice the cooked sausages into ¾-inch pieces.

5. When the wine and broth have reduced by half, season the mushrooms and onions with salt and pepper. Return the sausage slices to the skillet along with any accumulated juices, and continue to cook the liquid down until mostly evaporated, another 5 minutes. There should be about ½ cup of thin liquid remaining in the skillet. Remove the skillet from the heat, stir in the parsley and butter, and adjust the seasoning. Serve immediately.

VARIATION

In step 4, substitute 2 Granny Smith apples, peeled, cored, and thinly sliced, for the onions; and substitute 1 cup hard apple cider for the red wine. In steps 3 and 5, instead of the parsley add 1 scallion, thinly sliced (white and green parts).

Spiced Sausage with Greens, Corn, and Apples

MAKES: *4 servings*
TIME: *20 to 25 minutes*

Select a spicy sausage to hold its own with the bite of the greens and the sweet tartness of the corn and apples. To save on time, make sure you choose a cooked sausage, which can be reheated in minutes.

3 quarts water
8 spicy smoked cooked chicken or
turkey sausages
(about 1½ pounds total)
1 tablespoon vegetable oil
2 Granny Smith apples
1 package (10 ounces) frozen corn
kernels, thawed
1 pound greens, such as escarole,
mustard greens, or kale

1. Bring the water to a boil in a large pot.

2. Cut the sausages into ½-inch rounds. Heat the oil in a 12-inch skillet over medium heat. Add the sausage rounds and cook them about 4 minutes, while you peel, core, and cut the apples into ½-inch dice.

3. Stir the sausages, add the apples and corn, and cover the skillet. Simmer over low heat 10 to 12 minutes, while you prepare and blanch the greens.

4. Fill a large bowl with cold water. Remove and discard the thick stems of the greens, and tear the leaves into 2-inch pieces. Soak them in the bowl of water; then lift them out, leaving the grit behind in the bowl. Repeat this step once more with fresh water.

5. Plunge the greens into the boiling water and cook for 1 minute to soften. Drain, and add the blanched greens to the skillet. Stir, cover, and simmer for 5 minutes. Serve in deep bowls.

Chicken Sausages over Red Lentil Purée

MAKES: *4 servings*
TIME: *25 to 30 minutes*

When planning a quick meal, lentils don't exactly come to mind as an ingredient that is speedy to cook. Red lentils, however, can be done in 15 minutes and provide a terrific, rarely used Monday-to-Friday alternative to pasta and potatoes. This recipe was inspired by the Italian New Year's dish of *cotechino*—a lightly cured fresh pork sausage that is usually boiled or steamed—served with lentils. Here I have substituted the quicker-cooking red lentils for green ones, and a smoked chicken sausage for the *cotechino*.

1¼ cups red lentils
2½ cups water or chicken
  broth
2 cloves garlic, minced
⅛ teaspoon turmeric
¼ teaspoon ground sage
6 smoked chicken or turkey sausages
  (about 1½ pounds total)
¾ pound escarole
1 tablespoon olive oil
1 tablespoon tomato paste
2 tablespoons water
Salt and freshly ground black pepper
2 teaspoons balsamic vinegar

1. Combine the lentils with the water, garlic, turmeric (which helps keep the color of the lentils red), and sage in a 4-quart saucepan. Slowly bring the liquid to a simmer over medium heat. Partially cover the saucepan and simmer over very low heat (so the lentils don't foam over) until tender, about 10 minutes.

2. Meanwhile, slice the sausages into ½-inch rounds. Rinse the escarole leaves, shake off the excess water, and cut the leaves crosswise into ¾-inch slices.

3. Heat the oil in a 12-inch skillet over medium heat. Add the sausages and cook, covered, for 2 to 3 minutes. Turn them over and cook until slightly browned, another 2 to 3 minutes. Add the escarole to the skillet, cover, and simmer over low heat until the escarole begins to release its liquid, 3 minutes. Stir the sausages and escarole together and continue to cook over medium heat, stirring every now and then, until almost all of the liquid has evaporated, about 1 minute. Combine the tomato paste with the water and add it to the skillet; mix with the sausages and escarole. Season to taste with salt and pepper.

4. Season the lentils to taste with salt and pepper, and if you have an immersion blender, purée them right in the pot. (If you don't have such a tool, leave the lentils whole.) Stir in the balsamic vinegar. Spoon the lentil purée into shallow bowls, and arrange the sausages and escarole in the middle.

ESPECIALLY GOOD FOR CHILDREN

This is great to serve to kids, provided you braise the escarole separately and serve it on the side. To do so, gently heat it in 1 tablespoon olive oil in a covered skillet. Uncover the skillet and cook off the liquid. Season to taste with salt and pepper.

COMPLETE MEALS

Alessia's Favorite Chicken Supper

MAKES: *4 servings*
TIME: *20 to 25 minutes*

Take heart, all you mothers out there with picky eaters. When she was very young, my daughter's diet consisted primarily of potatoes, peanut butter, pasta, the occasional tuna fish sandwich, and lots of chocolate. Now an adolescent, Alessia has become a good eater with such a sophisticated palate that she is the one who suggested the quantity of ripe olives to add to this recipe.

2 tablespoons butter

2 whole skinless, boneless chicken breasts (about 1½ pounds total), halved, "tenders" removed and reserved for another use

8 to 10 ounces mushrooms

4½ cups water or chicken broth

Salt

1 cup instant polenta

2 cloves garlic, minced

1½ cups canned plum tomatoes, chopped, with their juices

¾ cup sliced pitted olives packed in olive oil, preferably Kalamata or "country-style" green olives

Freshly ground black pepper or dried red pepper flakes

1. Melt the butter in a large skillet over medium heat. When the foaming subsides, add the chicken breasts and cook until almost completely cooked through, about 4 minutes per side. Remove the chicken to a plate.

2. While the chicken is cooking, wipe the mushrooms clean with a damp paper towel, trim about ¼ inch off the ends of the stems, and cut the mushrooms into ¼-inch-thick slices.

3. Bring the water to a boil and add 1 teaspoon salt. Add the polenta, cover, and simmer over very low heat, stirring occasionally, until done, 5 minutes. Remove from the heat and keep covered until ready to serve.

4. After removing the chicken to the plate, add the garlic and mushrooms to the skillet and sauté, just until you get a whiff of the garlic. Then add the tomatoes with their juices and the olives and bring the liquid to a simmer, about 30 seconds. Cover and simmer until the mushrooms are cooked through, 5 minutes. Season to taste with salt and pepper, and return the chicken, and any juices it has given off, to the sauce. Simmer, uncovered, for a minute or so to fully heat the chicken.

5. Divide the polenta evenly among 4 plates. Top each serving with chicken and sauce, and serve.

VARIATION

Instead of polenta, cook ¾ cup quick-cooking white hominy grits in 2¾ cups salted water to which you have added 1 clove garlic. When the grits are done, remove the garlic clove and stir in ½ to ¾ cup grated sharp Cheddar cheese.

Pantry Chicken Dinner

A BLUEPRINT RECIPE

MAKES: *4 servings*
TIME: *15 to 25 minutes*

This recipe yields a remarkably delicious dinner, especially considering that it is fashioned out of pantry ingredients. First you start the starch to serve with the chicken—pasta, polenta, rice, or potatoes. While the starch is cooking, dice the chicken and cook it until halfway done. Then finish cooking it in 2 cups of a frozen vegetable combined with a seasoning sauce, such as salsa, pesto, or another homemade goodie you've got stashed in the freezer. Take a look at the variations below to figure out how to create your own version.

4½ cups water
Salt
1 cup instant polenta
3 tablespoons olive oil
1½ cups (loosely packed) freshly grated
* Parmesan cheese*
1 pound skinless, boneless chicken
* breasts or thighs*
1 package (10 ounces) frozen mixed
* vegetables, thawed*
1 cup mild salsa
Freshly ground black pepper

1. Bring the water and 1 teaspoon salt to a boil in a saucepan over moderate heat. Slowly pour in the polenta, cover, and simmer over low heat, stirring occasionally, until the polenta is cooked through, about 5 minutes. Remove from the heat, and stir in 1 tablespoon of the olive oil and the cheese. Keep warm, covered, until the chicken is done.

2. While the polenta is cooking, cut the chicken into ¾-inch cubes. Heat the remaining 2 tablespoons olive oil in a 12-inch skillet over medium heat. Add the chicken and cook, stirring, until partially cooked, 3 minutes.

3. Add the vegetables and stir for 1 minute more. Then add the salsa, cover, and cook over low heat until the chicken is cooked through and the vegetables are hot, 5 minutes more. Remove the chicken from the heat and season to taste with salt and pepper. Serve over the polenta.

VARIATIONS

■ In step 1, instead of cooking the polenta, bring 1¼ cups long-grain rice and 2 cups water to a boil. Or boil 2 pounds scrubbed new potatoes, cut into ½-inch dice. Or bring 4 quarts of water to a boil in which to cook 1 pound of spaghettini or linguini fini.

■ In step 3, instead of the mixed vegetables, substitute 1 package thawed frozen corn, "petite" peas, or chopped artichokes. And, instead of the salsa, use 2 to 4 tablespoons pesto or olive paste (good with potatoes or pasta and peas), or ¼ to ½ cup cilantro purée (good with rice and peas), or ½ to 1 cup tomato sauce (good with pasta and corn or artichokes).

Chicken and Apple Toss over Polenta

MAKES: *4 servings*
TIME: *25 to 30 minutes*

Some of the flavors of Thanksgiving inspired this dish of sautéed chicken, onions, apples, and raisins. It's served over polenta, the Italian version of cornmeal mush. The instant dry polenta, imported from Italy, towers over the reconstituted variety (which comes packaged in a plastic tube, is ready to be slicedw and reheated, and tastes absolutely dreadful).

½ cup golden raisins
2 tablespoons balsamic vinegar
1 onion
1¼ pounds skinless, boneless chicken "tenders," breasts, or thighs
2 to 4 tablespoons butter
3 Granny Smith apples
5¼ cups chicken broth or water
¼ teaspoon dried red pepper flakes
1 bay leaf
Salt
1¼ cups instant polenta
Freshly ground black pepper

1. Combine the raisins and vinegar in a bowl and set aside. Finely dice the onion. Cut the chicken into ½-inch dice.

2. Melt the butter in a large skillet over medium heat. Add the onion and sauté, stirring now and then, until it is golden and smells wonderful, 3 to 4 minutes. While the onion is cooking, peel the apples and cut them into ½-inch cubes.

3. Add the apples to the onion and sauté over low heat, stirring so they don't stick, until they begin to turn golden and tender, 3 to 4 minutes.

4. Meanwhile, combine 5 cups of the broth, the red pepper flakes, bay leaf, and 1 teaspoon salt in a medium saucepan and bring to a boil over high heat. In a slow steady stream add the instant polenta to the liquid. Cover, lower the heat to medium-low, and cook, stirring every now and then so the bottom doesn't scorch, for 5 minutes.

5. Add the chicken to the apples and onion, and stir for a minute. Add the raisins and vinegar and the remaining ¼ cup chicken broth, and bring to a simmer. Cover and cook over low heat until the chicken is just cooked through, 5 minutes. Season to taste with salt and pepper. Remove and discard the bay leaf.

6. Add another 2 tablespoons butter to the polenta if you wish, and adjust the seasoning. Serve the polenta in the bottom of a deep dish, and spoon the chicken and apples on top.

ESPECIALLY GOOD FOR COMPANY *Turn this into a spectacular dish, worthy of serving to company, by adding 3 to 4 tablespoons sour cream or mascarpone to the polenta right before serving. Dust the chicken with a sprinkling of chopped parsley to make the dish look more attractive, and serve with hard apple cider.*

Chicken Satay-Style with Couscous

MAKES: *4 servings*
TIME: *35 to 40 minutes*

"Sinfully delicious" would be appropriate words to describe this superb combination of chicken, coconut milk, peanuts, and lime juice. The recipe does take 35 minutes to prepare, but, boy, is it worth it! While the chicken is cooking and the couscous reheating, cut strips of Kirby cucumbers or bell pepper as a crisp refreshing vegetable accompaniment. Fresh mangoes or sliced pineapple would make a terrific dessert.

> 1½ cups water
> ¾ cup unsweetened coconut milk
> 4 tablespoons lemon or lime juice
>   (from 2 lemons or 3 limes)
> Salt
> 1¾ cups (10-ounce box) couscous
> 1 clove garlic, minced
> 1 teaspoon curry powder
> ¼ cup peanut butter, preferably chunky
> 1¼ pounds skinless, boneless chicken
>   (breasts or thighs), cut into strips about
>   ½ inch wide and 3
>   inches long
> 4 tablespoons (½ stick)
>   butter
> Freshly ground black
>   pepper

1. Combine the water, ¼ cup of the coconut milk, 2 tablespoons of the lemon juice, and 1 teaspoon salt in a mixing bowl. Add the couscous and steep for 15 minutes while you proceed to the next step.

2. In another mixing bowl, combine the garlic, curry powder, and peanut butter. Whisk in the remaining ½ cup coconut milk and 2 tablespoons lemon juice. Season the mixture with 1 teaspoon salt, and marinate the chicken strips in it while the couscous is steeping.

3. Melt the butter in a large wide skillet over medium heat. Add the chicken with its marinating liquid and cook, stirring frequently, until the chicken turns opaque, about 3 minutes. Cover and simmer over low heat until the chicken is just cooked through, 5 minutes.

4. Scatter the couscous over the chicken and simmer, covered, over low heat until the couscous has heated and the chicken is cooked through, 8 minutes. Take care to do this over low heat so the chicken does not burn. Mix the ingredients together, adjust the seasoning, and serve immediately.

SECOND TIME AROUND

For each 1 cup of leftovers, sauté 1 cup julienned or grated vegetable, such as carrot, snow peas, bean sprouts, red bell pepper, or cabbage, in 1 tablespoon vegetable oil. Add the leftovers and cook just until warmed through. To wake up the flavor, season to taste with drops of rice vinegar or fresh lemon juice and dried red pepper flakes. (If the leftovers stick to the skillet, add drops of water to release them.) Garnish with chopped fresh parsley or cilantro leaves.

Chicken and Chickpeas over Couscous

MAKES: *4 servings*
TIME: *25 to 30 minutes*

....

Another good recipe for calorie counters, but few calories doesn't have to mean little flavor. This combination of chickpeas and chicken is seasoned with the full-bodied flavors of cinnamon, ginger, and garlic. The raisins add a natural sweetness, and the squash adds body. Because no fat is used in the dish, I prepare it in a saucepan instead of a skillet.

> 2½ cups water
> 1 teaspoon ground cinnamon
> Salt
> 1 cup couscous
> 1 can (16 ounces) chickpeas, drained
> ½ teaspoon ground ginger
> ¼ teaspoon ground turmeric or paprika
> 1 clove garlic, minced
> 1 package (10 ounces) frozen sliced
>   carrots, thawed
> 1 package (10 ounces) frozen cooked
>   winter squash, thawed
> 1 pound skinless, boneless chicken breasts
> 2 large lemons
> ¼ cup (packed) fresh cilantro leaves
> ⅔ cup raisins
> Freshly ground black pepper
> Chopped fresh parsley or cilantro,
>   for garnish (optional)

1. Combine 1½ cups of the water, ½ teaspoon of the cinnamon, and ½ teaspoon salt in a saucepan and bring to a boil. Add the couscous, stir, remove from the heat, and cover. Set aside.

2. Combine the chickpeas, ginger, turmeric, garlic, carrots, squash, and remaining 1 cup water in another saucepan. Cover and bring to a simmer over medium-low heat. Simmer gently for 10 minutes.

3. While the chickpeas simmer, cut the chicken into ½-inch cubes, juice the lemons (you need 4 tablespoons), and mince the cilantro.

4. Add the chicken and raisins to the chickpeas, cover, and continue to simmer over low heat until the chicken is cooked through, 5 minutes. Season to taste with salt and pepper, and stir in 2 tablespoons of the lemon juice.

5. Give the couscous a stir, add the remaining 2 tablespoons lemon juice, and adjust the seasoning. Spoon the chickpeas and chicken into deep bowls and top with a portion of couscous. If you wish, garnish with chopped parsley.

VARIATION

Right before serving, off the heat, spoon ½ cup sour cream into the chickpeas and chicken. In a small skillet, sauté ½ cup sliced almonds or chopped pecans in 2 tablespoons butter until they give off a toasted aroma, 1 to 2 minutes. When the almonds turn golden, sprinkle them with 1 tablespoon sugar and continue to cook until they look glazed, about 1 minute more. Immediately remove from the heat. Top the couscous with the almonds.

Thai-Style Chicken Skillet

MAKES: *4 servings*
TIME: *35 minutes*

Given how easy it is to execute, this stew is unbelievably delicious. The complex flavor of this recipe derives from blending many and varied spices and seasonings, so don't cut down the quantities or on the number of ingredients.

1¼ cups long-grain rice, preferably
    converted
Salt
2 cups water
1 package (10 ounces) frozen "petite"
    peas, thawed
2 tablespoons butter
3 small cloves garlic, minced
¾ teaspoon ground cumin
½ teaspoon ground ginger
2 teaspoons nuoc mam (bottled Asian
    fish sauce) or 1 teaspoon anchovy
    paste (optional)
2 tablespoons all-purpose flour
1 cup coconut milk
1¼ cups chicken broth
1¼ pounds skinless, boneless chicken
    (breasts or thighs), cut into thin
    1-inch strips
1 tablespoon unsweetened
    unhomogenized peanut butter
½ teaspoon cayenne pepper
1 cup fresh cilantro leaves, finely chopped
4 lime wedges

1. Combine the rice, salt, and water in a saucepan and bring to a simmer over low heat. Cover and cook until the rice is barely tender, 15 minutes. Add the peas and simmer until the rice is tender and the peas are warmed through, another 2 to 3 minutes. Keep the rice warm, covered, until the chicken is done.

2. While the rice and peas are cooking, melt the butter in a large deep skillet over medium heat. Add the garlic, cumin, and ginger and sauté, stirring, for a few seconds. Then add the nuoc mam and flour and cook, stirring with a wooden spoon, until the flour taste is cooked out a bit, about 1 minute.

3. Stir in the coconut milk and broth, and, whisking continuously, slowly add to the skillet over medium heat. Bring the liquid to a simmer. Season with ½ teaspoon salt. When the coconut sauce has thickened after 1 minute, stir in the chicken strips and simmer, uncovered, until cooked through, 3 minutes. Whisk in the peanut butter. (Work it in from the edge of the skillet so it is easier to blend into the sauce). Stir the ingredients together to evenly distribute the peanut butter in the sauce.

4. Remove the skillet from the heat, stir in the cayenne and cilantro, and adjust the seasoning. Serve over the rice and peas, and garnish each portion with a lime wedge.

Chinese Chicken and Broccoli Sauté

MAKES: *4 servings*
TIME: *25 to 30 minutes*

What a difference a stash of exotic pantry ingredients can make in everyday fare! This is basically a sauté of chicken and broccoli, seasoned beautifully with Chinese spices that keep on your shelves for months. Serve a soothingly cool fruit dessert, such as chunked fresh pineapple or mangoes mixed with sliced bananas.

1¾ cups water
Salt
1 cup long-grain rice, preferably
   Texmati
1¼ pounds skinless, boneless chicken
   (breasts or "tenders")
½ head broccoli
2 cloves garlic
1 quarter-size slice peeled fresh ginger
½ cup chicken broth
1 tablespoon soy sauce
¼ cup hoisin sauce
2 teaspoons cornstarch
2 teaspoons water
2 tablespoons vegetable oil
2 tablespoons Asian sesame oil
Freshly ground black pepper
½ cup dry-roasted peanuts or cashews,
   finely chopped (optional)

1. Bring the water and some salt to a boil. Add the rice, cover, and simmer over low heat for 15 to 17 minutes or until just cooked through. Keep the rice warm, covered, off the heat.

2. While the rice is cooking, cut the chicken into ¾-inch cubes. Separate the broccoli florets from the stalks and cut the florets into bite-size pieces. Peel the stalks and cut them into ½-inch slices. Mince the garlic and ginger. Combine the chicken broth with the soy and hoisin sauces. Dissolve the cornstarch in the water, and stir in the broth. Set aside.

3. Heat the vegetable and sesame oils in a wok or deep 14-inch skillet over high heat until hot. Add the chicken and sauté, stirring continuously, until the pieces turn opaque, about 1 minute. Add the sliced broccoli stems and sauté, stirring continuously, about 1 minute more. Then add the florets and sauté until the broccoli is bright green, 1 minute longer.

4. Add the garlic and ginger and sauté until their aromas are released, about 15 seconds. Stir the soy mixture to recombine it with the cornstarch, add it to the skillet, and bring the liquid to a boil. Cover the skillet and simmer over low heat until the ingredients are cooked through and the sauce is thick, 2 minutes. Remove the skillet from the heat, and season with salt and pepper. Serve over the rice. Garnish with the chopped peanuts, if desired.

VARIATION

In step 3, instead of the broccoli use 4 carrots, peeled and cut into ¼-inch rounds, or 6 cups finely shredded cabbage or romaine lettuce.

SECOND TIME AROUND

Leftovers can be turned into a hot-and-sour soup: For 2 cups of leftovers (including the rice) add 2 cups chicken broth, 1 tablespoon soy sauce, 1 tablespoon white vinegar, and 1 teaspoon sesame oil. Bring to a simmer and season with dried red pepper flakes and 1 scallion (white and green parts), sliced.

Curried Chicken over Aromatic Rice

MAKES: *4 servings*
TIME: *25 to 30 minutes*

Indian food is my favorite among all ethnic cuisines in the world. I adore the complexity of its heady spicing and aromas. But to develop the intense yet subtle interplay of tastes in an Indian curry takes time, and so I was delighted when this quick curry turned out to be so delicious and authentic tasting.

1¼ cups converted long-grain rice
2 cups water
Salt
1¼ pounds skinless, boneless chicken (breasts or thighs)
1 onion
2 cloves garlic
1 quarter-size slice peeled fresh ginger
½ teaspoon ground cardamom
½ teaspoon ground cinnamon
½ teaspoon ground coriander
½ teaspoon turmeric
1 teaspoon ground cumin
1 tablespoon vegetable oil
2 tablespoons butter
1 package (10 ounces) frozen spinach, thawed
½ cup evaporated milk
1 tablespoon tomato paste
Freshly ground black pepper or dried red pepper flakes, to taste

1. Combine the rice and the water in a saucepan and bring to a simmer over low heat. Season to taste with salt, cover, and cook until just tender, 15 to 17 minutes. Keep the rice warm, covered, off the heat until the chicken is done.

2. While the rice cooks, cut the chicken into ½-inch cubes. Coarsely chop the onion in a food processor. Add the garlic and ginger and chop fine. Combine all of the spices in a little bowl.

3. Heat the oil and butter in a 12-inch skillet over medium heat. When the foam subsides, add the onion mixture and cook, stirring occasionally, until the onion is tender and a little golden, 5 minutes. Add the spices and cook, stirring, until you can smell the toasted spices, about 1 minute. Add the chicken and continue to cook, uncovered, stirring occasionally, until the chicken is partially cooked, about 5 minutes.

4. While the chicken is cooking, purée the

DELICIOUS PRETEND RISOTTO

This is a quick-cooking alternative to the traditional way of making risotto. The only thing that must remain the same is the rice: use medium- or short-grain rice, preferably an imported one such as Arborio.

Bring 4½ cups chicken or vegetable broth or ¼ cup dry white wine mixed with 4 cups broth, to a boil in a saucepan. Turn off the heat and season to taste with salt and freshly ground black pepper. In a separate saucepan sauté ¼ cup finely chopped onion in 1 tablespoon butter or olive oil until tender but not browned, about 2 minutes. Add 1½ cups rice and stir for half a minute or until the kernels are coated with the oil. Add one-third of the hot liquid to the rice and bring it swiftly to a boil over high heat. Reduce the heat to a simmer and cook the rice, covered, over low heat for 5 minutes. Give the rice a stir, add another one-third of the liquid, bring it swiftly back to a boil over high heat, then reduce the heat and simmer, covered, over low heat for another 5 minutes. Give the rice a stir, add the remaining liquid, bring it back to a boil, and cook over medium heat, uncovered this time, for another 10 minutes, stirring after 5 minutes to make sure the rice does not scorch. Add more liquid if too much has evaporated. You want to cook the rice just until it is tender and creamy and has absorbed almost all of the liquid. Season to taste with salt and pepper, 1 tablespoon butter, and ½ cup (or more) grated cheese, such as Parmesan. Stir until the cheese has melted in, and serve immediately. Makes 4 servings.

spinach with the evaporated milk and the tomato paste in a food processor. Add this to the chicken and cook, uncovered, stirring occasionally, until the chicken is cooked through and most of the moisture has evaporated, another 5 minutes. Remove the skillet from the heat, season to taste with salt and black or dried red pepper.

5. Arrange the rice in a ring on each plate, and spoon the chicken and spinach in the center.

SECOND TIME AROUND

Curried Chicken can be turned into a terrific soup: Combine the leftover rice and chicken mixture with water, broth, or tomato juice until it achieves a souplike consistency. Heat until hot. To freshen the taste, dust the soup with lots of chopped fresh cilantro.

Quick Chicken Mole over Rice

MAKES: *4 servings*
TIME: *30 minutes*

This incredibly easy recipe is rich with fragrance and calls to mind an authentic *mole*, which is a complexly spiced sauce from Mexico. Don't let the list of spices alarm you.

The whole dish, including the rice, is done in 30 minutes, even though it tastes as if you had spent hours in the kitchen.

1¼ cups long-grain rice, preferably
    Texmati
2 cups water
Salt and freshly ground black pepper
    to taste
2 cloves garlic
⅛ teaspoon ground cloves
¼ teaspoon ground cinnamon
¾ teaspoon dried oregano
1 teaspoon ground cumin
1 tablespoon chili powder
1 can (14½ ounces) Mexican-style or
    regular stewed tomatoes
2 tablespoons olive oil
1 tablespoon red wine vinegar
1 cup chicken broth
¼ cup canned chopped green chiles
8 skinless, boneless chicken thighs or
    2 whole skinless, boneless chicken
    breasts (1½ to 2 pounds total)
½ ounce unsweetened chocolate,
    finely chopped
½ cup sour cream (optional)
¼ cup chopped fresh cilantro,
    for garnish (optional)

1. Combine the rice and the water in a saucepan and bring to a simmer over low heat. Season to taste with salt and pepper. Cover and cook until just tender, 15 to 17 minutes. Keep the cooked rice warm, covered, until the chicken is done.

2. Meanwhile, mince the garlic. Combine the cloves, cinnamon, oregano, cumin, and chili powder in a little bowl. Drain the tomatoes, reserving the juices, and chop the solids. Return the chopped tomatoes to the juices.

3. Heat the oil in a nonreactive 9- to 10-inch skillet over medium heat. Add the garlic and cook, stirring, until it emits a lovely aroma, 10 seconds. Add the spice mixture and cook until it gives off its fragrance, 10 seconds. Add the vinegar and cook it for 5 seconds. Add the tomatoes, broth, and green chiles. Cook, un-covered, over low heat to thicken the sauce, 10 minutes.

4. While the sauce is cooking, remove any skin and fat from the chicken thighs and cut the meat into 2 × ⅓-inch strips. If you are using chicken breasts, separate the tenderloins and cut the breast pieces into strips about 2 inches long and ⅓ inch wide.

5. Add the chicken to the sauce and simmer, uncovered, over low heat until it is just cooked through, about 8 minutes for thigh meat and about 5 minutes for breast meat.

6. Season the sauce with salt and stir in the chopped chocolate. Keep stirring until the chocolate is dissolved. Serve over the rice, with a topping of sour cream and cilantro if you wish.

ESPECIALLY GOOD FOR COMPANY

To make the dish taste even more authentic, try this extra step. It will add subtle complex flavor to the sauce and only 5 minutes to your work. In step 4, after you have prepared the chicken, toast 2 tablespoons each of sesame seeds and raw peanuts in a dry cast-iron skillet for 30 seconds or until the sesame seeds are quite golden brown. Immediately transfer the seeds and nuts to a little bowl to cool. Combine the nuts, seeds, and ¼ cup golden raisins in a food processor or blender and purée with 2 to 3 tablespoons water until the mixture forms a paste. In step 6, stir this paste into the sauce right after you add the chocolate.

Saffron Chicken over Creamy Rice

MAKES: *4 servings*
TIME: *35 minutes*

The consistency of the rice in this recipe is similar to that of an Italian risotto, but the way I prepare it is a lot simpler. The creamy rice acts as a sponge to absorb the saffron-laden juices from the chicken. Use dark rather than white meat because it is moister, and be sure you use a short-grain rather than a long-grain rice, so that the texture is appropriately creamy.

4 cups chicken broth
Salt and freshly ground black pepper
4 tablespoons olive oil
1½ cups short-grain rice, such as the
    imported Italian arborio
1½ pounds boneless chicken thighs
½ teaspoon crushed saffron threads
¼ cup dry white wine or dry white
    vermouth
2-ounce chunk of fresh Parmesan cheese
2 cloves garlic
1 package (10 ounces) frozen "petite"
    peas, thawed
¼ teaspoon dried red pepper flakes

1. Combine the broth with salt and pepper to taste in a large saucepan and bring to a boil. Turn off the heat. In a separate 3-quart saucepan, heat 1 tablespoon of the oil. Add the rice and cook for 1 minute over low heat, stirring, until the kernels are coated with oil and are beginning to turn translucent. Add 2 cups of the hot broth and bring to a boil over high heat. Reduce to a simmer and cook over low heat, uncovered, for 5 minutes. Give the rice a stir and continue to cook until the rice has absorbed the broth, 5 minutes.

2. Meanwhile, remove the skin and all fat from the chicken, and cut the meat into ½-inch dice. Dissolve the saffron in the white wine. Grate the cheese and chop the garlic.

3. Heat the remaining 3 tablespoons oil in a 12-inch skillet over medium heat. Add the chicken and cook, stirring continuously, until it turns opaque around the edges, about 1 minute. Add the garlic and cook, stirring occasionally, until the chicken is almost cooked through, 1 minute more. Add the peas and cook until they are warmed through, about 1 minute. Add the white wine and saffron and cook over medium heat until the chicken is just cooked through, 2 to 3 minutes more. Season to taste with salt and red pepper flakes.

4. Add the remaining 2 cups broth to the rice, and bring back to a boil over high heat. Reduce the heat and simmer, uncovered, for another 10 minutes, stirring after 5 minutes. Cook until the rice is tender and creamy, and there are only a couple of spoonfuls of unabsorbed broth surrounding the grains, 3 to 4 minutes more.

5. Right before serving, stir the cheese into the rice and adjust the seasoning. Spoon some rice in the middle of shallow bowls and spoon a portion of chicken, peas, and liquid in the middle; the saffron liquid will pool around the rice in a gorgeous way.

VARIATIONS

- Instead of Parmesan cheese, stir ¼ cup crumbled soft goat's cheese into the rice just before serving.
- For a more Latin version, in step 1, bring 3 cups chicken broth and 1 cup unsweetened coconut milk to a boil. Omit the cheese, and in step 3 add ¼ cup golden raisins when you add the peas to the chicken.

ESPECIALLY GOOD FOR CHILDREN

For the kids, sauté half of the chicken and peas in a second skillet. Season with some tomato sauce or ketchup instead of the saffron and white wine.

Pulled Chicken over Rice

MAKES: *4 servings*
TIME: *25 minutes*

You may have guessed that this recipe is an adaptation of pulled pork sandwiches, a favorite barbecue recipe in which slow-cooked shoulder of pork is "pulled" into shreds and reheated in a fabulous barbecue sauce; the mix is then spooned over squishy buns. To make the meal more ample, I ladle this chicken version over a mix of rice, corn, and scallions rather than over hamburger buns.

1¼ cups converted rice
2 cups water
Salt
¼ cup barbecue sauce
2 cups canned stewed tomatoes, drained and chopped
1 cup chicken broth
1 tablespoon red wine vinegar
1 teaspoon Worcestershire sauce
1 teaspoon yellow mustard
2 scallions
1 pound skinless, boneless cooked chicken (breast or thigh meat)
1 tablespoon butter
1 package (10 ounces) frozen corn kernels, thawed, at room temperature
Cayenne pepper or Tabasco sauce to taste
Sour cream, for garnish (optional)

1. Combine the rice and water in a medium saucepan, add a pinch of salt, and bring to a simmer over medium-high heat. Cover and cook over low heat until almost tender, 10 minutes.

2. Meanwhile, combine the barbecue sauce, tomatoes, broth, vinegar, Worcestershire sauce, and mustard in a 9-inch nonreactive skillet. Slowly bring the mixture to a simmer over low heat, and cook gently, uncovered, for 5 minutes.

3. While the rice and sauce are cooking, trim and finely slice the scallions (green and white parts). With your fingers gently "pull" the

chicken into shreds, or simply cut it into 1 × ¼-inch lengths.

4. Place the butter, corn, and scallions on top of the rice. Cover and cook until the rice is tender and the corn has heated through, another 5 minutes.

5. While the rice, corn, and scallions are cooking, add the chicken to the sauce and cook, uncovered, over low heat until it is warmed through. Season with salt and cayenne pepper to taste. Mix the rice, corn, and scallions together and adjust the seasoning. Serve the chicken over the rice, and garnish with sour cream, if you wish.

Curried Braised Wings

MAKES: *4 servings*
TIME: *45 minutes*

....

This delicately balanced dish bubbles with complex tastes, but not a single spice or particular flavor emerges to overwhelm the others. Make this on a day you have leftover cooked rice on hand.

> 12 chicken wings (about 3 pounds)
> 2 tablespoons vegetable oil
> 1 onion
> 2 teaspoons ground cumin
> ¼ teaspoon ground cinnamon
> ¼ teaspoon ground ginger
> 2 tablespoons tomato paste
> ½ cup unsweetened coconut milk
> ½ cup water
> Salt
> Dried red pepper flakes
> ½ cup (packed) fresh mint leaves
> ½ cup plain regular or low-fat yogurt
> 1½ to 2 cups leftover cooked rice, reheated

1. Remove the wing tips and discard them or save them for making stock. With scissors, cut out the V-shaped flap of skin at the joint to create a neater, meatier wing.

2. Heat the vegetable oil in a wide nonstick skillet over medium-high heat. Add the wings and sauté them until golden, 3 minutes per side. (If you don't have a large enough skillet, do this in two batches, which will add 7 or 8 minutes to your cooking time.) During this time, finely slice the onion; combine the cumin, cinnamon, and ginger together in a small bowl; and measure out the remaining ingredients.

3. Remove the wings to a plate, and add the onion slices to the skillet. Sauté over high heat until tender, golden brown, and caramelized,

5 minutes. If they begin to stick, just add a tablespoon of water.

4. Add the spice mixture, and whisk in the tomato paste and coconut milk. Remove the skillet from the heat, add the water, and whisk the ingredients together to blend them. Season with 1 teaspoon salt and red pepper flakes to taste.

5. Bring the liquid to a boil, return the wings to the sauce, and cover. Simmer over low heat, turning the wings once until cooked through, 15 to 20 minutes. While they are cooking, finely chop the mint.

6. Remove the wings to a plate. Add the yogurt and mint to the sauce, and adjust the seasoning; spoon the sauce over the wings and serve immediately.

Spanish-Style Chicken and Rice

Makes: *4 servings*
Time: *35 minutes*

The taste of this great-looking dish is punched up by pimiento-stuffed olives. I cook this in a large deep saucepan so that I can brown all of the wings at once and save

some time. However, if you don't have a large saucepan, simply brown the wings in a couple of batches and then return all of them to the saucepan before adding the liquid. I use canned corn rather than frozen because I like its more pronounced sweetness.

1¼ *cups long-grain rice,*
  preferably converted
Salt
2 cups water
12 chicken wings (about 3 pounds)
4 tablespoons olive oil
4 small cloves garlic
1 can (15 to 16 ounces) corn kernels
1 can (14 to 16 ounces) stewed
  tomatoes
½ cup bottled pimientos or roasted
  red peppers
½ cup pitted or pimiento-stuffed
  green olives
½ teaspoon dried red pepper flakes

1. Combine the rice, salt, and water in a saucepan and bring to a simmer over low heat. Cover and cook until the rice is just tender, 15 to 17 minutes. Set aside, covered, until the chicken is done.

2. Using a sharp knife, cut through the wing joints of the chicken to separate each one into three parts. Save the bony wing tips for stock or discard them.

3. Heat the oil in a large deep saucepan over medium-high heat. Add the chicken wings, lower the heat and sauté until the skin stiffens, about 4 minutes on each side. Meanwhile, mince the garlic and drain the corn.

4. When the wings are golden, add the garlic and cook until you get a whiff of its aroma, 10 seconds. Then add the tomatoes and their juices. Break up the tomatoes by pressing them against the bottom of the skillet with the side of a wooden spoon.

5. Add the corn. Cover and simmer over medium heat until the wings are cooked through, 15 minutes. During this time chop the pimientos and add them to the skillet. Slice or chop the olives and set them aside.

6. When the chicken is cooked through, stir in the olives, cover, and simmer 5 minutes longer. Then stir the stew, season with red pepper flakes and salt to taste, and serve over the rice.

SECOND TIME AROUND

■ *Remove and discard the skin from the chicken wings, and chop the meat fine. Combine it with the remaining sauce and toss over spaghetti.*

■ *If the leftovers are too thick to be used as a sauce, thin them with more stewed tomatoes or a spaghetti sauce, and freshen the flavor by garnishing the leftovers with chopped scallions or parsley.*

Refried Chinese Chicken

MAKES: *2 to 3 servings*
TIME: *10 minutes*

....

Fried rice is the perfect way to recycle Chinese leftovers of any sort, especially dishes made with chicken. The egg softens the day-old rice and camouflages any "refrigerated" flavor.

> *2 tablespoons vegetable oil*
> *1½ to 2 cups leftover cooked rice*
> *1 large egg, lightly beaten*
> *½ cup frozen mixed vegetables or "petite" peas, thawed*
> *1½ to 2 cups leftover Chinese chicken*
> *2 tablespoons chopped fresh parsley, mint, or cilantro leaves (optional)*
> *Salt and freshly ground black pepper*

1. Heat the oil in a large skillet over medium-high heat until very hot. Add the rice and stir continuously until it is coated with the oil, 1 minute. Make a well in the center of the rice and add the egg. Immediately stir the egg and continue stirring until it is almost scrambled. Then, stirring, incorporate the egg into the rice.

2. Add the mixed vegetables and leftover chicken and cook, stirring continuously, until all the ingredients are hot, 1 minute. Add the parsley, remove the skillet from the heat, and season to taste with salt and pepper.

MORE IDEAS FOR LEFTOVER CHINESE CHICKEN

If you have no cooked rice on hand, reheat the leftovers on the stovetop or in a microwave oven. Spread warm tortillas with hoisin or duck sauce, and spoon the leftovers in the center of the tortillas. Roll up and eat.

■ Or spoon the leftovers on top of tortillas or pita bread and heat them in a 400°F oven. Eat as Chinese chicken pizza.

■ Or bake a potato and top it with leftover Chinese chicken.

■ Or mince whatever leftovers you have, reheat them with some thawed frozen "petite" peas, and toss the mixture over fresh ribbon noodles.

Pan-Roasted Herbed Potatoes and Chicken

MAKES: *4 servings*
TIME: *45 minutes*

Given its complexity—in both the depth of flavor and the intricacy of the textures—it's hard to believe this meal takes only 45 minutes to prepare. Don't be lazy and dice the potatoes into larger chunks—they won't cook properly.

> 2 whole skinless, boneless chicken breasts (about 1½ pounds total)
> ½ cup Basic Vinaigrette (page 64) or bottled salad dressing of your choice
> 4 large all-purpose or new red potatoes (1½ pounds)
> ⅓ cup olive oil
> 2 cloves garlic
> 4 bay leaves, or 1 teaspoon dried oregano or rosemary
> Salt and freshly ground black pepper
> 4 ripe tomatoes (1¼ pounds)

1. Remove the chicken tenderloins from the breast meat. Cut the breast meat in half horizontally, to create thin cutlets. Pound the tenderloins and cutlets between sheets of plastic wrap, until they are ¼ inch thick. Place them in a shallow bowl, add ¼ cup of the dressing, and set them aside to marinate.

2. Scrub the potatoes and cut them into ½-inch dice. Heat the oil in a 12-inch skillet over medium heat until very hot, about 1 minute. Add the potatoes, turning them with a slotted spoon until well coated with oil. Turn the heat down to medium-low and cook, uncovered, until the potatoes are a little crusty on the bottom, about 10 minutes. While the potatoes are cooking, mince the garlic.

3. Turn the potatoes over, and using a metal spatula, scrape and stir the crusty bits that are sticking to the bottom of the skillet. Add the garlic and bay leaves, and season with 1 teaspoon salt and some freshly ground black pepper. Cover and cook until the potatoes are tender, another 10 minutes. During this time, core the tomatoes, cut them into ¼-inch slices, and marinate them in the remaining ¼ cup dressing.

4. When the potatoes are almost soft and cooked through, lay the chicken and its marinating juices on top. Cover and simmer over low heat until the chicken is just cooked through, about 5 minutes on each side.

5. Spoon some tomatoes and dressing in the center of each dinner plate, and place a chicken breast over and slightly to one side of the tomatoes. Discard the bay leaf, and scrape the crusted potato bits from the skillet back into the potatoes; adjust the seasoning. Spoon some potatoes on the other side of the tomatoes, and moisten the chicken with the remaining tomato dressing.

VARIATIONS

Other delicious marinades for the chicken:
- ½ teaspoon grated lemon zest mixed with 3 tablespoons lemon juice and 1 tablespoon olive oil
- ¼ cup plain yogurt or buttermilk seasoned with ½ teaspoon ground cumin

Potatoes with Cabbage and Chicken

MAKES: *4 servings*
TIME: *25 to 30 minutes*

Despite my short-cut approach, this dish, inspired by a traditional Hungarian stew of pork and sauerkraut is so delicious I believe my Hungarian mother-in-law would approve.

2 pounds new red potatoes
Salt
4 slices bacon, pork, or turkey
8 skinless, boneless chicken thighs
(about 2½ pounds total)
3 cups shredded Savoy or green
cabbage
2 tablespoons dry vermouth
or white wine
2 teaspoons paprika
½ teaspoon caraway seeds
¼ cup (packed) fresh dill
leaves
Freshly ground black
pepper
¼ cup sour cream (optional)

1. Scrub the potatoes and cut them into 1-inch chunks. Transfer them to a 4-quart saucepan and cover them with water. Season with ½ teaspoon salt, cover, and bring the water to a boil over high heat. Simmer over moderate heat until just tender, 10 to 15 min-

utes. Do not overcook or the potatoes will fall apart.

2. While the potatoes cook, dice the bacon into ½-inch pieces. Cook the bacon in a 12-inch skillet over medium heat until partially cooked, 3 to 4 minutes. Meanwhile, remove as much fat as possible from the chicken and cut it into 1½ × ⅓-inch strips. Add the chicken to the skillet and continue to cook over medium heat, uncovered, stirring occasionally until the chicken is partially cooked, about 5 minutes more.

3. Meanwhile, add the vermouth to the chicken, scraping up any browned bits from the bottom of the pan. Stir in the paprika and caraway seeds. Mix the cabbage into the chicken in small batches. Cover and cook until the chicken is cooked through and the cabbage has wilted but still has some crunch to it, another 10 minutes. While the cabbage is cooking, mince the dill.

4. Drain the potatoes and return them to the saucepan. Toss them with the dill and season to taste with salt and pepper. Remove the chicken and cabbage from the heat and season to taste with salt and pepper. Stir in the sour cream, if desired. To serve, center the cabbage and chicken in the middle of a dinner plate and surround it with the dilled potatoes.

VARIATIONS

- Instead of making the potatoes, heat cornbread or muffins and split them open; spoon the cabbage and chicken with some sauce over the bread.
- Make some polenta to serve with this instead of the potatoes.
- Add 1 pound of rinsed, drained sauerkraut to the chicken instead of the cabbage. If you do, then be sure to use the sour cream to tame the tangy taste of the sauerkraut.

PAPRIKA TIP

Unbeknownst to most people, paprika should be stored in the refrigerator; otherwise it loses its flavor and can become infested with tiny bugs.

Chicken, Tomatoes, and Portobellos over Penne

MAKES: *6 servings*
TIME: *20 minutes*

As much as I, a lover of butter, cream, and olive oil, hate to admit it, this super-lean sauce is as delicious and moist as any sauce loaded with fat. The natural aromatic juices of the mushrooms and tomatoes coat and flavor each bite of pasta.

Salt
12 ounces short-shaped pasta, such as
    penne or fusilli
4 portobello mushrooms, stemmed
¼ cup water
4 tomatoes
½ cup red wine or chicken broth
1 pound skinless, boneless chicken breasts
½ cup (packed) flat-leaf parsley
Freshly ground black pepper

1. Bring a large pot of salted water to a boil. Add the pasta and cook until it is tender but still firm to the bite, 8 to 10 minutes.

2. While the pasta is cooking, wipe the portobello mushrooms clean with a damp paper towel. Cut each in half, then across into ¼-inch-thick slices. Heat a large nonstick skillet over medium-high heat. Add the mushrooms and cook, stirring, until they begin to stick to the pan, 2 minutes. Then add the water and continue to cook until they are tender, about another 3 minutes.

3. While the mushrooms are cooking, core and dice the tomatoes.

4. Add the tomatoes and the wine to the mushrooms. Cover and simmer over medium heat until they have given off their juices, about 3 minutes. During this time, cut the chicken into ½-inch dice.

5. Add the cubed chicken to the tomatoes and mushrooms, cover, and cook until just cooked through, 5 minutes. During this time finely chop the parsley.

6. Season the sauce well with salt and pepper (take care in the seasoning, or the dish will taste flat).

7. Drain the pasta and return it to the cooking pot off the heat. Toss the pasta with the mushrooms, chicken, and parsley, and adjust the seasoning before serving.

SECOND TIME AROUND

Add to the leftovers a 15-ounce can of white beans, rinsed and drained, a pinch of dried or fresh sage, and enough chicken broth to turn this into a soup. Sprinkle with grated Parmesan.

Salsa Chicken with Pasta

MAKES: *4 servings*
TIME: *30 minutes*

What's left in my refrigerator at the end of the week often inspires a recipe. In this case, I wanted to use up some ground chicken in a pasta sauce, but I had only a smidgen of spaghetti sauce on hand. However, there were several jars of salsa, so I combined the salsa with the spaghetti sauce and voilà—a scrumptious pasta topping as well as a chance to clean out the fridge! If you like your sauce spicy, use 2 cups of salsa and skip the spaghetti sauce.

> Salt
> 1 pound penne or fusilli
> 2 carrots
> 4 small cloves garlic
> ¼ cup olive oil
> 1 pound ground chicken or turkey
> 1 cup mild or hot salsa
> 1 cup spaghetti sauce or tomato purée
> Freshly ground black pepper
> 1 cup grated extra-sharp Cheddar or
>   Monterey Jack cheese (optional)

1. Bring a large pot of salted water to a boil. Add the pasta and cook until tender but still firm to the bite, about 10 minutes.

2. Meanwhile, finely chop the carrots in a food processor. Add the garlic cloves and process until the garlic is minced, a few seconds longer.

3. Heat the oil in a large skillet over medium-high heat. Add the carrots and garlic, lower the heat to medium, and simmer until the carrots begin to soften, about 3 minutes. Add the ground chicken and cook until crumbled and no longer pink, about 5 minutes. Break up the clumps of meat by mashing them against the bottom of the skillet with the side of a wooden spoon.

4. While the chicken is cooking, chop or purée the salsa in the food processor or blender. When the chicken is cooked, add the salsa and the spaghetti sauce. Cover and simmer over low heat for 5 minutes. Season to taste with salt and pepper.

5. Drain the pasta and divide it among 4 plates. Spoon the sauce over each portion and serve immediately. Pass the grated cheese separately, as you like.

SECOND TIME AROUND

Combine each 2 cups of leftovers with ½ cup ricotta cheese, 1 beaten egg, and ¼ cup grated Cheddar cheese. Transfer the mixture to a baking pan and bake in a preheated 350°F oven for 40 minutes or until the egg has set. Serve with a salad of watercress and Boston lettuce.

Roasted Red Pepper and Chicken Fusilli

MAKES: *4 servings*
TIME: *30 minutes*

Both the texture and the flavor of ground turkey stand up better than ground chicken to the bold taste of roasted peppers. To round out the meal, serve a tangy side dish, such as a simple green salad with mustard vinaigrette or cucumbers in lemon vinaigrette—or follow the main course with a fruit salad of banana mixed with pineapple, mango, or berries.

Salt
12 ounces of fusilli, penne, or
  elbow macaroni
3 cups (10 ounces) mushrooms
¼ cup olive oil
4 small cloves garlic, minced
2 cups (12 ounces) roasted red peppers
  or pimientos
4 ounces grated Parmesan or mild fresh
  goat's cheese
Salt and freshly ground black pepper
1 to 1¼ pounds ground turkey or chicken

1. Bring a large pot of salted water to a boil over medium heat. Add the pasta and cook until it is tender but still firm to the bite, about 10 minutes.

2. Meanwhile, wipe the mushrooms clean with a damp paper towel, trim ¼ inch off the bottom of the stems, then cut the mushrooms into ¼-inch-thick slices.

3. Heat the oil in a large skillet over medium heat. Add the mushrooms and sauté just to coat them with the oil, about 1 minute. Add the garlic, cover, and simmer until the mushrooms are tender, about 5 minutes.

4. While the mushrooms are cooking, purée the roasted peppers with the cheese in a blender or food processor. Season with salt and pepper, and set aside.

5. When the mushrooms are tender, add the turkey to the skillet and sauté over medium heat, uncovered, stirring constantly to break up the clumps, until cooked through, about 5 minutes. Remove from the heat and season to taste with salt and pepper.

6. Drain the pasta and return it to the cooking pot, off the heat. Add the mushroom and turkey mixture to the pasta and toss until well combined. Adjust the seasoning. When serving, top each portion of pasta with some of the roasted pepper and cheese mixture.

VARIATION

Ground turkey is sold in packages of a pound or more. Single people or couples should make the full recipe for the ground turkey and mushroom mix, but only half of the pepper and cheese purée. Freeze half of the ground turkey mix for another day. The second time around, instead of topping the pasta and mushroom mix with the roasted pepper and cheese purée, top it with spoonfuls of fresh ricotta cheese mixed with Olive Paste (page 231) or Sun-Dried Tomato Paste (page 232).

Turkey and Pasta with Parsley Sauce

MAKES: *4 servings*
TIME: *25 to 30 minutes*

With the vibrant flavors of garlic, black olives, capers, and parsley, I prefer the meatier taste of ground turkey to the blander one of chicken. These quantities should be enough to satisfy your appetite, but if they aren't, serve this with a green bean salad and fresh melon for dessert.

Salt
1 cup pitted green olives
6 tablespoons extra-virgin olive oil
1 small jar (3 ounces) capers,
   rinsed and drained
2 cups canned plum tomatoes, drained
2 large ribs celery
1 cup (packed) flat-leaf parsley leaves
1 pound penne, ziti, or rigatoni
1 pound ground turkey or chicken
1 large clove garlic, minced
Dried red pepper flakes
Grated Parmesan or Romano cheese,
   for serving

1. Bring a large pot of salted water to a boil for the pasta.

2. While the water is heating, purée the olives and 4 tablespoons of the olive oil in a blender; transfer the purée to a large bowl and add the capers. With scissors, cut the plum tomatoes lengthwise into ½-inch-wide strips over a bowl to catch the juices, and add the tomatoes and their juices to the olives. Cut the celery into ¼-inch dice and finely chop the parsley. Add these to the olives.

3. Add the pasta to the boiling water. At the same time, heat the remaining 2 tablespoons olive oil in a large skillet over medium heat. Add the turkey and sauté, stirring and mashing the turkey with the side of a wooden spoon to break it up into clumps, until opaque, 2 to 3 minutes. Add the garlic and continue to sauté until the turkey is cooked through, 3 to 4 minutes.

4. Remove the skillet from the heat and add the turkey and any juices to the sauce in the bowl. Toss thoroughly to combine, and season to taste with salt and red pepper flakes.

5. Drain the pasta and toss it with the turkey and sauce. Adjust the seasoning. Serve the grated cheese on the side.

VARIATION

If you have olive paste or sun-dried tomato paste in the house, you can omit pitting and chopping the cup of green olives. In step 2, add ¼ cup of the paste of choice to the capers and tomatoes.

Delicious-with-Everything Chicken Sauce

MAKES: *4 servings*
TIME: *30 minutes*

Nothing is easier than creating a sauce with ground poultry, and once you know the basic drill (page 160), your repertoire can expand infinitely. There is one caveat, however: When you begin to sauté ground chicken, it is distressingly pasty. Persevere, however, because with enough cooking and mashing, the pasty mass turns crumbly.

Serve the sauce over cooked pasta or whatever else you fancy.

> 4 slices bacon, finely chopped
> 1 small onion, finely chopped
> 1 large clove garlic, minced
> 1 to 1¼ pounds ground chicken
>   or turkey
> 1 can (28 ounces) plum tomatoes,
>   drained
> ½ cup pitted Kalamata olives
> ½ cup (packed) fresh parsley leaves
> 1 tablespoon drained small capers
> ¼ teaspoon dried red pepper flakes
> ½ teaspoon dried oregano
> Salt

1. Sauté the bacon in a large skillet over medium heat until it begins to render its fat, 3 to 5 minutes. Add the onion, cover, and cook until soft, 5 minutes. Uncover the skillet and cook until the moisture has evaporated and the onion is beginning to sizzle in the bacon fat, about 1 minute.

2. Add the garlic and chicken, and over medium heat mash and stir the chicken constantly until it begins to crumble, about 2 minutes. Stop stirring, let the chicken cook for 2 to 3 minutes, and then mash it again. Proceed this way until the chicken is no longer pink

and is fully broken up, 10 minutes. While the chicken is cooking, chop the tomatoes, slice the olives, and mince the parsley.

3. Add the tomatoes, olives, capers, red pepper flakes, and oregano to the chicken. Cover and simmer for 5 minutes. Remove the skillet from the heat, add the parsley, and season to taste with salt.

HERB PUREES, HERB ICE CUBES

Every now and then, when I find I have overloaded on fresh herbs and am not quite sure when I will get to use them, I prolong their life in a couple of ways. I remove the leaves from the stems, rinse them well, purée them in a food processor, and then use cheesecloth to squeeze out the excess moisture. I transfer the herb purée to a jar, cover it with vegetable or olive oil, and store it in the fridge, where it will keep for a week. This way, I can spoon out a dose of chopped fresh herbs in oil to season any number of dishes like soups, stews, and salads—even those made with ingredients other than chicken!

Another way to preserve herbs is to chop them up and put little amounts in ice-cube trays. Cover the herbs with water and freeze them to create herb ice cubes, perfect to use in soups and stews or other dishes where the ice can melt.

VARIATIONS

Greek-Style Sauce: In step 1, substitute 2 tablespoons olive oil for the bacon. In step 3, omit the capers and olives. Instead, after you add the tomatoes, add the red pepper flakes and 1 teaspoon dried oregano along with ¾ teaspoon ground cinnamon, ½ teaspoon grated lemon zest, and 2 tablespoons lemon juice. Substitute fresh mint for the parsley.

Indian-Style Sauce: Omit the olives, capers, red pepper flakes, and oregano. In step 2, right after you add the ground chicken, add the following mixture of spices: ½ teaspoon each of ground cardamom, cinnamon, and coriander, 1 teaspoon each of dried mint and ground turmeric, and 1½ teaspoons ground cumin. In step 3, after you simmer the tomatoes, remove the skillet from the heat and stir in ½ cup plain yogurt; adjust the seasoning. Omit the parsley; if you wish, add ½ cup chopped fresh mint or cilantro instead.

Utterly Lazy Person's Sauce: In a nonstick skillet, sauté the ground chicken or turkey in 1 tablespoonful oil until crumbled and the meat has lost its raw color. Add ½ cup barbecue sauce and remove from the heat. Stir in ½ cup sour cream (regular or low-fat), and season to taste with salt and pepper.

Dieter's Dream Chicken Sauce: In a nonstick skillet, sauté the ground chicken or

THE BLUEPRINT FOR CHICKEN SAUCE

Ground chicken (or ground turkey) cooks in record time. Combining it with different ingredients turns it into an infinitely variable sauce. In fact, you can change its nature so easily and frequently that you need never have the same sauce twice! What is marvelous about this recipe is that it is equally terrific spooned over pasta, bulgur, rice, cornmeal, potatoes, vegetables, or just plain bread. This is what you'll need for 4 servings:

1. The fat in which to sauté the ground meat: 2 tablespoons of vegetable or olive oil, butter, or rendered bacon fat.

2. The seasoning vegetables, which transform the ground meat into a tasty mixture: Quickest is a clove or two of garlic, crushed through a press, or 2 to 3 thinly sliced scallions (white and green parts). Less assertive is to add a chopped onion to the fat and cook it down for 5 to 10 min-

utes, until it is tender and sweet. At this point you can also add ¼ cup finely chopped celery, bell pepper, carrot, or some mixture thereof.

3. The meat itself: 1 to 1¼ pounds ground chicken or turkey. Both are readily available. The ground turkey is a bit easier to use because it crumbles in the pan more easily. The chicken tends to clump together, but move it around constantly and eventually it separates into a familiar crumbly texture.

4. The liquid and seasonings to turn the ground meat into a sauce: It can be 2 cups of chopped tomatoes, or 1 cup of broth mixed with something to give it body, such as hoisin sauce. The liquid can come from wine and broth or yogurt as well; the permutations and possibilities are endless.

5. The seasonings that give the sauce its distinctive character: These can include just about any dried herbs and spices, fresh herbs, pastes, and any condiments you can think of. After you have tried some of the sauces on pages 158 and 159, I'm sure you'll come up with your own variations.

turkey until crumbled and the meat has lost its raw color. Add 1 teaspoon grated lemon zest, ¼ cup each of chicken broth and lemon juice, and 1 cup of chopped fresh herbs such as mint, parsley, dill, or basil, or a mixture thereof. Season with salt and lots of freshly ground black pepper.

Hoisin-Glazed Chicken in Tortillas

MAKES: *4 servings*
TIME: *35 minutes*

To introduce surprise and variety into my Monday-to-Friday dinners, I mix and match various cuisines. In this recipe, I stuff warm tortillas with an Asian-flavored sautéed chicken and, borrowing from Vietnamese and Thai cuisine, add shreds of raw lettuce and lots of fresh mint and cilantro. It is a remarkably satisfying dish for one that is so lean. Because there is so little fat, you may find that the tortillas seem dry. To add moistness, take an extra 10 minutes to whip up Mango-Avocado Salsa.

8 large leaves Boston lettuce
1 cup fresh cilantro leaves
1 cup fresh mint leaves
4 small carrots
8 large burrito-style tortillas
    (10 inches in diameter)
2 large skinless, boneless chicken
    breasts (1½ to 2 pounds total)
1 tablespoon Asian sesame oil
1 clove garlic, minced
1 tablespoon rice vinegar
1 tablespoon honey
1 tablespoon soy sauce
1 tablespoon hoisin sauce
Salt and freshly ground black pepper
Mango-Avocado Salsa (page 165)
    or Ginger Soy Sauce (page 228)
    (optional)

1. Rinse and dry the lettuce leaves and stack them on a plate. Rinse and dry the cilantro and mint leaves, and place them in separate bowls. Grate the carrots.

2. Preheat the oven to 400°F.

3. Arrange the tortillas, overlapping, on a baking sheet and cover with aluminum foil. Cut the chicken into ½-inch chunks.

4. Heat the sesame oil in a 9-inch skillet over medium heat. Sauté the chicken, stirring continuously with a slotted spoon, just until it stiffens, 1 minute. Put the tortillas in the oven.

5. Add the garlic, vinegar, honey, soy sauce, and hoisin sauce to the skillet and bring to a simmer. Cook until the chicken is cooked through, 2 minutes. Push the chicken to one

side of the skillet, and set the half of the skillet with the liquid over medium-high heat. Boil the liquid away until it reduces to a glaze, about 30 seconds (keep your eye on this because it can burn quickly). When the liquid looks syrupy, remove the skillet from the heat and combine the reduced sauce with the chicken; season to taste with salt and pepper.

6. To assemble the tortillas, center a leaf of lettuce in the middle of each tortilla. Top with chicken, grated carrot, and mint and cilantro leaves. Roll up and serve.

Paprika Chicken over White Beans

MAKES: *4 servings*
TIME: *30 minutes*

....

The white beans add body and texture to this authentic-tasting Hungarian stew. It is so filling that a salad to start, or bread to serve alongside the stew, is more than enough to round out the meal. More ferocious appetites might welcome some additional rice or egg noodles, but I think the dish then becomes too heavy.

8 skinless, boneless chicken thighs
   (about 2½ pounds total)
2 red bell peppers (8 ounces each),
   stemmed and seeded
4 tablespoons olive oil
2 or 3 cloves garlic, minced
2 cups stewed or plum tomatoes with
   their juices
1 teaspoon caraway seeds
1 tablespoon paprika
1 can (16 ounces) white beans
   (cannellini), drained and rinsed
Salt and freshly ground black pepper
½ cup sour cream or plain yogurt
   (optional)

1. Cut the fat out of the chicken thighs, and cut them into ¾-inch pieces. Finely julienne the bell peppers.

2. Heat the oil in a deep wide skillet over medium heat. When the oil is hot, add the peppers and chicken and sauté for 1 minute to coat with the oil. Cover, and cook over medium heat until the chicken is partially cooked, 3 to 4 minutes. Using tongs, turn the chicken over and mix it with the peppers as best you can. Cover and simmer until the chicken is cooked through, another 4 to 5 minutes.

3. While the chicken and peppers are cooking, combine the garlic with the plum tomatoes and their juices in a mixing bowl. Break up the tomatoes with the side of a spoon. Add the caraway seeds, paprika, and 1 teaspoon salt. Mix to combine.

4. Add the tomato mixture and the beans to

the skillet. Cover and simmer until beans are hot and the flavors have had a chance to come together, 10 minutes. Season to taste with salt and pepper, and serve in deep bowls garnished with sour cream, if you wish.

VARIATION

I had no white beans one day when I had intended to make this stew, but did find a can of white hominy on my pantry shelf. I substituted the hominy for the white beans and presto, an original recipe was born. It tasted even more delicious than I had anticipated and is as good as the original one with white beans.

Chili Chicken

MAKES: *4 servings*
TIME: *30 to 35 minutes*

....

Roasted, grilled, sautéed, and even sauced chicken can be transformed into a chili with spices that are distinctive enough to give the leftovers a new identity. Chili tastes better when you give it time to simmer so the flavors mellow and blend. However, when time is of the essence, as it is here, a pinch of sugar will round out any unfinished flavor. A good easy accompaniment is a stack of baked or steamed corn tortillas.

> ¼ cup olive oil
> 1 onion, finely chopped
> 2 red bell peppers, stemmed, seeded, and finely chopped
> 10 ounces mushrooms, trimmed and cut into ¼-inch-thick slices
> 1 tablespoon chili powder
> 2 teaspoons ground cumin
> 2 cups (8 ounces) diced leftover cooked chicken
> 1 can (16 or 19 ounces) chickpeas or hominy, rinsed and drained
> 2 cups canned plum tomatoes with their juices
> ½ teaspoon sugar
> 1 tablespoon red wine vinegar
> Salt and freshly ground black pepper

1. Heat the oil in a large saucepan over medium heat. Add the onion, peppers, and mushrooms, cover, and cook over low heat, stirring occasionally, until tender, 5 to 6 minutes.

2. Add the chili powder and cumin and sauté for a few seconds to release the flavors of the spices. Add the chicken, chickpeas, and tomatoes with their juices. With the side of a spoon, break the tomatoes into pieces. Cover and simmer over low heat for 10 minutes so the flavors blend together.

3. Uncover the saucepan and cook over medium heat to evaporate some of the liquid, about 1 minute. Stir in the sugar, vinegar, and season with salt and black pepper to taste.

ON THE GRILL

Indoor Grilled Chicken Breasts

MAKES: *4 servings*
TIME: *20 minutes*

This method of cooking creates a bit of smoke, but the flavor makes it worthwhile. I like to grill chicken thighs (see page 166 for recipe) because they don't char and dry out as easily, but grilled chicken breasts are a great favorite with most people. Be sure to keep the skin on to protect the delicate breast meat; you can always remove it later, although you'll lose some of the charred flavor. So open the windows wide and grill away.

To further season and moisten the chicken, serve it topped with one of the salsas that follow.

1 tablespoon olive oil
1 tablespoon lemon or lime juice
Salt and freshly ground black pepper
2 whole chicken breasts, halved
    (2½ to 3 pounds total)
Vegetable oil for the grill
Mango-Avocado Salsa or Tomato-Avocado-
    Cilantro Salsa (recipes follow)

1. Combine the olive oil with the lemon juice, and season with salt and pepper. Rub this into and under the chicken skin.

2. Lightly oil a 12-inch stovetop grill pan and heat over high heat until it is very hot, 1 to 2 minutes.

3. Grill the chicken over medium-high heat until just cooked through, 4 to 5 minutes on each side. Season to taste with salt and pepper.

Mango-Avocado Salsa

Peel, pit, and cut 2 mangoes and 1 Hass avocado into ½-inch chunks; combine them in a mixing bowl. Halve 1 lime and juice it over the mangoes and avocado. Remove the skin and pith from 1 lemon. Cut between the membranes to loosen the segments, and cut the segments into fine dice. Add the lemon segments to the bowl and squeeze whatever juice is left in the membranes into the bowl. Finely cut a small bunch of chives and add them to the bowl. Toss the ingredients to thoroughly combine, and season with salt to taste and about ¼ teaspoon dried red pepper flakes. Refrigerate, covered, until serving time.

Tomato-Avocado-Cilantro Salsa

Peel, pit, and dice 2 Hass avocados. Dice 4 small tomatoes and combine with the avocados in a mixing bowl. Add ¼ cup chopped cilantro leaves and 2 tablespoons lime or lemon juice; season well with salt and a bit of cayenne pepper. Refrigerate, covered, until serving time.

GRILLED OR FRIED CHICKEN REDUX

You know how the best part of grilled or fried chicken is lost when you refrigerate the leftovers because the crisp skin gets all soggy? Well, don't despair. Here's a tip on how to re-create the crisp skin and reheat the chicken at the same time. Preheat the oven to 450°F. Put the leftover chicken on a cake rack set in a baking pan, and reheat for 10 minutes. The interior will be warm but not dry, and the skin will be crisp again. I like to zap up the recycled chicken by sprinkling it with drops of vinegar, as the British do their fish and chips.

Grilled Chicken over Red Cabbage

MAKES: *4 servings*
TIME: *30 minutes*

Like most Americans, I love the flavor of grilled foods, especially when I am trying to lose a few pounds and am desperate for flavor without fat. Because I am an apartment dweller, I have had to find ways to grill indoors. The best tool for this task is the cast-iron stovetop grill pan. Keep all the windows open while you grill, because the smoke created by this technique is quite something. What is so satisfying in this dish is the cool crunch of the cabbage against the warm grilled chicken—as well as the surprising notes of fresh ginger and sweet plump raisins.

2 whole skinless, boneless chicken breasts,
*   halved (about 1½ pounds total)*
6 tablespoons lime juice
½ cup plain yogurt
1 teaspoon minced fresh ginger
½ teaspoon minced garlic
½ cup golden raisins, soaked in water
*   to plump up*
4 cups finely sliced red cabbage
Salt and freshly ground black pepper
1 small red onion, sliced

1. Marinate the chicken in 2 tablespoons of the lime juice in a nonreactive bowl while you make the cabbage salad.

2. Blend the yogurt with 3 tablespoons of the remaining lime juice, the ginger, garlic, and raisins in a mixing bowl. Toss this with the cabbage, and season to taste with salt and pepper. Add the remaining 1 tablespoon lime juice if need be. Refrigerate, covered, until the chicken is done.

3. Preheat a stovetop grill, and oil it, if necessary, according to the instructions. Place the onion slices on the outside edges of the grill and the chicken in the middle. Grill the chicken, turning it once, for about 8 minutes.

4. Divide the cabbage salad among 4 plates. Place each chicken breast over the cabbage, and garnish with slices of grilled red onion.

ESPECIALLY GOOD FOR CHILDREN

Buy or make some mayonnaise-dressed coleslaw for the kids, and serve it with the chicken in place of the cabbage salad.

GETTING THE MOST FROM FRESH GINGER

A neat way to extract the flavor of fresh ginger is to chop it fine and then pass it through a garlic press. What comes out is pure smooth ginger juice. This is a wonderful way to infuse a dish with just a nuance of ginger.

Indoor Grilled Chicken Thighs

MAKES: *2 servings*
TIME: *25 to 30 minutes*

With the advent of great stovetop grills, indoor grilling has become a popular technique. Covering the grill makes this a somewhat unorthodox method, but it works. I like to sprinkle gremolata—the parsley, garlic, and lemon zest garnish traditionally associated with braised veal shanks—over the chicken to serve; it adds a sharp freshness that marries well with the grilled flavor of the chicken.

1 lemon
1 clove garlic, minced
1 teaspoon coarse salt
½ teaspoon dried ground sage
4 skinless, boneless chicken
     thighs (1 to 1¼ pounds)
¼ cup (packed) flat-leaf parsley
     leaves
Salt and freshly ground black pepper

1. Lightly oil a 12-inch stovetop grill pan and heat over medium heat. Grate enough of the lemon peel to give you 1 teaspoon grated zest; set it aside. Then squeeze the lemon to make 1 tablespoon juice.

2. With the tip of a chef's knife, make a paste by rubbing the garlic with the coarse salt and

sage in a small bowl. Mix this paste with the lemon juice. Make shallow slashes on both sides of the chicken thighs and rub the garlic mixture into the flesh.

3. Set the chicken thighs on the grill, turn the heat to medium-low, and grill, uncovered, for 5 minutes.

4. While the chicken is grilling, finely chop the parsley and combine it with the lemon zest; set aside.

5. Cover the chicken with a lid or bowl that is large enough to cover all the pieces, and cook for another 5 minutes. Turn the chicken over with tongs or a spatula, cover and cook 10 minutes longer.

6. Uncover and cook the chicken until just cooked through (it will look brown-red at the bone), 5 minutes. Remove the chicken to a plate and let it rest for 5 minutes. Season with salt and lots of coarsely ground black pepper, and serve topped with the gremolata.

Grilled Chicken Over Chestnut Compote

MAKES: *4 servings*
TIME: *30 to 35 minutes*

This sumptuous winter dish has a fabulous flavor and is a breeze to make. What makes it special is the contrast between the charred taste of the grilled chicken and the sweetness of the chestnuts and dried fruit. Chicken thighs are better for grilling than chicken breasts because they remain moister. This unusual cooking technique solves the problem of how to cook chicken thighs so that the interior is cooked through and the exterior is not overdone.

2 cloves garlic
Salt, preferably coarse
1 teaspoon dried
ground sage
1 tablespoon balsamic
vinegar
8 skinless chicken thighs
(about 3 pounds total)
1 cup dried apricots
1 cup pitted dried prunes
2 cans (8 ounces each) chestnuts
packed in water, drained
¼ cup Madeira or Port
1 tablespoon butter
Freshly ground black pepper

1. Preheat a 12-inch stovetop grill pan.

2. Mince 1 of the garlic cloves, and with the tip of a chef's knife, make a paste by rubbing the garlic with 1 teaspoon salt and ½ teaspoon of the sage. Mix this with the vinegar in a small bowl. Make shallow slashes on both sides of the thighs, and rub the garlic mixture into the flesh. Set the chicken thighs on the grill, turn the heat to medium-low, and grill, uncovered, for 5 minutes.

3. Crush the remaining garlic clove with the flat side of a large knife. Combine the apricots, prunes, chestnuts, Madeira, butter, the crushed garlic clove, and the remaining ½ teaspoon sage in a 4-quart saucepan. Cover and simmer over low heat, stirring every now and then, until the chicken is done, about 20 minutes.

4. Meanwhile, cover the chicken after it has grilled for 5 minutes, and continue to cook for another 5 minutes. Turn the chicken over (use tongs or a spatula) and cook, covered, for 10 minutes longer. Then uncover and grill until just cooked through, 5 minutes longer. (The meat will look brown-red at the bone). Remove the chicken to a plate and let it rest for 5 minutes.

5. Remove and discard the crushed garlic clove from the chestnut mixture and season the mixture with lots of freshly ground black pepper. Serve 2 chicken thighs per person, with the chestnut-fruit compote on the side.

ESPECIALLY GOOD FOR COMPANY

This is fabulous and festive enough to serve to company. The only change I would make is to add 2 tablespoons of heavy cream to the chestnut compote at the end of the cooking time—to make it silkier and even more luxurious.

Mushroom-Lover's Chicken

MAKES: *2 servings*
TIME: *30 minutes*

Slivers of raw cultivated mushrooms under the chicken and grilled portobello mushrooms on top make this a mushroom-lover's dream. The layers are drizzled with extra-virgin olive oil, balsamic vinegar, and shavings of Parmesan cheese. The flavors are crisp and fresh, light yet bold. The recipe is for only two people because skillet-type stovetop grills don't come larger than 12 inches in diameter and cannot accommodate more ingredients. However, if you can cook this on an outdoor grill, you can double the recipe to serve four people.

*1 whole skinless, boneless chicken
breast, halved (12 ounces)*
Salt and freshly ground black pepper
*4 large portobello mushrooms, stemmed,
wiped clean, and halved*
2 cups cultivated mushrooms
Extra-virgin olive oil, to taste
Balsamic vinegar, to taste
*4 large basil leaves, rinsed and
patted dry*
*Chunk of good-quality Parmesan
cheese*

1. Heat a 12-inch stovetop grill pan over medium-high heat. Place the chicken breast between two sheets of plastic wrap and lightly flatten the halves with a meat pounder or heavy iron skillet. Season lightly with salt and pepper. Dry the chicken with paper towels.

2. Place the chicken breasts in the center of the grill pan, and surround them with the portobellos. Grill at medium heat for 3 minutes on one side. Turn the chicken and mushrooms over, and grill until the chicken is just cooked through, 4 minutes on the other side.

3. Meanwhile, using a damp paper towel, wipe off the caps of the cultivated mushrooms. Remove ¼ inch from the bottoms of the stems, and then cut the mushrooms into ¼-inch-thick slices. Divide the mushrooms between two large dinner plates. Season them with salt and pepper, and drizzle with 2 teaspoons of olive oil and 2 teaspoons balsamic vinegar. Cut the basil into shreds with scissors, and scatter over the mushrooms. Using a vegetable peeler, shave some thin slices of Parmesan over the mushrooms and basil.

4. When the chicken and portobellos are done, transfer them to a cutting board. Cut the chicken into ½-inch-thick diagonal slices, and arrange them on top of the raw mushrooms. Drizzle the chicken with more olive oil and balsamic vinegar to taste, and more shavings of Parmesan cheese. Season to taste with salt and pepper. Cut the portobellos into thick slices and scatter them over the chicken. Serve immediately.

**SECOND
TIME
AROUND**

Leftovers are perfect for a chicken salad: Toss with some mayonnaise, and add some crunch with diced raw celery, carrot, fennel, or bell pepper. A handful of chopped fresh parsley wouldn't hurt, either.

No-Tend Oven Cooking

The answer to Monday-to-Friday dinners doesn't always have to be a meal made in 30 minutes or less. While I can appreciate the fact that after a busy day, most people are unwilling to spend a lot of time making dinner, in certain situations it's easier to spend just 15 or 20 minutes preparing a dish and then let it cook in the oven for 40 minutes or so. During the time it takes to cook the chicken, you can do small chores, balance your checkbook, help your kids with their homework, or put your feet up and relax.

Another advantage to having a few easy longer-cooking recipes on hand is that it allows for some variety—and it lets you prepare some meals that feature the juicier and more flavorful dark meat or quartered chicken.

While most of these recipes are substantial and you'll need little else to round out the meal, I have added a couple of recipes for times when plain chicken on its own is all you want to eat and you're satisfied with a cooked frozen vegetable served on the side.

Added to this "oven" category are also a few recipes designed for a special kind of oven—the microwave—which is a very helpful tool for meals that serve 1 or 2 people. So for those evenings when you have a bit more time, here is a selection of delicious oven-cooked chicken dishes and chicken suppers.

OVEN MEALS

Mediterranean Casserole

MAKES: *4 servings*
TIME: *15 minutes preparation*
1 hour no-work baking time

It's unseemly to brag, but I have to boast about the fabulous taste of this recipe. The play of flavors between the fennel, lemon juice, and green olives is heavenly—and I promise you'll leave the table feeling happy and satisfied. The mix of chickpeas and red beans makes the dish attractive and gives it texture, but in

Monday-to-Friday fashion, use one type of bean if that's all you have on hand.

>   *4 small or 3 large fennel bulbs*
>   *¼ cup olive oil*
>   *1 chicken, cut into 8 pieces*
>   *(about 3½ pounds)*
>   *½ cup dry white wine or hard apple cider*
>   *2 lemons*
>   *1 cup chicken broth*
>   *2 cloves garlic, minced*
>   *1 teaspoon dried oregano*
>   *1 bay leaf*
>   *1 can (15 ounces) chickpeas,*
>   *drained and rinsed*
>   *1 can (15 ounces) small red kidney beans*
>   *or pink beans, rinsed and drained*
>   *½ cup green pimiento-stuffed Spanish*
>   *olives*
>   *½ cup (packed) fresh parsley or dill leaves*
>   *Salt and freshly ground black pepper*

1. Preheat the oven to 375°F.

2. Halve and core the fennel bulbs and cut them into ¼-inch-thick slices.

3. Heat the oil in a deep 6-quart flameproof casserole over medium-high heat. Sauté the chicken just to stiffen the skin, about 2 minutes per side.

4. Remove the chicken to a bowl, and add the fennel and wine to the casserole. Cover and cook over low heat until the fennel starts to become tender, 3 to 5 minutes. While this is cooking, grate 1 teaspoon lemon zest and squeeze ¼ cup lemon juice.

5. Add the lemon zest and juice, broth, garlic, oregano, and bay leaf to the fennel. Return the dark meat and chicken wings to the casserole, and bring the liquid to a simmer over high heat. Cover, transfer to the oven, and bake for 30 minutes.

6. Add the breast meat, chickpeas, and red beans to the casserole. Cover and bake until the chicken is cooked through, 15 minutes more. While this is cooking, chop the olives and parsley and mix them together.

7. Remove the chicken to a platter and let it rest for 10 minutes. When it is cool enough to handle, remove and discard the skin and the fat underneath the skin (leave the skin on the chicken wings; it's just too hard to remove it). Bring the beans and juices in the casserole back to a simmer, add the olives and parsley, and season to taste with salt and pepper. Remove and discard the bay leaf. Spoon the juices and beans over the chicken and serve.

SECOND TIME AROUND

Remove the chicken meat from the bones and cut into small dice. Warm the chicken in the remaining beans and juices, and serve over pasta or rice.

Kay McEnroe's Old-Fashioned Casserole

MAKES: *4 servings*
TIME: *20 minutes preparation*
1 hour no-work baking time

....

My friend Helen Kahn, who is a friend of Kay McEnroe (the mother of John McEnroe, the famous tennis player), passed this recipe on to me. When Kay was a young mother and on a tight budget, this casserole was a dinner stand-by and a favorite in her household. It fits into the Monday-to-Friday scheme of things and has become a favorite of mine as well, because it is so unbelievably easy to assemble and delicious to eat.

1 large onion
2 carrots
1 rib celery
4 cloves garlic
1 can (28 ounces) peeled Italian tomatoes
2 tablespoons vegetable oil
1 chicken, quartered (3 to 3½ pounds)
½ teaspoon dried oregano
Salt and freshly ground black pepper
2 cups elbow macaroni

1. Preheat the oven to 350°F.

2. Finely chop the onion, carrots, and celery. Mince the garlic. Drain the tomatoes, reserving the juices, and chop the solids.

3. Heat the oil over high heat in a large deep flameproof casserole. When it is very hot, add the chicken, skin side down. Lower the heat to medium and cook, without stirring, until the skin is stiff and golden, 3 to 4 minutes. Turn the chicken over and cook, again without stirring, for another 3 minutes.

4. Remove the chicken to a bowl and set aside. Add the onion, carrots, celery, and garlic to the casserole and cook over medium-high heat, stirring frequently, until the vegetables are soft, 7 to 8 minutes. Add the tomatoes, their reserved juices, and the oregano. Bring the liquid just to a boil and season to taste with salt and pepper.

5. Remove the tomatoes and vegetables to another bowl and set aside. Add the elbow macaroni to the emptied casserole (off the heat) and top with the reserved chicken. Spoon the vegetables and tomatoes over the chicken.

6. Cover the casserole tightly and bake until the chicken is tender and the macaroni is cooked, 1 hour. Serve directly from the casserole.

SECOND TIME AROUND

Remove the chicken meat from the bones and combine it with all the other leftovers in enough tomato juice or chicken broth to create a soup. Bring the soup to a simmer and season to taste with salt and pepper. To brighten the color and taste, add some chopped fresh basil right before serving. Serve with a dusting of Parmesan cheese.

Garlic Chicken with Peppers and Beans

MAKES: *4 servings*
TIME: *15 minutes preparation*
1 hour no-work baking time

One could cook this on the stove and reduce the time by 10 minutes, but oven baking gives the chicken time to thoroughly absorb the flavors of the peppers and garlic.

¼ cup olive oil
2 red bell peppers, stemmed, seeded, and cut into ¼-inch strips
1 chicken, cut into 8 pieces (3½ pounds)
1 cup dry white wine
1 cup chicken broth
6 garlic cloves
1 teaspoon dried sage leaves, or 8 large fresh leaves, snipped
Salt and freshly ground black pepper
1 can (15 ounces) white cannellini beans, rinsed and drained
1 can (15 ounces) small red kidney beans, rinsed and drained
¼ cup (packed) flat-leaf parsley leaves

1. Preheat the oven to 375°F.

2. Heat the oil in a deep 6-quart flameproof casserole over medium-high heat. Add the bell peppers, cover, and cook over low heat until

tender, 5 minutes. While these are cooking, re-move the skin from the chicken pieces (except for the wings, where it is just too hard).

3. Push the peppers to the side and add the chicken. Cook over medium heat just to stiffen the flesh, 2 minutes on each side. Remove the breast pieces from the casserole and set them aside. Add the wine, broth, garlic, and sage and bring the liquid to a simmer. Add 1 tea-spoon salt and pepper to taste. Cover, transfer the casserole to the oven, and bake for 30 minutes.

4. Return the breast meat to the casserole, and add the white and red beans. Continue to bake, uncovered, until the chicken is cooked through, 15 minutes. While the chicken is cooking, coarsely chop the parsley.

5. Serve the chicken in deep bowls, sprinkled with fresh parsley and swimming in all its lovely fragrant juices. Or, using a slotted spoon, transfer the chicken and beans to a serving plate. Boil the juices down until only 2 cups remain, 3 to 4 minutes. Adjust the sea-soning, stir in the parsley, and ladle the sauce over the chicken and beans.

SKINNING CHICKEN

It's easiest to remove the skin when the chicken is cold. If the skin still slips and slides, grab hold of it with paper tow-els and pull hard.

Beer-Braised Chicken

MAKES: *4 servings*
TIME: *20 minutes preparation*
45 minutes no-work baking time

One of the best traditional dishes in Belgium (where I spent a good portion of my childhood) is beef braised in beer. In this recipe, I've borrowed from this idea and made it work with chicken. If you can't find a rich Belgian beer, then make it with a good American ale. There is a lot of sauce, so be sure to serve bread to sop it up—a good hearty rye or pumpernickel will stand up to the bold flavors of the stew.

2 tablespoons vegetable oil
1 chicken, cut into 8 pieces (about 3½
    pounds total)
1 onion
2 carrots
2 ribs celery
1 tablespoon butter
1 bottle (12 ounces) imported Belgian beer
1 teaspoon sugar
1 teaspoon dried thyme leaves
1 bay leaf
Salt and freshly ground black pepper
20 ounces mushrooms
⅓ cup (packed) fresh parsley leaves

1. Preheat the oven to 350°F.

2. Heat the oil in a deep 6-quart flameproof casserole over medium-high heat. Add the

chicken and sauté, skin side down, until the skin has stiffened a bit, 3 to 4 minutes. While the chicken is browning, chop the onion, carrots, and celery in a food processor.

3. When the chicken is slightly golden, remove the pieces to a plate. Melt the butter in the casserole, and add the onion, carrots, and celery. Sauté until softened slightly, 2 to 3 minutes. Return the drumsticks, thighs, and wings to the casserole (save the breast meat for later). Add the beer, sugar, thyme, bay leaf, 1 teaspoon salt, and pepper to taste. Bring the liquid to a simmer, cover, and transfer the casserole to the oven. Bake for 30 minutes.

4. While this is cooking, trim the mushrooms and wipe the caps clean with damp paper towels. (Or if the mushrooms are very dirty, peel them.) Cut the mushrooms into ¼-inch-thick slices.

5. Add the breast meat and the mushrooms to the casserole, cover, and bake until all the chicken is cooked through, 20 minutes more. Chop the parsley.

6. Remove the chicken pieces to a plate and let rest for 10 minutes. When they are cool enough to handle, remove and discard the skin and the fat underneath the skin (don't bother with the chicken wings). With paper towels, blot off the surface fat from the liquid in the casserole. Remove the bay leaf, adjust the seasoning, and stir in the parsley. Arrange the chicken on a platter, ladle the sauce and mushrooms over it, and serve.

SECOND TIME AROUND

You'll probably have sauce, rather than meat, left over. Use the sauce as the base for a homemade soup.

Stuffed Chicken Rolls over Zesty Vegetables

MAKES: *4 servings*
TIME: *20 minutes preparation*
1 hour no-work baking time

This recipe is so easy to make and to vary, you'll come to rely on it as a good old stand-by. It has lots of flavor, and while it takes time, it takes no effort to cook. What I like especially is how the cheese melts almost entirely into the flesh of the chicken to moisten and enrich it. Thanks to all the vegetables, this ends up being a light meal, despite the cream cheese inside the chicken.

2 medium zucchini (¾ pound)
1 yellow squash (½ pound)
1 can (14½ ounces) stewed tomatoes or
"pasta-style" tomatoes
1 can (6 ounces drained weight) pitted
jumbo black olives, drained and chopped
1 bag (16 to 20 ounces) frozen corn
kernels, thawed
Salt and freshly ground black pepper
½ cup finely chopped Black Forest ham,
(4 ounces)
½ cup whipped cream cheese
½ cup finely snipped fresh chives
8 thin-sliced chicken breast cutlets
(about 1½ pounds total)

1. Preheat the oven to 425°F.

2. Trim off the ends of the zucchini and yellow squash. Cut them in half lengthwise, remove the seeds if they are big, and cut them into ½-inch chunks.

3. Combine the zucchini and yellow squash in a mixing bowl with the tomatoes, olives, and corn. Season with 1 teaspoon salt and black pepper to taste. Transfer this mixture to a 13 × 9-inch nonreactive baking dish. Cover and bake for 15 minutes.

4. While the vegetables are baking, combine the ham, cream cheese, and chives; season with salt and pepper. Using your fingers, press some of the mixture over each chicken slice. Roll up and secure with toothpicks.

5. Remove the baking dish from the oven, and arrange the chicken rolls in a row over the vegetables. Re-cover the dish and bake until the chicken is just cooked through, another 30 to 35 minutes. Serve 2 chicken rolls per person, and surround them with the vegetables and natural juices.

VARIATIONS

- In step 2, add 4 ounces chopped canned green chiles. In step 4, substitute ½ cup grated Monterey Jack cheese for the cream cheese.
- In step 4, substitute goat cheese for the cream cheese, and chopped fresh basil leaves for half of the chives.
- In step 4, substitute ¼ cup blue cheese for ¼ cup of the cream cheese.

Papillotte Chicken
A BLUEPRINT RECIPE

MAKES: *4 servings*
TIME: *20 minutes preparation*
30 minutes no-work baking time

This recipe, which is one of my favorites in this book, is an adaptation of fish *en papillotte,* a French method of baking individual portions of fish and vegetables wrapped in parchment. In this version, each package of chicken can be flavored individually, so the possibilities and permutations are endless and allow the cook to customize each portion to suit different needs. The technique is a great way to infuse the chicken with lots of flavor without unwanted calories. And what is fabulous, too, is that the method works as well for the single person as it does for the family of six.

4 skinless, boneless chicken breast halves
   (about 1½ pounds total)
3 tablespoons green or black olive paste
3 new potatoes (12 ounces)
4 small tomatoes, cored
1 tablespoon vegetable oil
Salt and freshly ground black pepper

1. Preheat the oven to 450°F.

2. Remove the tenderloins from the chicken halves and reserve them for some other use. Rub the olive paste on both sides of each chicken breast half.

3. Cut the potatoes into ¹⁄₁₆-inch-thick slices, and thinly slice the tomatoes. Set four 12-inch squares of aluminum foil on the counter. Lightly oil the center of each piece of foil, and spread some potato slices in the middle; sea-

son them with salt and pepper. Cover the potatoes with a chicken breast half, then cover with more potato slices, salt and pepper, and the tomato slices. Wrap the chicken airtight, and set the packages on a baking sheet. Bake until all is cooked through, 30 minutes.

4. When the chicken is done, unwrap the packages carefully (steam will escape when you open the packages). Transfer the chicken, potatoes, tomatoes, and the natural juices to shallow bowls.

VARIATIONS

General seasoning ideas:
■ Rub 1 tablespoon or so of a flavored oil or vinegar, salsa, Homemade Tandoori Paste (page 230), or any of the herb pastes in the Exotic Homemade Pantry (page 222), onto each chicken breast before baking.
■ Instead of the potatoes, tuck ½ cup cooked beans, lentils, rice, or couscous underneath the raw chicken.
■ Instead of the tomatoes, top the chicken with ½ cup thinly sliced zucchini or red onion, or sliced peeled, seeded cucumbers.
■ Add ¼ cup prepared caponata, sliced roasted red peppers, or chopped marinated artichoke hearts to each package.

Italian Style: Instead of the potatoes, spread ½ cup drained canned white beans, 2 slivers fresh garlic, a leaf or two of fresh sage, and 1 teaspoon extra-virgin olive oil underneath the chicken. Top the chicken with the tomatoes.

In-a-Major-Hurry Style: Center half a cup of cooked black beans underneath each chicken breast half. Season each chicken breast with lemon juice and top with ½ cup thawed mixed frozen vegetables and a few slices of fresh garlic.

Asian Style: Spread each chicken breast half with 1 teaspoon each of Asian sesame oil, soy sauce, and rice vinegar. Top each piece with ½ cup sliced jicama, 1 cup fresh spinach, and 1 sliced scallion. After baking, open the package and garnish with sesame seeds.

ESPECIALLY GOOD FOR CHILDREN

Instead of the olive paste and tomatoes, season each chicken breast half with mild barbecue sauce or ketchup and top with ½ cup frozen corn kernels. Top with the tomatoes.

Crisp Chicken with Cabbage and Apples

MAKES: *4 servings*
TIME: *20 minutes preparation*
1 hour no-work cooking time

In the 1980s, it was fashionable to crumb poultry and seafood with instant mashed potato buds to create a crisp topping that tasted like flaked potato chips. This practice has disappeared from restaurants but remains a constant in my house. The cabbage and ap-ples provide a juicy, gorgeous-looking sweet-and-sour counterpoint to the crackling chicken.

½ cup red Zinfandel
1 teaspoon ground cumin
½ teaspoon ground cinnamon
Salt
4 slices bacon, finely chopped
4 cups (packed) finely
    sliced red cabbage
2 Granny Smith apples,
    peeled, cored, and
    finely chopped
4 large skinless, boneless
    chicken breast halves,
    "tenders" removed, pounded thin
    (about 1½ pounds total)
2 tablespoons butter, melted
1 tablespoon cider vinegar
Freshly ground black pepper
1 cup instant mashed potato buds
1 small bunch fresh chives

1. Preheat the oven to 400°F.

2. Whisk together the wine, ½ teaspoon of the cumin, ¼ teaspoon of the cinnamon, and 1 teaspoon salt in a nonreactive 4-quart flame-proof casserole.

3. Add the bacon, cabbage, and apples. Bring to a boil over high heat (push the cabbage aside and look at the liquid on the bottom). Cover, transfer the casserole to the oven, and bake for 30 minutes.

4. Meanwhile, in a shallow dish, combine the

melted butter, vinegar, remaining ½ teaspoon cumin and ¼ teaspoon cinnamon, and salt and pepper to taste. Coat the chicken in the marinade and set aside, covered, in the refrigerator, 30 minutes.

5. Dip the chicken in the potato buds, making sure the pieces are completely covered. Set them on a rack placed on a baking sheet, put the baking sheet in the oven next to the casserole, and bake 30 minutes (the chicken should be cooked through and barely golden brown). While this is cooking, finely snip the chives (you need about ⅓ cup).

6. Remove the cabbage from the oven and mix to evenly distribute the apples and bacon. Taste and adjust the seasoning. Set a portion of cabbage and apples on each dinner plate, center some chicken in the middle, and garnish the chicken with the chives.

Roasted Stewed Chicken with Vegetables

MAKES: *4 servings*
TIME: *10 minutes preparation*
1 hour no-work cooking time

It would make sense to say that if you roast something you can't stew it at the same time—the two techniques are on opposite ends of the culinary spectrum. However, I have combined the two in this recipe by first roasting the sweet potatoes, onions, and garlic to develop that characteristic charred flavor, then finishing the dish by adding tomatoes, zucchini, and chicken and its marinade, so the ingredients do end up stewing in their own juices. This recipe will be a boon to any cook who is on a diet because the flavors are fabulous yet the fat is kept to a minimum. As with all roasted food, the appearance isn't as spectacular as the flavor.

> 2 medium sweet potatoes
> 2 medium onions
> 6 cloves garlic
> 1 tablespoon vegetable oil
> Salt
> 1¼ pounds skinless, boneless chicken breasts
> ⅓ cup lime juice
> ⅓ cup orange juice
> ⅓ cup lemon juice
> Freshly ground black pepper
> 2 beefsteak tomatoes, cored
> 2 medium zucchini, trimmed

1. Preheat the oven to 500°F.

2. Peel the sweet potatoes, cut them into 1-inch rounds, and set them in a large roasting pan. Roast, uncovered, for 15 minutes.

3. Meanwhile, peel the onions and cut each

one into 8 wedges. Toss the onion wedges and garlic with the vegetable oil in a mixing bowl, and season to taste with salt. Add these to the roasting pan and roast for 30 minutes more.

4. Meanwhile, cut the chicken into ½-inch cubes and toss them with the lime, orange, and lemon juices. Season with 1 teaspoon salt and ½ teaspoon pepper.

5. Cut each tomato into 6 wedges. Halve each zucchini lengthwise, and if the seeds are large, scoop them out with a spoon. Cut into 1-inch-thick slices.

6. Add the tomatoes, zucchini, chicken, and citrus juices to the roasting pan (carefully, as the juices will steam). Toss all the ingredients together with a spoon, and return the pan to the oven. Roast, uncovered, until the chicken is cooked, about 15 minutes.

7. Transfer the vegetables and chicken to shallow bowls, and spoon the natural juices over the top. Serve immediately.

VARIATION

This dish is even more special if, right before serving, you drizzle the vegetables and chicken with extra-virgin olive oil or with an herb-flavored oil. To make the dish look more attractive, sprinkle each portion with minced fresh herbs, such as parsley or cilantro.

Baked Spaghetti Squash and Chicken

MAKES: *4 servings*
TIME: *15 minutes preparation*
1 hour no-work baking time

I don't prepare spaghetti squash often because it takes a while to cook, but when I do, I am reminded of how delicious it is. I like to serve it with this chicken in cream sauce because the sauce envelops each strand of the spaghetti squash as it would pasta. I have discovered that it is easier to remove the seeds when the squash is partially cooked, before it becomes too hot to handle.

> 1 spaghetti squash (3 to 3½ pounds)
> 2 tablespoons butter
> 2 tablespoons all-purpose flour
> 1 cup chicken broth
> 12 ounces skinless, boneless chicken
>   breasts, cut into ½-inch cubes
> ½ cup milk or heavy (or whipping) cream
> Salt and freshly ground black pepper
> ½ cup (packed) fresh basil leaves
> ⅓ cup grated Parmesan cheese

1. Preheat the oven to 375°F.

2. Using a sharp knife, prick the squash in two or three places. Set it on a baking pan and bake for 30 minutes. Remove the pan from the oven, cut the squash in half lengthwise, and scoop out the seeds. Return the squash halves, cut side down, to the pan

and bake until tender, 30 minutes more.

3. Meanwhile, melt the butter in a medium-size saucepan over medium-low heat. Add the flour and cook, stirring continuously, for 1 minute. Whisk in the broth and bring the mixture to a boil, whisking all the while. Add the chicken and simmer, uncovered, over low heat until it is cooked through, 3 to 5 minutes. Remove from the heat and stir in the milk. Season with 1 teaspoon salt and pepper to taste.

4. Chop the basil. Ten minutes before the squash is done, gently reheat the chicken in the sauce. Stir the basil and Parmesan into the sauce and adjust the seasoning.

5. Remove the squash from the oven. Use a fork to rake the interior of the squash until it separates fully into strands and only the shell remains. Transfer the squash strands to a serving dish, and top with the chicken and cheese sauce.

VARIATION

To make the sauce more elaborate and the entire meal more filling, in step 3, right after the chicken is cooked, add 1 package (10 ounces) frozen "petite" peas, thawed.

SECOND TIME AROUND

Chances are, you will have leftover spaghetti squash. If you do, chop the leftovers and reheat them with 1 can (15 ounces) black beans, rinsed and drained, ½ cup chili sauce, and enough water to make a stewlike consistency. Serve over rice, and garnish with chopped fresh cilantro and a dollop of plain yogurt.

Two-Cup Chicken Casserole

MAKES: *4 servings*
TIME: *15 minutes preparation*
30 minutes no-work baking time

Two cups each of four ingredients form the foundation of this delicious quick dinner. What is so amazing is that the sophisticated flavors belie how simple it is to pull this casserole together. The big taste surprise is to be found in the juicy, crunchy salsa of chopped Asian pear, cilantro, and red onion—a delicious counterpoint to the smoky heat of chipotle peppers and the cooling richness of the sour cream. If Asian pears are hard to find, substitute a fresh Barlett pear or very fine dice of peeled Granny Smith apple.

2 cups (15-ounce can) small red beans,
  rinsed, drained
2 cups (15-ounce can) hominy, rinsed,
  drained
2 cups (10-ounce package) frozen corn,
  thawed
2 cups chopped drained, canned plum
  tomatoes
2 tablespoons olive oil
12 ounces skinless, boneless chicken
  breasts, cut into ½-inch cubes
2 tablespoons canned chipotle peppers
  packed in adobe sauce
Salt
½ fresh Asian pear
½ cup (packed) fresh cilantro leaves
Small wedge of red onion
Sour cream or crumbled fresh goat cheese,
  for garnish (optional)

1. Preheat the oven to 400°F.

2. Combine the red beans, hominy, corn,
tomatoes, oil, chicken, and chipotle peppers
in a mixing bowl. Transfer the mixture to a 2-
quart baking pan and season with salt to taste.
Cover and bake until the chicken is cooked
through and the other ingredients are hot, 30
minutes.

3. While this is cooking, peel and dice the

Asian pear (you need ½ cup), chop the
cilantro, and mince enough red onion to
give 2 tablespoons. Combine these ingredients in a mixing bowl and set aside in the refrigerator.

4. Serve portions of the casserole in deep
bowls, topped with sour cream, if you like,
and the Asian pear salsa.

ESPECIALLY GOOD FOR CHILDREN

Omit the chipotle peppers and just top the kids' portions with plain yogurt or sour cream and leave the delicious salsa for mom and dad.

Lazy Day Chicken

Makes: *4 servings*
Time: *15 minutes preparation*
1 hour no-work baking time

This is the perfect recipe for days when
how much energy you have left at the end
of a day is more the issue than how much time.
I came up with the idea when my best friend
was musing about how, in spite of her great sophisticated palate, she longed for the taste and
ease of the casseroles of yore but without all
the fat they used to call for. This request of
hers led me to this ridiculously easy recipe,
which is relatively fat-free.

1 jar (15 ounces) whole boiled onions,
   rinsed and drained
1 package (10 ounces) frozen mixed
   vegetables, thawed
1 package (10 ounces) frozen "petite"
   peas, thawed
2 cans (6 ounces drained weight each)
   sliced mushrooms, drained
Salt and freshly ground black pepper
2 whole chicken breasts, split in half
   (about 3 pounds total)
1 can (10¾ ounces)
   cream of
   mushroom soup
½ cup water
1 tablespoon paprika
1 tablespoon Dijon
   mustard

1. Preheat the oven to 400°F.

2. In a nonreactive baking pan combine the onions, vegetables, peas, and mushrooms. Season to taste with salt and pepper.

3. Remove the skin from the chicken; trim and discard any excess fat from the chicken. Salt and pepper the meat and bury each piece, flesh-side down, into the vegetables.

4. Combine the soup with the water, paprika, and mustard in a mixing bowl. Season with 1 teaspoon of salt and freshly ground black pepper to taste. Pour this over the chicken and vegetables and cover the baking dish. Bake for 30 minutes, then uncover and bake until the chicken is done, 30 minutes more.

VARIATION

In step 2, instead of the mixed vegetables, peas, and mushrooms, substitute 2 packages (10 ounces each) frozen corn, thawed, 4 ounces canned chopped green chiles, and 1 can (6 ounces) pitted jumbo black olives, drained and chopped.

Paprika-Braised Chicken with Fruity Sauerkraut

MAKES: *4 servings*
TIME: *15 to 20 minutes preparation*
45 minutes no-work baking time

Polenta is a fantastic side dish to serve with this boldly flavored stew because it provides a smooth and creamy counterpoint to the pungent earthy tones of the caraway and the sauerkraut. To save time, use instant imported Italian polenta and cook it in the microwave following the package instructions. If polenta is out of the question, then make rice as a side dish, or at the very least, serve a hunk of good bread on the side.

2 tablespoons vegetable oil
1 onion, chopped
1 large red bell pepper, stemmed, seeded,
    and cut into thin strips
1 clove garlic, slivered
1 tablespoon Hungarian sweet
    paprika
¼ cup dry white wine
½ cup tomato purée
Salt and freshly ground black
    pepper
8 to 10 skinless chicken thighs
    (2½ to 3 pounds total)
1 package (2 pounds)
    prepared sauerkraut
2 jars (4 ounces each) baby-food fruit
    purée, such as pear, apple, or apricot
1 teaspoon caraway seeds
½ cup sour cream

1. Preheat the oven to 375°F.

2. Heat the oil in a 4-quart enameled cast-iron casserole over medium heat. Add the onion, bell pepper, and garlic and sauté, stirring continuously, until the onion begins to turn golden, 4 to 5 minutes.

3. Remove the casserole from the heat and stir in the paprika. Add the wine and return the casserole to high heat. Boil the wine until it has almost completely evaporated, 2 to 3 minutes. Add the tomato purée and season with 1 teaspoon salt and black pepper to taste. Add the chicken thighs, and bring the liquid to a simmer. Cover and transfer the casserole to the oven. Bake until the chicken is cooked through, 45 minutes.

4. Meanwhile, rinse the sauerkraut and squeeze it to press out all the moisture. In a nonreactive casserole (or even a deep glass pie plate), combine the sauerkraut with the fruit purée and the caraway seeds. Season to taste with salt and pepper. Cover and heat in oven for the last 15 minutes the chicken is cooking.

5. Remove both dishes from the oven. Stir the sour cream into the sauerkraut. Remove the chicken thighs from the sauce and transfer them to the sauerkraut. Spoon off the fat from the sauce in the casserole and adjust the seasoning. To serve, spoon the sauce over the chicken and sauerkraut.

Indian-Spiced Chicken, Chickpeas, and Couscous

MAKES: *4 servings*
TIME: *15 minutes preparation*
1 hour no-work baking time

In the past 20 years, Americans have developed sophisticated palates but have less time than ever to cook what they have come to appreciate. Thanks to these newly demanding but time-crunched palates, we have more exotic prepared foods at our disposal. One such "kitchen helper" is a prepared tandoori paste or spice mixture, which comes in a jar or can. Dust or rub some of this mixture on your chicken and your house will smell heavenly, just like an Indian restaurant. If you're a purist, you can make your own paste (see Homemade Tandoori Paste, page 230).

8 to 10 skinless chicken thighs (2½ pounds)
1 cup plain yogurt
2 tablespoons prepared tandoori spices or paste
1 clove garlic, minced, or 1 teaspoon garlic paste
¾ cup very hot water
½ cup orange juice
Salt
½ teaspoon ground cinnamon
1 cup couscous
1 can (16 ounces) chickpeas, rinsed and drained
2 tablespoons butter
½ cup (packed) fresh cilantro leaves
½ cup sour cream or plain yogurt (optional)

1. Preheat the oven to 375°F.

2. With a sharp paring knife, slash the chicken thighs in several places, going down to the bone. Set the chicken in a baking pan. Combine the yogurt, tandoori mixture, and garlic and pour it over the chicken. Turn the chicken in the mix several times to thoroughly cover it. Bake, uncovered, for 30 minutes.

3. While the chicken is baking, combine the hot water, orange juice, 1 teaspoon salt, and the cinnamon in a 2-quart baking dish. Add the couscous, give it a stir with a fork, and let it steep until the couscous has plumped up somewhat, 15 minutes. Stir the chickpeas into the couscous, and dot the top with the butter. Cover the dish and set aside.

4. Turn the chicken pieces over, and return the baking pan to the oven. Set the couscous in the oven as well. Increase the heat to 450°F, and bake until the chicken is done and the couscous and chickpeas are heated through, another 30 minutes. While these are cooking, chop the cilantro.

5. Place the couscous and chickpeas in individual deep bowls, and top with the chicken and pan juices. Sprinkle with the cilantro, and add a spoonful of sour cream if you wish.

Saffron Chicken and Rice

MAKES: *4 servings*
TIME: *15 minutes preparation*
25 minutes no-work baking time

Inspired by paella, this chicken and rice dish is a lot easier to prepare and thus is feasible for Monday-to-Friday meals. Baking it in the oven rather than cooking it on the stovetop allows the rice and chicken to cook evenly without the bottom burning. The saffron colors and flavors the dish beautifully, and the surprise addition of crisp fresh grapes adds just the right note of sweetness.

> ¼ cup extra-virgin olive oil
> 1 clove garlic, slivered
> 1½ cups jasmine or Texmati long-grain rice
> 12 ounces skinless, boneless chicken thighs or breasts, cut into ½-inch dice
> 1 tablespoon white wine vinegar
> ½ teaspoon saffron threads
> 2 cups chicken broth
> 1 teaspoon salt
> ¼ teaspoon dried red pepper flakes
> 1 cup seedless grapes, preferably green
> ⅓ cup bottled roasted red peppers or pimientos

1. Preheat the oven to 375°F.

2. Heat the oil in a 4-quart flameproof enameled cast-iron casserole over medium heat. Add the garlic and rice and cook, stirring continuously, until some of the rice kernels begin to turn translucent, about 3 minutes.

3. Add the chicken and cook until the chicken has mostly turned opaque, 1 minute more. Add the vinegar and cook until almost entirely evap-

orated, a few seconds. Add the saffron and broth, the salt and dried red pepper flakes. Bring the liquid to a boil over high heat.

4. Cover the casserole and transfer it to the oven. Bake until the rice is soft and has absorbed all of the liquid and the chicken is cooked through, 25 minutes. While the rice and chicken are cooking, cut the grapes in half and finely chop the roasted peppers.

5. Remove the casserole from the oven, and stir in the grapes and peppers. Cover and let stand for 5 minutes to warm the grapes and peppers.

VARIATION

Instead of grapes and roasted peppers, add 1 cup thawed frozen "petite" peas or 1 cup finely diced marinated artichokes in step 4.

Oven-Baked Potatoes and Chicken in Vinegar

MAKES: *4 servings*
TIME: *15 minutes preparation*
1 hour no-work baking time

What else can I say about this recipe other than the fact that it is delicious and worth every second it takes to cook. The

potatoes, which bake separately alongside the casserole, are the perfect foil for the fragrant sauce, which gets a unique and tangy flavor from the vinegar.

> 4 Idaho or russet potatoes
> 8 boneless chicken thighs
>   (about 2½ pounds total)
> ¼ cup olive oil
> 6 carrots, cut into ½-inch rounds
> ¼ cup red wine
> ¼ cup red wine vinegar
> 1 cup canned plum tomatoes,
>   with some of their juices
> Salt
> 1 clove garlic
> ¼ teaspoon dried rosemary
> ¼ teaspoon dried thyme
>   leaves
> 1 bay leaf
> ½ cup (packed) fresh pars-
>   ley leaves
> Freshly ground black pepper

1. Preheat the oven to 500°F.

2. While the oven is preheating, scrub the potatoes and prick them with a fork. Set the potatoes directly on the oven rack and bake until soft, 1 hour.

3. While the potatoes are baking, remove the skin from the chicken. Heat the oil in a medium-size flameproof casserole over medium heat. When the oil is hot, add the carrots and sauté for 2 to 3 minutes just to get them cooking. Add the wine, vinegar, tomatoes and their juices, 1 teaspoon salt, the garlic, rosemary,

thyme, and bay leaf. Bring the liquid to a boil, pressing the tomatoes against the sides of the casserole with a spoon to break them up. Boil to reduce the liquid somewhat and evaporate the alcohol, 5 minutes.

4. Add the chicken to the casserole and bring the liquid back to a boil. Cover, and transfer the casserole to the oven. Bake until the chicken is done, 45 minutes. While this is cooking, chop the parsley.

5. Remove the potatoes and the casserole from the oven. Remove and discard the bay leaf and garlic clove. Stir the parsley into the chicken, and season to taste with salt and pepper.

6. To serve, cut each potato into 6 rounds and spread them out on a dinner plate. Center 2 thighs in the middle of the potatoes, and spoon some sauce on top.

Chinese Chicken Casserole

MAKES: *4 servings*
TIME: *15 minutes preparation*
25 minutes no-work baking time

I love the mysterious taste of Chinese five-spice powder, the essential flavor in this delicate yet flavorful dinner. A fruit salad made with mango, pineapple, or kiwi is great after this meal, as is any fruit sorbet.

¼ cup vegetable oil
1 clove garlic, chopped
1 quarter-size piece fresh ginger,
* minced*
1½ cups long-grain converted rice
1¼ pounds skinless, boneless chicken
* thighs, cut into ½-inch pieces*
2 tablespoons rice vinegar
2¼ cups chicken broth
¼ cup light soy sauce
½ teaspoon Chinese five-spice powder
2 teaspoons sugar
Salt
Dried red pepper flakes
½ cup unsalted cashew nuts
8 ounces fresh snow peas

1. Preheat the oven to 375°F.

2. Heat the oil in a 4-quart enameled cast-iron casserole over medium heat. Add the garlic, ginger, and rice. Cook, stirring continuously, until the rice kernels turn translucent, about 2 minutes. Add the chicken and cook, stirring, until the chicken is almost cooked through, 1 minute more.

3. Add the vinegar and cook until it is almost entirely evaporated, just a few seconds. Then add the broth, soy sauce, five-spice powder, sugar, 1 teaspoon salt, and ¼ teaspoon dried red pepper flakes. Bring the liquid to a boil over high heat, cover, and transfer the casserole to the oven.

4. Bake until the rice is soft and has absorbed all the liquid and the chicken is cooked through, 25 minutes. While the rice and

chicken are cooking, chop the cashews. Bring 2 quarts salted water to a boil and blanch the snow peas for 1 minute; drain and set aside.

5. Remove the casserole from the oven, stir in the snow peas, and adjust the seasoning. Garnish each portion with cashews.

SECOND TIME AROUND

Turn leftovers into a tasty salad by adding strips of raw red bell pepper, and by refreshing it with chopped cilantro, lime juice, and more chopped cashews.

Green Chile Chicken Pie

Makes: *4 to 6 servings*
Time: *20 minutes preparation*
35 minutes no-work baking time

In its unapologetic use of canned goods, this sinfully delicious casserole reminds me of the best of 1950s cooking. In this recipe, corn tortillas are layered with a mix of cooked chicken, tomatoes, chiles, and canned creamed corn. And as if this were not lush enough, a generous dose of sour cream and cheese is introduced as well (this last little touch makes it a great hit with kids).

> 2 tablespoons olive oil
> 1 onion, finely chopped
> 1 tablespoon chili powder
> 1 teaspoon ground cumin
> 1 can (15 ounces) creamed corn
> 1 can (14½ ounces) stewed or
>   "pasta-style" tomatoes
> 1 can (4 ounces) chopped green
>   chiles
> 3 cups skinless, boneless diced
>   cooked chicken
> 1 package (about 12) corn tortillas
> Salt and freshly ground black pepper
> 1 cup sour cream
> 4 ounces Monterey Jack cheese

1. Preheat the oven to 375°F.

2. Heat the oil in a large skillet over medium heat. Add the onion and cook until somewhat translucent, about 5 minutes. Add the chili powder and cumin and sauté for a few seconds just to release the aroma. Add the corn, tomatoes, chiles, and chicken and bring the mixture to a simmer.

3. While this is coming to a simmer, stack the tortillas and cut them into strips about ¾ inch wide. When the chicken mixture is at a simmer, season to taste with salt and pepper. Layer one-third of the tortilla strips in a 9-inch square baking pan, and top with one-

third of the sour cream and one-third of the chicken mixture. Repeat with two more layers of tortilla strips, sour cream, and chicken. Cover and bake for 30 minutes. While it is baking, grate the Monterey Jack cheese.

4. When the chicken has finished baking, uncover the baking pan, sprinkle the cheese over the top, and bake, uncovered, until the cheese has melted, 5 minutes more.

Leftover Chicken Pot Pie

MAKES: *About 3 servings*
TIME: *10 minutes preparation*
30 minutes no-work baking time

A made-from-scratch chicken pot pie takes hours to prepare, and the process is unthinkable in a Monday-to-Friday kitchen. The idea of a pot pie, however, is not so impractical if you use it as a clever way to reheat leftovers. I combine leftover chicken, plain or mildly sauced, with cooked vegetables, seasonings, and ricotta cheese, and top it all with a refrigerated pie crust. (I use ricotta rather than a homemade white sauce to bind and moisten the leftovers because it is less wet than a

white sauce, and refrigerated pie crust never bakes completely if it is in contact with as wet a medium as a sauce.)

> 1 cup ricotta cheese
> ½ cup spaghetti sauce
> 1 clove garlic, minced or passed through a garlic press
> 1½ to 2 cups cut-up cooked chicken, plain or in a sauce
> 2 cups chopped leftover vegetables
> 1 can (4 ounces) chopped green chiles
> Salt and freshly ground black pepper
> 1 refrigerated pie crust (9 inches round)

1. Preheat the oven to 425°F.

2. Combine the ricotta, spaghetti sauce, garlic, chicken, vegetables, and chiles in a mixing bowl. Season to taste with salt and pepper, and transfer the mixture to a round ovenproof baking dish, between 9 and 10 inches in diameter and 1½ inches deep.

3. Place the refrigerated pie crust loosely over the rim of the baking dish, and with the tip of a knife make some slashes in the dough to allow the steam to escape. Bake for 25 minutes, then raise the heat to 450°F and bake 5 minutes more for the crust to completely bake through. Let the pie rest for 5 minutes, then cut into wedges and serve.

VARIATION

Instead of using pie crust, cut 4 corn tortillas into wide strips with kitchen shears. Strew the strips over the ingredients and bake for 20 minutes only, to heat the ingredients.

Oven Entrées

Surprise Chicken Packets

MAKES: *4 servings*
TIME: *10 minutes preparation*
30 minutes no-work baking time

The little bit of stuffing in the middle of each chicken breast is both a flavor surprise and a moistening agent. The trick to creating a pocket is to use a sharp slender knife and to make a short slit on the side of the chicken breast so the filling can't seep out of the pocket: Make a 1-inch cut, and carefully work the knife inside the chicken to cut it in half without opening the side further. The lettuce around the chicken gets a bit crinkled when it is baked, but it is there to keep the chicken moist.

*2 thick whole skinless, boneless chicken
    breasts (2 to 3 pounds total), halved,
    "tenders" removed*
8 large fresh basil leaves
¼ cup low-fat ricotta cheese
Juice of ½ lemon
Salt and freshly ground black pepper
*¼ cup finely sliced scallions (white and
    green parts)*
8 to 12 large Boston lettuce leaves
*4 large beefsteak
    tomatoes, cored*
*¼ cup vinaigrette
    (optional)*

1. Preheat the oven to
400°F.

2. Hold the chicken flat with one hand, and
with the other use a slender boning knife to
make a 1-inch slit on the thicker side of one
breast half. Take care not to pierce through
the top or bottom of the chicken. Work the
tip of the knife first to one side of the breast,
up to ½ inch from the edge, and then toward
the other side. This way you will have cut the
breast in half on the interior without making a
long slit along the side. With your fingers
work 2 basil leaves and 1 tablespoon ricotta
into the pocket. Repeat with the remaining
chicken, basil, and ricotta.

3. Season the outside of the chicken with the
lemon juice and salt and pepper to taste.
Sprinkle the pieces with scallions, then wrap
each in 2 or 3 lettuce leaves. Set the packets
on a baking sheet and bake until the chicken
is cooked through, about 30 minutes.

4. While the chicken is baking, cut the tomatoes into fine dice and toss with the vinaigrette, if using. Center a portion of tomatoes
in the middle of each dinner plate, reserving a
bit for garnish.

5. Place the cooked chicken over the tomatoes, spoon the remaining tomatoes over the
top, and serve.

VARIATION

Instead of the ricotta, work into each pocket 1
tablespoon olive paste, salsa, caponata, or
mixed chopped fresh herbs, such as tarragon,
mint, dill, chives, and parsley.

Baked Herbed
Chicken

MAKES: *4 servings*
TIME: *15 minutes preparation*
1¼ hours no-work baking time

The little culinary trick that makes this
easy dish so uncommonly delicious is the
flour, which is
worked into
the butter,
garlic, herbs,
and lemon juice
and "glues" their
flavors to the chicken.

¼ cup olive oil
2 tablespoons butter, melted
2 cloves garlic, minced
¼ cup lemon juice
½ cup (packed) chopped fresh parsley, dill,
    or basil, or 2 tablespoons dried
Salt and freshly ground black pepper
3 tablespoons all-purpose flour
1 chicken, quartered or cut into 8 pieces
    (3½ to 4 pounds)

1. Preheat the oven to 375°F.

2. Combine the olive oil, butter, garlic, lemon juice, and herbs in a medium-size bowl. Season well with salt and pepper. Work in the flour with a spoon, and spoon this herb paste under and into the skin of the chicken.

3. Place the legs and thighs in a baking pan large enough to accommodate all the chicken in a single layer, and bake for 20 minutes. Add the breast and wing parts and bake until all the pieces are cooked through and the juices of a thigh run clear with a hint of pink when it is pricked with a fork, 40 to 45 minutes. Turn the heat up to 400°F and bake until the skin develops a golden color, 5 minutes more.

4. Remove the chicken from the oven and serve with the pan juices and browned bits spooned over the top. Or, discard the fat from the roasting pan, add 1 cup water to the pan, and bring it to a simmer, on top of the stove, scraping up the browned pit with a wooden spoon. Boil the juices down until they have thickened slightly. Season with salt and black pepper to taste, and spoon over the chicken.

VARIATION

Instead of the herb mixture, purée ¼ cup crumbled fresh goat cheese, 1 minced clove garlic, 12 sun-dried tomatoes packed in oil, 2 tablespoons olive oil, and salt and pepper to taste in a food processor. Spread this mixture under and into the chicken skin and bake as directed. Omit the pan sauce.

QUICK ROUND-OUT

To round out a chicken main dish, while the chicken is cooking, sauté 1 thinly sliced onion and 2 julienned red bell peppers in 2 tablespoons olive oil in a skillet over medium heat. When the onion and peppers are soft, add 8 to 10 ounces sliced fresh mushrooms and sauté for another 2 to 3 minutes. Add 1 package (10 ounces) thawed frozen corn kernels, cover, and simmer until heated through, 3 minutes. Season with salt and pepper to taste.

If you are so inclined, cook up some rice, couscous, or quinoa to go with the meal; otherwise, just serve a high-quality French bread so you have a vehicle with which to mop up any juices.

Asian Chicken, Breaded and Baked

MAKES: *4 servings*
TIME: *15 minutes preparation*
1 hour no-work baking time

Here's a delicious recipe for health-minded cooks. The skin is removed before baking to minimize the calories and fat. The chicken is then coated with a hot and spicy paste and dipped in dried bread crumbs to give the finished dish some crunch. To compensate for the loss of flavor that occurs when you remove the fat, the paste is boldly flavored with the tang of lime, the heat of red pepper, and the perfume of garlic.

A lovely side dish to serve as a counterpoint would be a salad of bean sprouts, Boston lettuce, and arugula leaves dressed lightly with a lemon vinaigrette.

2 large limes
¼ cup unsweetened coconut milk, preferably "light"
1 teaspoon ground cumin
1 teaspoon dried red pepper flakes
½ teaspoon ground cinnamon
¼ teaspoon ground coriander
1 large clove garlic
Salt
1 chicken (3½ to 4 pounds), quartered or cut into 8 pieces, skin removed
½ cup dried bread crumbs

1. Preheat the oven to 375°F.

2. Wash one of the limes, and using a sharp paring knife, remove a 1 × ¼-inch piece of zest. Be sure to leave all white pith behind. Juice the lime; you should have about 2 tablespoonfuls of juice.

3. In a blender combine the coconut milk, cumin, red pepper flakes, cinnamon, coriander, garlic, lime zest, lime juice, and 1 teaspoon salt. Blend until thoroughly mixed.

4. Score the chicken flesh with a sharp knife, then rub the coconut milk mixture onto the chicken. Dip the chicken in the bread crumbs, patting so they adhere on both sides.

5. Set the leg and thigh pieces on a baking pan and bake for 15 minutes. Add the breast and wing pieces, bone side down, and bake until all parts are cooked through, 50 minutes more. Cut the remaining lime into wedges and serve with the chicken.

VARIATIONS

■ To make this leaner still, use plain low-fat yogurt instead of the coconut milk.
■ In step 3, add ½ teaspoon curry powder to the spices.
■ Instead of this spice paste, rub the skinless chicken with 2 tablespoons of a commercial or Homemade Tandoori Paste (page 230) mixed with ¼ cup yogurt or unsweetened coconut

milk. Then dip the chicken in the bread crumbs.

ESPECIALLY GOOD FOR CHILDREN

Save the spicy rub for the adults. Rub the kids' chicken with mild barbecue sauce or ketchup before dredging it in bread crumbs.

Oven-Fried Chicken

MAKES: *4 servings*
TIME: *15 minutes preparation*
1 hour no-work baking time

If at all feasible, prepare the chicken ahead of time so it can fully absorb the flavors of the yogurt marinade. Marinating the chicken for the full hour intensifies the flavor, but of course this dish tastes fine even if you can't spare the hour. Good old-fashioned creamy coleslaw makes a great side dish and can be assembled in the time it takes to bake the chicken.

1 clove garlic, minced
1 tablespoon brown sugar or honey
½ cup plain regular or low-fat yogurt
Salt and freshly ground black pepper
1 chicken, quartered or cut into 8 pieces
    (3½ to 4 pounds total)
½ cup all-purpose flour
1 teaspoon paprika
1 tablespoon vegetable oil

1. Combine the garlic, brown sugar, and yogurt in a mixing bowl. Season to taste with salt and pepper. Turn the chicken pieces in the yogurt mixture, and if you have the time, cover and set aside in the refrigerator for 1 hour.

2. Preheat the oven to 375°F.

3. Combine the flour with the paprika, 1 teaspoon salt, and 1 teaspoon pepper in a shallow plate.

4. Lightly oil a baking dish large enough to accommodate the chicken without crowding. Coat the chicken with the seasoned flour and shake off any excess. Set the chicken, skin side down, in the dish and bake for 25 minutes.

5. Turn the chicken over and bake until cooked through, another 35 minutes. Serve immediately, or set on a rack to cool to room temperature.

VARIATIONS

■ In step 3, instead of the paprika, combine the flour with ½ teaspoon chili powder or cayenne pepper.

■ For a Creole touch, in step 3 add ¼ teaspoon each of garlic salt, dried thyme, and cayenne pepper to the flour and paprika.

MORE IDEAS FOR OVEN-FRIED CHICKEN

Cut a whole chicken into 6 or 8 pieces. Pull off the skin. Marinate the pieces in ⅓ to ½ cup yogurt, Basic Vinaigrette (page 64), Basil and Garlic Purée (page 224), or Homemade Tandoori Paste (page 230). Coat each piece with one of the following coating mixes:

- ½ cup dried plain bread crumbs mixed with ½ cup finely chopped or ground nuts, such as peanuts or almonds.
- 1 cup pulverized tortilla chips, Ritz crackers, or saltine crackers, mixed with 1 teaspoon paprika and cayenne pepper to taste.

Meltingly Marvelous Chicken

MAKES: *4 servings*
TIME: *20 minutes preparation*
45 minutes no-work baking time

The dark meat of the chicken is by nature moister than the white meat, and this recipe makes it moister still by cooking the chicken thighs in their own juices. This dish takes a little more time than usual, but the richly complex flavor makes the wait worthwhile.

2 tablespoons butter
8 skinless chicken thighs (3 pounds total)
2 cloves garlic, minced
¼ cup Dijon mustard
¼ cup lemon juice
2 tablespoons dark or light brown sugar
Salt and cayenne pepper
¼ cup (packed) parsley leaves

1. Preheat the oven to 350°F.

2. Melt the butter in a 4-quart flameproof enameled cast-iron saucepan over medium heat. Add the thighs and sauté just until the skin stiffens slightly, 2 minutes per side. Remove them to a plate.

3. Add the garlic to the saucepan, along with the mustard, lemon juice, and brown sugar. Season lightly with salt and cayenne pepper. Return the chicken to the pan and turn the thighs well in the mixture to coat on all sides.

4. Bring the mixture to a simmer over medium heat. Cover, and transfer the pan to the oven. Bake until the chicken is cooked through, 45 minutes. Meanwhile, finely chop the parsley.

5. When the chicken is done, place the thighs on a plate and keep them warm. Discard the surface fat from the juices in the pan, and boil the juices down over high heat until only ½ cup remains. Adjust the seasoning, and remove the pan from the heat. Add the parsley and spoon the sauce over the chicken.

VARIATION

In step 3, after you add the garlic, add ⅓ cup of green salsa or an herb purée (see pages 224 and 225) instead of the mustard, lemon juice, and brown sugar. In step 5, add ½ cup plain yogurt to the reduced juices, and substitute chopped cilantro for the parsley.

Feta-Stuffed Chicken

MAKES: *4 servings*
TIME: *10 minutes preparation*
45 minutes no-work baking time

This dish has an "ugly duckling" look but a real "swan" taste. The garnish of fresh herbs helps, but if you don't have any, don't worry. The flavor of the dish will be just as marvelous without them.

8 ounces feta, mild goat cheese, or Boursin cheese
2 teaspoons dried oregano
1 tablespoon butter, at room temperature
1 teaspoon grated lemon zest
¼ cup lemon juice
Salt and freshly ground black pepper
2 whole bone-in chicken breasts, skin on, split in half
¼ cup (packed) flat-leaf parsley leaves or fresh dill (optional)

1. Preheat the oven to 425°F.

2. Combine the cheese, oregano, butter, lemon zest, and lemon juice in a small bowl. Season to taste with salt and pepper.

3. Loosen the chicken skin from the flesh without completely detaching it, and stuff as much of the cheese mixture under the skin as possible. Spread the remaining mixture over the skin. Place in a baking pan and bake for 30 minutes. Raise the heat to 450°F and bake until the chicken breasts are cooked through and slightly golden on top, 15 minutes longer.

4. While the chicken is baking, chop the parsley. Remove the chicken from the oven, sprinkle it with chopped parsley, and serve immediately.

VARIATION

In step 2 make a stuffing with 4 ounces shredded Monterey Jack cheese, 4 ounces cream cheese, 1 teaspoon grated lime zest, ¼ cup lime juice, ¼ cup soft bread crumbs, and 1 teaspoon each of chili powder and ground cumin. In step 3, seed and mince 2 fresh jalapeño peppers; sprinkle them over the cooked chicken in step 4. Serve with lime wedges if you wish.

Chicken in the Microwave

Microwave Chicken for Two

A Blueprint Recipe

MAKES: *2 servings*
TIME: *25 minutes*

I'm not hugely fond of the microwave oven because when all is said and done, it doesn't save you a lot of time if you are cooking an entire meal for four people. However, many people like the convenience and cleanliness of cooking everything in a single washable dish, and so for them I offer this blueprint recipe of chicken and vegetables for two. (A recipe for more people would take longer than the usual 30-minute Monday-to-Friday time frame.) The chicken and vegetables aren't enough for a complete meal, so during the time it takes to prepare and cook the dish, make a side dish such as couscous or rice or one of the starch accompaniments I recommend in my Hearty Skillet Suppers (see page 101).

1½ tablespoons olive oil
½ onion, finely chopped
1 clove garlic, finely chopped
1 green or red bell pepper, stemmed, seeded, and finely chopped
2 cups mushrooms
1 tablespoon tomato paste
12 ounces skinless, boneless chicken (thigh or breast)
¼ teaspoon dried oregano
Salt and freshly ground black pepper

1. Combine the oil, onion, garlic, and bell pepper in a 2-quart microwaveable casserole. Cover with microwaveable plastic wrap (turned back at one corner to prevent steam buildup), and microwave at 100% power for 3 minutes.

2. Meanwhile, wipe the mushrooms with a damp paper towel and trim ¼ inch off the stems. Cut the mushrooms into ¼-inch-thick slices.

3. Unwrap the dish, give the ingredients a stir, and add the mushrooms and tomato paste. Rewrap as before and microwave at 100% power for another 3 minutes. During this time cut the chicken into ½-inch cubes.

4. Unwrap the casserole, add the chicken and oregano, and season with ½ teaspoon salt and pepper to taste. Stir the ingredients well and re-cover the casserole (with a new piece of plastic wrap, if need be, turning it back at one corner as before). Microwave at 100% power for another 3 minutes for white meat or 5 minutes for dark meat. Remove the casserole from the oven and let it stand for 5 minutes. Stir, adjust the seasoning, and serve.

VARIATIONS

With Other Vegetables: In step 1 combine the onion and garlic with 1 cup chopped fresh celery or fennel.

For a Southwest Accent: In step 4, when you add the chicken, add 1 teaspoon chili powder and ½ teaspoon ground cumin in addition to the oregano.

For an Indian Accent: In step 4, stir ½ teaspoon curry powder, a sprinkling of dried red pepper flakes, and ¼ cup golden raisins into the ingredients instead of the oregano. When done, serve with sour cream.

For a French Accent: In step 3, instead of the tomato paste, stir in 1 teaspoon prepared mustard. In step 4, stir ¼ teaspoon dried tarragon into the ingredients instead of the oregano.

Microwave Pantry Chicken

MAKES: *2 servings*
TIME: *15 minutes*

To make a chicken-and-pantry dinner in the microwave oven, all you need is a thawed 10-ounce package of frozen vegetables, 12 ounces of diced chicken, and anywhere from ¼ to ½ cup of a seasoning sauce such as a salsa. Take a look at the variations below to get some ideas, then go ahead and create your own. You can also make this dish with all the ingredients still frozen; it will just take a little longer to cook.

> 1 package (10 ounces) frozen corn
>   kernels, thawed
> ½ cup prepared green or red salsa,
>   mild or hot
> 12 ounces skinless, boneless chicken
>   (thigh or breast), cut into ½-inch dice
> Salt and freshly ground black pepper
> Sour cream or grated Monterey Jack
>   cheese (optional)

1. Combine the corn, salsa, and chicken in a mixing bowl. Season to taste with salt and pepper.

2. Transfer this mixture to a microwaveable dish, cover (turned back at one corner) with plastic wrap, and microwave at 100% power for 3 to 4 minutes. Give the mix a stir, cover again, and microwave for another 2 minutes. Let the dish stand for 5 minutes to complete the cooking before serving.

3. Serve in deep bowls, garnished with sour cream if you wish.

VARIATIONS

Two other good combinations:
- 1 package (10 ounces) frozen sliced carrots, thawed, 12 ounces chicken, and ½ cup Coconut Peanut Sauce (page 226).
- 1 package (10 ounces) frozen "petite" peas, thawed, 12 ounces chicken, and ½ cup Cilantro Purée (page 225).

THE FORGETFUL COOK

Don't worry if you've forgotten to thaw the vegetables and the cubed chicken. Plunk the block of frozen chicken cubes in a microwaveable dish and cook, uncovered, at 100% power for 2 minutes. Separate the chunks of chicken. Set the frozen vegetables (it's all right if they are still in a block) on top of the chicken and cook, uncovered, for 2 minutes more. Stir the ingredients—by now the vegetables and chicken will be mostly thawed.

Add ½ cup salsa or tomato sauce, cover with plastic wrap with a corner pulled back, and cook at 100% power for 3 minutes. Add 1 tablespoon of olive oil, and salt and freshly ground black pepper if the salsa is not especially fiery. Stir the ingredients, moving those from the outside edge of the plate toward the middle and the ones from the center toward the outside edge.

Again, partially cover and cook for 4 minutes. Then stir the ingredients and if all the chicken is not cooked through, continue to cook, checking and stirring at 2-minute intervals, until it is done (dark meat will take longer).

Let stand for 2 minutes before serving.

Zesty Herbed Chicken

MAKES: *2 servings*
TIME: *30 minutes*

This recipe is so fast and quick, you'll have plenty of time to make the incredible citrus salsa to use as a topping. This recipe yields a lot of fragrant juice, so it is well worth cooking some rice to serve alongside.

> ¼ cup lemon or lime juice
> 1 clove garlic, minced
> 1 teaspoon chili powder
> Salt and freshly ground black pepper
> 1 whole chicken breast (1¼ pounds)
> Citrus Salsa Topping (recipe follows)

1. Combine the lemon juice, garlic, chili powder, and salt and pepper to taste in a round microwaveable dish. Rub this mixture onto the chicken and marinate for at least 10 minutes.

2. Cover the dish tightly with plastic wrap, poke a few holes in it for steam vents, and microwave at 100% power for 10 minutes. Uncover, turn the chicken over, re-cover, and microwave until just cooked through, another 6 to 7 minutes. Let the chicken stand for 3 minutes (it will cook a bit more upon standing). Spoon the juices over the top, and serve with the salsa.

Citrus Salsa Topping

MAKES: *About 3 cups*
TIME: *15 minutes preparation time*

....

1 red or pink grapefruit
2 oranges
1 Hass avocado
1 scallion, trimmed
3 jalapeño peppers, seeded and chopped
1 bunch chopped fresh cilantro,
    rinsed and patted dry
Salt

1. With a sharp knife, peel the grapefruit and oranges, removing all of the skin and white pith. Holding each fruit over a bowl to catch the juices, cut between the membranes to loosen the segments and drop them into the bowl. Remove any seeds from the fruit.

2. Peel and dice the avocado and add it to the bowl. Thinly slice the scallion (both white and green parts) and seed and chop the jalapeños, adding both to the bowl. Remove and chop enough cilantro leaves to make ¼ cup (loosely packed). Add them to the bowl and toss. Season to taste with salt.

Sunday Start-ups and Quick Fixes

In my *Monday-to-Friday Cookbook* I explained how I take advantage of the time I have on a Sunday afternoon to roast enough chicken so that I have leftovers for a meal later on in the week—which I use to enrich a soup, concoct a speedy chicken salad, or effortlessly create a main-course pasta salad.

In this chapter I've brought together all the recipes that require more time than a typical weekday may allow for. Here are serious Sunday Start-up recipes that are perfect to make on the weekend when you have more time—roasted chickens, game hens, turkey breast, and a couple of long-simmering soups made in such large quantities that you are sure to have leftovers. You will also find recipes that will give you a head start on dinners you can fix up easily and quickly later on in the week when you are short on time.

I thought a good way to end this chapter would be with the comforting Grandma Helen's Jewish Chicken Soup, which takes a bit more time than the Monday-to-Friday cook may have, making it a perfect inclusion to the Sunday Start-ups. After all, what chicken cookbook would be complete without an old-fashioned chicken soup recipe?

Roasted Chickens, Two at a Time

MAKES: *3 to 4 servings per chicken*
TIME: *15 minutes preparation*
1¼ to 1½ hours no-work cooking time

Like all cooks, I am constantly changing the way I do things. I used to roast all chickens untrussed, and I couldn't be bothered with basting. I've discovered, however, that a bit of string tied around the bird's ankles, as well as basting now and then, does indeed yield a tastier, juicier bird.

2 whole chickens (3½ to 4 pounds each)
1 onion, coarsely chopped
1 teaspoon dried thyme
1 teaspoon dried rosemary
1 teaspoon dried tarragon
2 tablespoons butter, at room temperature
2 tablespoons olive oil
Salt and freshly ground black pepper
2 tablespoons butter, melted

1. Preheat the oven to 475°F.

2. Remove the giblet package and excess pieces of fat from the cavity and neck of each chicken. Pat them dry. (For easier carving, remove the wishbone; see box, page 204.)

3. In a bowl, combine the onion, herbs, room-temperature butter, olive oil, 1 tablespoon salt, and pepper to taste. Stuff the mixture into the cavities of the birds, and strew whatever does not fit in the bottom of a roasting pan large enough to accommodate both birds without crowding.

4. Wrap a length of string around the tail, then bring it up around the legs and tie again. Set the chickens, breast side up, on the onion mixture. Season the skin with salt, and roast for 30 minutes. Lower the heat to 350°F.

5. Remove the pan from the oven (making sure to close the oven door), brush the breasts with the melted butter, and return the chickens to the oven. Roast for another 45 minutes to 1 hour, for a total of about 22 minutes per pound. Remove the chickens from the oven and prick the thighs with a knife; the juices should run clear without a trace of pink.

Remove one bird to a cutting board and let sit for 10 minutes before carving. Carve the bird and strain the pan juices into a saucepan or bowl (to remove any bits of onion that have browned too much). Spoon the strained juices over the carved chicken and serve.

6. Let the second bird cool to room temperature. Once the second bird is cool enough to handle, remove the skin and discard. Then remove the meat from the bones. Tightly wrap the meat in plastic wrap and store for up to 3 days in the refrigerator.

VARIATION

Roasted Chickens à l'Indienne: In step 3, instead of the onion, herbs, butter, and oil, make a paste of 2 tablespoons tomato paste, 3 tablespoons lemon juice, 1 teaspoon ground cumin, 1 teaspoon chili powder, 1 teaspoon ground cinnamon, ½ teaspoon ground coriander, ½ teaspoon ground ginger, and salt and pepper to taste. Slide your fingers between the skin and flesh of the chicken to loosen the skin. Rub some of the paste on the flesh, underneath the skin, and some on top of the skin. Set the birds on a rack in the roasting pan, and proceed to step 4.

Roasted Chicken and Veggies Too

MAKES: *8 servings*
TIME: *10 minutes preparation*
1¾ hours no-work cooking time

When I want to have roasted vegetables along with my roasted chicken, I roast bird and veggies, in different pans, at a high heat in the same oven. A bird roasted at a high heat cooks in a shorter time and yields a crispier skin, but it doesn't develop the well-tended infused flavor it does when you cook it more slowly and baste it as you go. To compensate for this, be sure to make the pan sauce for extra flavor. To minimize the smokiness this roasting method can produce, make sure your oven is clean, use a heavy-duty roasting pan, and open the windows wide.

1 roasting chicken (7 to 7½ pounds)
Salt
1 cup chopped fresh parsley or basil,
    or a mix of fresh herbs; or 1
    teaspoon each dried thyme,
    rosemary, and tarragon
6 cloves garlic, unpeeled
¼ cup dry white wine
¾ cup water or chicken broth
1 tablespoon butter
Freshly ground black pepper
Roasted Vegetables (recipes follow)

1. Place an oven rack in the center of the oven. Preheat the oven to 475°F.

2. Remove the giblet package and excess pieces of fat from the cavity and neck of the chicken. For easier carving, remove the wishbone (see box, this page). Pat dry and season the cavity with salt only (pepper burns at such a high heat). Stuff the cavity with the herbs and garlic. It is not necessary to truss the bird.

3. Place the bird, breast side up, in a roasting pan and roast for 15 minutes. Remove the pan from the oven (close the door) and move the bird around in the pan so it will be less likely to stick to the bottom. Return the pan to the oven and roast, without opening the door, until done, another 1½ hours. Prick the thighs with a knife; the juices should run clear without a trace of pink. Remove the bird to a cutting board and let it rest for 30 minutes.

CARVING TRICK

It is easier to carve the breast if you take an extra step and remove the wishbone before roasting. With your fingers, feel for the wishbone. Using a paring knife, make slits above the wishbone so you can see it. Slip the knife underneath and scrape away the flesh below the bones. Cut the wishbone at its base, where the bones join in a flatter end. Cut out that bone, then bend the wishbone away from you to break the two bones out of their joints.

4. Meanwhile, transfer the juices from the roasting pan to a bowl or degreaser, and skim off the surface fat. Return the degreased juices to the roasting pan. Remove the garlic and herbs from the cavity and add them to the juices in the roasting pan. Set the pan over medium-high heat and add the wine and water. Boil the liquid down over high heat until reduced by half, 1 to 2 minutes. Using a slotted spoon, remove and discard the garlic and herbs.

5. Carve the legs. Remove the breast from the bones and slice it across the grain. Right before serving, whisk the butter into the sauce and season to taste with salt and pepper. Serve with your favorite roasted vegetables.

Roasted Vegetables

So many vegetables taste great with roasted chicken. Here are preparation steps and cooking times for a dozen of them. The quantities listed will serve 4 people. Because roasted vegetables lose moisture and shrivel up at high heat, they may not win any beauty contest when they're done—but, boy, their flavor is hard to beat. All of these should be roasted at 475°F in a separate pan from the one in which you're roasting the chicken. Try to time their cooking so both the chicken and vegetables are ready at the same time (remember, the chicken rests for 30 minutes after you've removed it from the oven). If the vegetables are ready before the chicken, cover them with aluminum foil to keep warm.

Acorn Squash

Even though it takes less time to roast them halved, I roast acorn squash whole. Why? Because I have sustained too many little knife nicks in trying to cut them in half before cooking! Wash 2 medium-size squash, and with a sharp knife, prick the skin in several places. Set them in a baking pan and pour ⅛ inch of water into the pan. Roast for 45 minutes to 1 hour or until tender. Remove the squash from the oven, split them in half, and scoop out the seeds. To each half add butter and brown sugar to taste. Season with salt and pepper.

Beets

Scrub 2 pounds of beets clean, but leave them unpeeled with a bit of top attached. Rub them with vegetable oil and set them in a baking pan. Roast small beets for 30 to 45 minutes, medium ones for 45 minutes to 1 hour, larger ones for at least 1 hour.

Carrots, Parsnips, and Turnips

Peel 1½ pounds of carrots, parsnips, or turnips, and cut them into 2-inch chunks (or wedges for turnips). With your hands, rub a couple of teaspoonfuls of olive or vegetable oil over them. Season with salt. Set them in a pan large enough to hold them in a single layer; add ⅛ inch of water or chicken broth to the pan, and roast until tender, 30 to 45 minutes.

Garlic

There are a couple of ways to go here. To roast the head as a unit, cut a ¼-inch slice off the stem end, leaving the cloves attached. Rub the exposed part of the cloves

with a teaspoon or so of vegetable oil, and set the head in the roasting pan alongside your bird; cook for 30 minutes. Or loosen the cloves and roast them whole, unpeeled, in the pan with the chicken for 20 to 30 minutes.

Onions

Peel 2 pounds of onions and cut each one in half from stem to root. Cut each half again into 2 or 3 wedges. Rub the onion wedges with 1 teaspoon of vegetable oil and season with salt. Roast for 30 to 45 minutes.

Bell Peppers

Start roasting 8 small or 4 large bell peppers as soon as you put the bird in, because they need to cool a bit before you can remove the charred skin. Rinse and dry the peppers, and set them on a baking sheet. Roast, turning once, for 45 minutes or until the skins are almost burned. Remove the peppers from the oven and transfer them to a plastic bag and tightly close the bag. Leave until cool enough to handle, then remove the blackened skin and discard the stem and seeds.

Potatoes

Scrub 2 pounds of boiling or Yukon Gold potatoes. Set them, unpeeled, in a baking pan and add ⅛ inch of water to the pan. Roast for 1 to 1¼ hours or until tender.

To roast Idaho baking potatoes, scrub 4 potatoes, then prick them in several places and set them directly on the oven rack. Roast until tender, 1 to 1¼ hours.

THINK AHEAD

To save time tomorrow, cook all of what you have today. For example, cook the whole head of broccoli and put leftovers aside. Tomorrow night you'll have leftovers from which to start a salad or soup or vegetable stir fry.

Zucchini and Summer Squashes

Scrub 2 pounds of squash, trim off the ends, and cut them in half lengthwise. Using a small spoon, remove and discard the seeds. Cut the squash into 1- to 2-inch-long chunks, and rub them lightly with 2 teaspoons vegetable oil. Season with salt and set them in a baking pan large enough to accommodate them in a single layer. Add ⅛ inch of water to the pan and roast for 30 minutes.

Sweet Potatoes

Scrub 4 medium sweet potatoes clean, and prick them in several places with a sharp knife. Set them on a baking pan (to catch any oozing juices), and roast until tender, 45 minutes to 1 hour.

Tomatoes

Wash, core, and halve 2 large beefsteak tomatoes. Drizzle 1 teaspoon of vegetable oil on top, and set them in a small baking pan. Roast for 20 minutes.

ROASTING THE WHOLE CHICKEN

Relaxed Sundays are the perfect time to roast chickens. Once prepared, the roasted chicken is a boon to the Monday-to-Friday cook. Leftover chicken can easily star the rest of the week in delicious pasta meals, soups, salads, and sandwiches. There is a ton of controversy about how best to roast a bird so that the legs are cooked through while the breast remains moist. Theories and cooking tricks abound. Some people resort to roasting the chicken breast side down. Others swear that roasting chicken for 1 hour at 500°F will do the trick. Others believe that cooking the chicken for hours in a 300°F oven yields the most succulent roast. Many cooks adhere to the classic method of basting and turning the chicken every 15 minutes until it is done.

In reality, the white meat of the bird cooks at one rate, the dark meat at another. For a perfectly tender moist breast, the legs will be a little underdone, and for perfectly cooked drumsticks, the breast will be slightly overdone. If you can't tolerate these quirks of nature, then turn to recipes for quartered and cut-up chicken, in which the dark meat is started first and cooked longer than the white meat so both parts end up cooked properly.

For juicier flesh with lots of flavor, I roast two chickens at once. They fit tightly in one pan, so there is less dry air circulating around them. They also create more steam while they roast, in turn producing a moister, juicier bird. I start roasting them at 425°F, then continue to cook them between 350°F and 375°F, and baste the birds during the cooking time. However, when I roast chicken in this fashion, I can't roast vegetables at the same time because the heat isn't high enough.

When I want to roast vegetables too, I roast the bird at very high heat without basting. But when I use that method, I like to cook a larger bird, because at such high heat, the flesh of a plump bird will be juicier.

BEFORE YOU BEGIN

Remove as much of the interior fat as possible, do a quick truss at the ankles (or not, if you are roasting at high heat), and place the chickens in a baking pan. Then put the pan in the center of the preheated oven. I happen to find it easy to plunk the chickens right into the pan without a rack, but for drier, crispier skin all around, I use a rack.

BASTING

Basting, the spooning of melted butter, pan juices, or other liquids over a roast, helps keep the bird moist while it cooks and imparts a deeper flavor. One very important point: When you baste, remove the chickens from the oven and immediately close the oven door so the temperature does not get too low. If you baste with the door open, the temperature rapidly drops a hundred degrees and skews the roasting time. Instead, put the pans on top of the stove and baste the chickens with a long-handled shallow spoon. I find it is also easier to do a better job of basting with the roasting pan on top of the stove because I am not hunched over with my face in the scorching heat.

WHEN IS THE CHICKEN DONE?

The National Broiler Council recommends cooking a whole chicken to an internal temperature of 180°F. If you don't have a thermometer, the chicken is done when a paring knife is inserted in the thickest part of the thigh, without touching the bone, and the juices run clear, without a hint of pink.

LEFTOVER DIVIDENDS

One of the motivations for my Sunday chicken-roasting routine is the leftover dividends I plan for. But in order to make the most of those leftovers, take a bit of care in how you handle them. Rather than tossing the leftover carcass into the fridge to deal with at a later date, take the time to discard the skin and fat, remove the meat from the bones, and wrap the meat airtight. This preserves the flesh and keeps it moister for longer. You can also get extra dividends from the carcass itself; there is always enough delicious meat on the bones to yield a flavorful stock. If you don't have time that evening to make a quick broth from the bones (see page 234), store them in a plastic bag and freeze them for another day.

Game Hens with Pecan Rice Pilaf

MAKES: *4 servings*
TIME: *45 to 50 minutes*

The contrast of the sweetness of the raisins and peas is terrific against the spiciness of the ginger and tang of the lime juice here. The only little trick is to figure out how to cut the birds into quarters, but armed with a good pair of kitchen shears, you should have no trouble. Chances are you rarely will have 45 minutes during the week, so make this on a Sunday when you have a bit more time.

2 Rock Cornish hens (about 1½ pounds each)
4 teaspoons olive oil
1 teaspoon paprika
Salt and freshly ground black pepper
2 tablespoons butter
2 tablespoons sesame seeds
1 clove garlic, minced
½ teaspoon ground ginger
1 cup converted rice
1 teaspoon honey
2 cups chicken broth or water
½ cup pecans, walnuts, or blanched almonds
1 package (10 ounces) frozen "petite" peas, thawed
⅔ cup golden raisins
4 lime wedges

1. Preheat the oven to 375°F.

2. Remove the giblets from the interior of the hens. With heavy-duty kitchen shears, cut along either side of each backbone and remove it. Cut off and remove the first two joints of the wings, so only the fleshy joint is left on the breast. Also cut off and remove any excess neck skin. Pat the skin dry with paper towels.

3. Mix the oil with the paprika and season to taste with salt and pepper. With your fingers, rub this mixture into the birds. Set them, skin side down, in a baking dish  large enough to accommodate them without crowding. Bake for 20 minutes; turn over and bake until cooked through, 15 minutes more.

4. Meanwhile, melt the butter in a medium-size saucepan over medium heat until golden, about 1 minute. Add the sesame seeds, garlic, and ginger and sauté for a few seconds. Add the rice and sauté for 1 minute to coat the kernels with the butter. Stir in the honey and broth, and bring the liquid to a boil. Season to taste with salt and pepper, cover, and cook over low heat for 15 minutes. During this time coarsely chop the nuts.

5. Stir the peas and raisins into the rice, cover, and simmer until the rice is cooked through and the peas are warm, 5 minutes. Adjust the seasoning and keep warm, covered, until the game hens are done.

6. Right before serving, stir the nuts into the rice. Spoon a portion of rice on each plate. Arrange two halves of a hen over the rice, and garnish each plate with a wedge of lime to squeeze over the chicken.

Chicken Stew
Any Way
and Every Way

MAKES: *8 servings*
TIME: *30 minutes preparation*
1 hour no-work cooking time

The first time around, I flavor this stew with simple seasonings so that when I serve it again, I can vary its character in any number of ways. I deliberately leave the sauce light and soupy so there's lots of it to enjoy. Don't forget to remove all excess skin and fat from the chicken or you'll end up with a greasy stew.

1 onion, coarsely chopped
2 carrots, coarsely chopped
2 ribs celery, coarsely chopped
¼ cup vegetable or olive oil
2 chickens, quartered (3½ to 4 pounds each)
1 cup chicken broth
½ cup dry white wine or white vermouth
2 cloves garlic
1 bay leaf
Salt and freshly ground black pepper
10 ounces mushrooms
2 tablespoons butter
1 package (10 ounces) frozen "petite" peas, thawed
¼ cup (packed) fresh parsley leaves
¼ cup (packed) fresh dill

1. Combine the onion, carrots, and celery in a food processor, and pulse about 15 times until the vegetables are chopped, but not too finely. Heat the oil in a 5- to 6-quart casserole over medium heat. Add the vegetables, cover, and cook over low heat for 5 to 7 minutes. Meanwhile, pull the skin off the dark meat of the chicken (to help your grip, use a paper towel). Remove as much excess fat as possible.

2. Add the dark meat to the casserole along with the broth, wine, garlic, bay leaf, 1 teaspoon salt, and pepper to taste. Bring the liquid to a simmer over medium heat. Cover and cook for 15 minutes. While this is cooking, cut off the wing tips at the second joint. Remove the skin and excess fat from the white meat as well.

3. Add the white meat to the casserole. Cover and cook over low heat until all the chicken is cooked through, 20 minutes.

4. Meanwhile, trim ¼ inch off the ends of the mushroom stems, wipe the mushrooms clean with a damp paper towel, and cut into thin slices. Melt the butter in a skillet, and sauté the mushrooms over medium heat until they begin to soften, 3 to 4 minutes. Remove them from the heat and add the peas. Chop the parsley and dill.

5. When the chicken is done, remove half to one platter for the first night's dinner, and cover it with aluminum foil to keep warm. Transfer the other half to a freezer container. Let the sauce settle so the fat surfaces, then degrease the sauce. Season the sauce to taste with salt and pepper, and remove the bay leaf. Transfer half of the sauce to a bowl to cool. (When the extra chicken and sauce are thoroughly cooled, cover them well and freeze them separately.)

6. Return the remaining half of the sauce to the casserole and bring it to a simmer. Add the cooked mushrooms and peas. When the liquid is at a simmer, remove the casserole from the heat and add the parsley and dill; adjust the seasoning. Serve the chicken with the juices, peas, and mushrooms in deep bowls.

SECOND TIME AROUND

Southeast Asia style: In a 4-quart saucepan, combine the leftover sauce, ½ cup coconut milk, the zest of 1 lemon and 1 lime, and the stems of a small bunch of cilantro. Bring to a simmer over medium heat. Season to taste with salt and pepper, add the cooked chicken, cover, and simmer for 10 minutes or until the chicken is just heated through. Remove the cilantro stems and garnish with chopped roasted peanuts and chopped cilantro leaves. Serve over plain rice.

Southwest style: In a 4-quart saucepan, toast 1 tablespoon chili powder over medium heat for a few seconds or until you get a whiff of its aroma. Add the leftover sauce and whisk in 2 tablespoons tomato paste. Add 1 can (4 ounces) chopped green chiles, 1 package (10 ounces) thawed frozen corn kernels, and 1 can (6 ounces drained weight) pitted jumbo black olives. Bring to a simmer and add the chicken. Cover and simmer over low heat for 10 minutes or until the chicken is just heated through. Adjust the seasoning and garnish with sour cream or fresh goat's cheese and, if you wish, chopped cilantro. Serve over warm flour tortillas.

Italian style: In a 4-quart saucepan, combine 2 cups drained canned stewed tomatoes, the leftover sauce, ¼ cup finely sliced roasted red peppers (from a jar), 2 jars (6½ ounces each) drained marinated artichokes, coarsely chopped, ¼ cup sliced pitted good-quality olives, and 1 tablespoon drained nonpareil capers. Bring to a simmer over medium heat, add the chicken and cook, covered, over low heat for 10 minutes or until the chicken is just heated through. Adjust the seasoning. Serve with polenta.

Baked Chicken with Noodles, Plus

MAKES: *4 servings, plus 2 more meals*
TIME: *1 hour*

There's a simple "comfort food" quality to this dish and to its Second and Third Time Around variations that should make all of them appeal to even the pickiest of eaters. Baking 12 chicken breasts at once gives you enough for all three very different meals. Recipes for the variations follow this one.

12 boneless, skinless chicken breast
    halves (about 5 pounds total)
1 clove garlic, minced
¼ cup lemon juice
2 tablespoons olive oil
Salt
4 tablespoons (½ stick) butter
⅓ cup all-purpose flour
4 cups milk
¾ cup (2 ounces) freshly grated
    Parmesan cheese
Freshly ground black pepper
1½ pounds fettuccine
4 medium tomatoes, cored and cut
    into ¾-inch dice
1 bunch fresh chives, finely snipped

1. Preheat the oven to 375°F.

2. Arrange the chicken breasts on a large baking sheet. In a small bowl combine the garlic, lemon juice, oil, and 1 teaspoon salt. Rub this mixture into the chicken. Cover with foil and bake until the chicken is just done, 45 minutes.

3. Meanwhile, melt the butter in a medium-size saucepan over medium heat. When the foaming subsides, whisk in the flour and cook over low heat for 1 minute. Gradually, whisking vigorously so the mixture does not lump, work in 2 cups of the milk. Then add the remaining 2 cups milk. Bring to a simmer, whisking occasionally. When the sauce comes to a simmer (do not let it boil over), turn the heat to low and cook for 2 to 3 minutes. Remove from the heat and add 1 teaspoon salt, the Parmesan cheese, and pepper to taste.

4. Half an hour before the chicken is done, bring 4 quarts of water to a boil in a large pot. Add the fettuccine and cook until tender but still firm to the bite, 10 minutes. Drain and return half the noodles to the pot. Transfer the other half to a 13 × 9-inch baking pan and set aside for the Second Time Around (see next page). Add the diced tomatoes and chives to the noodles in the pot and toss them together.

5. Transfer some of the noodle mixture to a platter. Remove the chicken from the oven and arrange 4 chicken breast halves down the center of the noodles. Spoon about half of the sauce over the chicken. (You could also do this on individual dinner plates.) Reserve the remaining chicken for the Second (and Third) Time Around (see below).

SECOND TIME AROUND

After dinner, purée ½ cup oil-packed sun-dried tomatoes in a food processor and add them to the noodles along with 1 thawed package (10 ounces) of frozen "petite" peas and ⅓ cup fresh basil leaves, chopped. Season to taste with salt and pepper.

Cut 4 of the remaining chicken breast halves into ½-inch dice and add to the baking pan. Cover with aluminum foil and refrigerate for up to a week or freeze for up to 3 weeks.

Thaw the casserole, if it is frozen, in the refrigerator or microwave. Preheat the oven to 400°F and bake, covered, until heated through, 45 minutes. (You can bake it unthawed, but it will take 1½ hours to heat through).

THIRD TIME AROUND

Dice the remaining 4 cooked chicken breasts and combine with 1 cup chopped drained pimiento-stuffed Spanish olives or a prepared olive salad. Season with salt and pepper to taste. (This will keep in the fridge for 3 days.)

Make quick dinner sandwiches by stuffing this mixture into pita pockets along with shredded iceberg lettuce and chopped tomatoes, or by wrapping the mixture in warm flour tortillas which you first spread with mayonnaise. Top the stuffed tortillas with chopped tomatoes mixed with chopped fresh cilantro, and eat with a knife and fork.

Here's another way to use the chicken and olive mixture. Preheat the oven to 450°F. Spread pita bread or small prebaked pizza-type bread with tomato sauce. Dot with the chicken and olives, then top that with thin slices of fresh mozzarella cheese. Bake for 10 minutes.

One Turkey Breast, Three Meals

MAKES: *12 servings*
TIME: *15 minutes preparation for the turkey;*
15 minutes preparation for the potatoes
2½ hours no-work cooking time

It is handy to cook an entire turkey breast because out of one effort you get enough left over to rustle up at least two more meals. The two recipes that follow this one use the leftover cooked turkey.

4 tablespoons butter (½ stick), at room
temperature
½ cup (packed) fresh parsley leaves
½ cup (packed) fresh basil leaves
Grated zest of 2 lemons
Juice of 2 lemons
Salt and freshly ground
black pepper
1 bone-in turkey breast (7 to
9 pounds)
2 pounds russet or Yukon
Gold potatoes
2 red or yellow bell peppers
4 large tomatoes (about 1¼ pounds
total)
2 large cloves garlic
⅓ cup extra-virgin olive oil
½ cup dry white wine

1. Preheat the oven to 350°F.

2. Blend the butter, parsley, basil, lemon zest and juice, 1 tablespoon salt, and 1 teaspoon pepper in a food processor.

3. Remove the giblet package from inside the breast cavity (reserve it for making stock). Cut the wings off at the second joint and set them in the bottom of a roasting pan. With your fingers, gently lift the skin to loosen it from the breast meat, and rub the herb butter under the skin and into the flesh; rub some over the skin as well. Set the turkey breast alongside the wings in the roasting pan, and bake for 20 minutes per pound, about 2¾ hours.

4. While the turkey is baking, scrub the potatoes and cut them into ⅛-inch-thick slices. Stem and seed the peppers, and cut them into ¼-inch-thick strips. Core the tomatoes and cut them into ⅛-inch-thick slices. Thinly slice the garlic.

5. Drizzle 1 tablespoon of the oil in the bottom of a 3-quart oval or rectangular nonreactive baking dish. Arrange a layer of potatoes in the pan and season them with salt and pepper; then add a layer of bell peppers and a layer of tomatoes. Scatter one-third of the garlic, 2 tablespoons of the white wine, and 2 tablespoons of the olive oil over the tomatoes. Do another two layers of ingredients, ending with the tomatoes, remaining white wine, and remaining oil. Cover and bake for 1 hour. Then uncover and bake until the potatoes are tender, 30 minutes to 1 hour.

6. Remove the turkey breast and the vegetables from the oven and let the roast rest on a carving board for at least 15 minutes before slicing. Transfer the pan juices to a 1-quart measuring cup. When the fat floats to the surface, skim it off with a bulb baster. Whatever you don't catch with a bulb baster, blot off with paper towels.

7. Slice some turkey, moisten it with the degreased pan juices, and serve with the vegetables.

**SECOND
TIME
AROUND**

When dinner is done, remove and discard the turkey skin and bones. Dice the leftover turkey into 1-inch cubes and freeze them for another day. Or assemble the Southwest Turkey Casserole (facing page) and freeze that. You can also just wrap the turkey well and save it for later in the week, when you can use it in the Turkey and Stuffing Salad (below) or any Second Time Around roasted chicken soups.

Turkey and Stuffing Salad

MAKES: *4 servings*
TIME: *20 minutes*

It may not be usual to eat a cool salad with a warm stuffing, but the flavor and texture combination of the two work phenomenally well. This is a great favorite at my house because it's speedy to make and delightfully surprising in taste.

4 tablespoons (½ stick) butter
1 tablespoon dried tandoori seasoning, curry powder, or garam masala
3 cups diced cooked turkey breast
½ cup dried cranberries or raisins
1 package (6 ounces) unseasoned bread stuffing
1 cup unsweetened coconut milk
Salt and freshly ground black pepper
6 cups mesclun
10 ounces mushrooms
⅓ cup prepared salad dressing, such as Basic Vinaigrette (page 64)

1. Melt the butter in a large skillet over medium heat. When the foaming has subsided, add the tandoori seasoning, turkey, and cranberries. Cook over low heat until the ingredients are heated through, 3 to 4 minutes.

2. Add the bread stuffing and cook, stirring constantly, for 1 minute. Then add the coconut milk and cook just until the bread has absorbed the milk. Season to taste with salt and pepper. Set aside.

3. While the stuffing mixture is cooling down, rinse and dry the mesclun. Wipe the mushrooms clean with damp paper towels, trim ¼ inch off the stems, and cut them, across the caps, into ¼-inch slices. Mix the mushrooms with the mesclun and toss with the dressing. Make a wreath of salad on each plate, and center a portion of warm turkey stuffing in the center.

Southwest Turkey Casserole

MAKES: *4 servings*
TIME: *30 minutes, or 1¼ hours if frozen*

I like to assemble this casserole and pop it in the freezer the same night I cook the turkey breast. Then it's waiting for me when I need it.

1 cup long-grain rice
1 can (4 ounces) chopped green chiles
1 can (6 ounces drained weight) pitted jumbo black olives, coarsely chopped
2 cups chopped canned tomatoes with their juices
1 cup chicken or other broth
Salt
1 teaspoon ground cumin
3 cups cooked turkey in bite-size chunks
8 ounces Monterey Jack cheese, grated

1. In a 4-quart flameproof casserole, combine the rice, green chiles, olives, tomatoes and their juices, broth, 1 teaspoon salt, and the ground cumin. Add the turkey and mix the ingredients thoroughly. Cover and refrigerate for up to 5 days, or freeze for up to 3 months.

2. Thaw the casserole, if it is frozen, overnight in the refrigerator or in the microwave. Bring the ingredients to a boil over low heat, then simmer gently for 20 minutes or until the rice is cooked through and most of the liquid has been absorbed.

Alternatively, preheat the oven to 350°F and bake the casserole for 45 minutes. Then transfer it to the top of the stove and finish cooking it for 15 minutes or until the rice is cooked through and most of the liquid has been absorbed.

3. Sprinkle each portion with Monterey Jack cheese, and serve.

Turkey Soup and Soup and Soup

MAKES: *12 servings*
TIME: *20 minutes preparation
1¼ hours cooking time*

The biggest chore in making this soup will be to find a pot large enough to hold the turkey. The flavors of the broth are fabulous, thanks to the high dose of garlic and clever use of pickling spices. This first-night soup is magnificently potent in flavor and, believe it or not, low in fat. The second and third night's soups have different flavors altogether.

And of course, if the additional soup ideas don't appeal to you, then save the cooked turkey to use in salads and the turkey broth to use as a base for other soups.

> 1 bone-in turkey breast (5 to 7 pounds)
> 2 cups chicken broth
> 4 cloves garlic
> 2 tablespoons pickling spices, tied in
>   cheesecloth
> 2 ounces rice noodles
> 1 package (10 ounces) ready-to-eat
>   fresh spinach
> 4 carrots
> 1 Hass avocado
> Salt
> 2 limes, each cut in half
> Asian sesame oil
> Dried red pepper flakes
> ½ cup chopped fresh cilantro leaves
>   (optional)
> Black sesame seeds (optional)

1. Place the turkey, skin side up, in an 8-quart stockpot. Add the broth and enough cold water to cover the turkey (about 2 gallons). Bring the water to a simmer over medium heat. As the water heats, the turkey will throw off grayish foam, which you should remove with a shallow spoon. When the foam has been removed, add the garlic and pickling spices. Reduce the heat to low, cover partially, and simmer until the breast is cooked through, 1 hour.

2. Meanwhile, cover the rice noodles with warm water and let them stand for 30 minutes

to soften. Stem the spinach and rinse the leaves under cold water. Peel and grate the carrots. Drain the softened noodles and cut them into 4-inch lengths.

3. Remove the turkey to a cutting board and let it rest while you cook the rice noodles and vegetables. Degrease the broth and continue to simmer it gently until you are ready to ladle it out. Put the rice noodles in a 4-quart saucepan and cover with 4 cups water. Bring the water to a simmer over medium heat, and cook until the noodles are tender, 3 minutes. Add the grated carrots and simmer 1 minute longer. Add the spinach leaves, and when they are wilted, remove the saucepan from the heat (keep the noodles and vegetables in the hot water). Peel and pit the avocado, cut it into thin slices, and divide the slices among 4 soup bowls.

4. Remove and discard the turkey skin. Cut some thin slices from the breast. Cut them into smaller chunks and divide them among the soup bowls. Drain the rice noodles, carrots, and spinach and divide them equally among the soup bowls as well.

5. Season the turkey broth to taste with salt, and ladle some into each soup bowl. Let each diner season their portion to taste with lime juice, sesame oil, red pepper flakes, cilantro, and black sesame seeds.

WHAT TO DO WITH THE LEFT-OVER TURKEY AND BROTH

When the turkey has cooled down, remove the meat from the bones and cut into ¾-inch chunks. Discard the bag of pickling spices and the garlic cloves. Degrease the leftover broth. Divide the broth and the turkey chunks together between two 2-quart containers. Refrigerate for up to 4 days or freeze it for up to 3 months.

Second-Time-Around Turkey Soup with Dumplings

MAKES: *4 servings*
TIME: *10 to 15 minutes preparation*
45 minutes no-work cooking time

Making dumplings might seem like an odd thing to recommend during the week, but they are a delicious change of pace. The dough takes all of 3 minutes to assemble and the dumplings only 10 minutes to cook. Anyway, because the broth and turkey are already prepared, other than the dumplings all you have left to do is to simmer the mushrooms and carrots in the broth.

6 cups leftover turkey broth
4 cups diced leftover cooked turkey
6 carrots
10 ounces mushrooms
2 cups water
Salt
½ cup all-purpose flour
¾ teaspoon baking powder
1 large egg, lightly beaten
Freshly ground black pepper
¼ cup (packed) fresh dill or parsley
    leaves, chopped

1. Combine the broth and turkey in a 4-quart saucepan, cover, and bring to a simmer over medium heat. Meanwhile, peel the carrots and cut them into ¼-inch rounds; add them to the soup. Trim ¼ inch off the ends of the stems, then wipe the mushrooms clean with a damp paper towel and cut them into ¼-inch-thick slices. Add them to the soup as well. When the broth reaches a simmer, add the water and 1 teaspoon salt. Cover the saucepan and cook over low heat until the carrots are tender, about 15 minutes.

2. Five minutes before the soup is done, prepare the dumpling dough: Combine the flour, baking powder, and ¼ teaspoon salt in a small bowl. Make a well in the middle of the flour mixture and add the egg. Using a fork to work a little bit in at a time, blend the flour into the egg until you have formed a stiff but sticky dough. If the dough is too hard to work, drizzle in a tablespoonful or so of the simmering broth.

3. When the carrots and mushrooms are tender, season the soup to taste with salt and pepper. By teaspoonfuls (no larger—they will swell up to 1½ inches in diameter), drop the dumpling dough into the boiling soup and cook over medium heat, uncovered, until they take shape and float to the surface, about 1 minute.

4. Cover the pan and cook gently over medium heat for 10 minutes, or until the dumplings are swollen, airy, and cooked through. Season to taste with salt and pepper. Remove the soup from the heat and add the dill. Serve immediately.

Third-Time-Around Turkey Soup

MAKES: *4 servings*
TIME: *20 minutes*

This soup is delightfully original, fresh, and gorgeous to look at—hard to believe it's constructed from leftovers!

6 cups leftover turkey broth
4 cups diced leftover cooked turkey
1 package (10 ounces) frozen "petite" peas, thawed
2 cups torn romaine or Boston lettuce leaves
½ cup (packed) fresh mint leaves
½ cup (packed) flat-leaf parsley leaves
½ cup coconut milk (optional)
½ teaspoon ground ginger
Salt
8 slices sandwich bread
1 tablespoon sesame oil
1 tablespoon vegetable oil
Freshly ground black pepper
1 small red bell pepper

1. Combine the broth and turkey in a large saucepan and bring to a simmer over medium heat. Meanwhile, purée the peas with the lettuce, mint, parsley, coconut milk if using, ginger, and 1 teaspoon salt in a food processor. Transfer the purée to a bowl and set it aside.

2. Cut the bread into ½-inch cubes. Heat the sesame and vegetable oils in a large nonstick skillet. Add the bread cubes and sauté them until golden on all sides, 2 to 3 minutes. Season well with salt and pepper. While the bread is cooking, stem, seed, and finely dice the bell pepper.

3. When the soup is at a simmer, stir in the pea purée and bring the mixture to just under a simmer. Remove from the heat and serve; let each person garnish his or her portion with the croutons and the red pepper dice.

Grandma Helen's Jewish Chicken Soup

MAKES: *3 to 4 quarts*
TIME: *15 minutes preparation*
2½ hours no-work cooking time

A book of chicken recipes wouldn't be complete without an old-fashioned chicken soup. This one is made the way my grandmother made it, with a strong garlic taste and, thanks to the use of free-range birds, an intensely deep poultry flavor. To create a richly flavored stock using this recipe and the same method, omit the parsnip and substitute chicken backs and wings for the whole chicken.

1 chicken, preferably free-range,
    quartered (4 to 5 pounds)
4 quarts water
1 onion
2 carrots
1 parsnip
2 ribs celery
4 cloves garlic

1. Set the chicken in a large stockpot or soup pot and cover it with the water. Bring the water to just under a boil over high heat. As it heats, skim off the foam that surfaces. When all the foam has been skimmed off, simmer the chicken, partially covered, without letting it boil, until the chicken is partially cooked, 45 minutes. (If the water boils, the soup will be cloudy.) While this

TURNING THE SOUP INTO DINNER

Bring 1½ quarts degreased chicken soup to a boil over medium heat, and season to taste with salt and pepper. Add 2 cups of vermicelli that has been broken into 1-inch lengths or ½ cup rice, and cook until tender, 5 to 15 minutes. Add 1 package (10 ounces) thawed frozen peas or artichoke hearts and 2 cups cooked chicken, and simmer just to reheat, 2 to 3 minutes. Remove the soup from the heat and garnish with 2 tablespoons chopped fresh dill or parsley.

is cooking, cut the onion, carrots, parsnip, and celery stalks in half.

2. Add the vegetables to the pot along with the garlic, and simmer, partially covered, over low heat until the meat falls off the bone, another 1½ hours. Keep the level of the liquid constant by adding more water as it evaporates.

3. Remove the chicken and vegetables with a strainer. If the chicken has some flavor left, keep it for later. Discard the vegetables. Ladle the broth into a large bowl through a cheesecloth-lined sieve, and let it cool to room temperature. Refrigerate for at least 1 hour or overnight, then remove the congealed fat. Pull the meat off the bones in large chunks, discarding the skin, fat, and bones. The soup is now ready to be used.

Homemade Exotic Pantry

In the *Monday-to-Friday Cookbook,* I discussed at length the joys of having a pantry that is well stocked, not only with everyday condiments such as barbecue sauce, salsa, and pickles, but with more exotic ones such as pesto, olive paste, and sun-dried tomatoes. I demonstrated how, with a dab of these flavorful staples, the most ordinary salad or the simplest of pastas could be enlivened quickly and with little effort.

In my second book, *Monday-to-Friday Pasta,* I expanded slightly on this theme and included recipes for some of the pantry staples, such as pesto and olive paste. In both books I relied on a handful of pantry ingredients that were easy to make from scratch and/or commercially available.

Since then I've looked farther afield for pantry ingredients. Olive paste, pesto, and salsa are great, but why not have that same convenience with cilantro paste, or coconut paste, or Indian curry? With that in mind I've come up with a few more concoctions that bring depth of flavor to chicken dishes in a flash.

You'll see how, inspired by the idea of pesto, I've come up with a few other herb purées. My most recent culinary infatuation is with the flavors of Southeast Asia, so I've developed some Indonesian-style mixes. And because I have always been enamored of the heady spices of Indian food, I thought it would be handy to have a paste that was as handy as curry powder but a lot more authentic—and so Homemade Tandoori Paste was born. Dried porcini mushrooms are another favorite, so I figured out a way to always have them at the ready without having to wait 30 minutes to reconstitute them. I hope you explore the exotic pantry and that it increases your eating enjoyment as much as it does mine.

WAYS TO USE THE EXOTIC PANTRY

To make the best use of these pantry ingredients, think of them as instant flavor boosters that will add intriguing taste to a gamut of dishes from soups to sandwiches.

TO FLAVOR THE CHICKEN BEFORE COOKING

The whole bird: Rub a seasoned paste or herb purée under the skin of the bird before roasting.

The quartered bird: Marinate the chicken overnight in Basic Vinaigrette before baking or grilling. As with the whole bird, rub some herb purée, garlic paste, or vinaigrette over and under the skin before roasting or baking.

Chicken pieces: To create a marinade in which to soak chicken pieces before grilling, roasting, or baking, use the Basic Vinaigrette (page 64) as a base and change its character each time by adding a dab of a different herb purée or seasoning paste. Or use the Ginger Soy Dipping Sauce as a marinade. If you are grilling plain chicken, add a sauce or salsa from the pantry as an accompaniment. For example, the Roasted Garlic Paste, tossed with Basic Vinaigrette, cucumbers, and chopped fresh tomatoes, makes a terrific topping for grilled chicken thighs.

Ground chicken: To instantly season ground chicken for loaves and burgers, mix a dab or more of the Ancho Paste, Basil and Garlic Purée, Homemade Tandoori Paste, or an herb purée into the meat.

After cooking ground chicken, add a seasoning paste from the pantry along with some chicken broth and a thawed frozen vegetable. Toss this lively instant sauce over rice, pasta, or other grain of choice.

TO FLAVOR SOUPS AND STEWS

Instead of cooking seasoning vegetables, like onions, at the start, simply add a teaspoon of dried herbs or spices at the end of the cooking time.

TO FLAVOR SALADS AND SANDWICHES

A spoonful of an exotic pantry ingredient mixed into yogurt, mayonnaise, or a dressing you already have on hand livens up chicken salads and makes for a super-exotic sandwich spread.

STORING THE EXOTIC PANTRY

Because many of these exotic pantry ingredients include a high proportion of garlic and oil (which can breed bacteria), they don't keep for long in the fridge and ought to be stored in the freezer. My solution is to freeze the pantry ingredients in small portions so that they are usable in small doses. One way is to lay a piece of plastic wrap on a metal baking sheet. Place 2- to 3-tablespoon-size dollops of the paste or purée 1 inch apart. Lay a piece of plastic wrap over the top and press down; freeze. When the little portions are frozen solid, rewrap them individually and pack them in a self-seal plastic bag.

Another idea is to freeze small amounts of the paste or purée (or stock) in ice cube trays. The problem is that a plastic tray absorbs odors and flavors. My solution is to line each cube with plastic wrap before filling it. When they are frozen solid, lift the little plastic mounds out of the cubes, rewrap them, and store in a self-seal plastic bag.

Basil and Garlic Purée

MAKES: *About 2 cups*
TIME: *10 minutes*

Having boldly flavored condiments at the ready makes weekday cooking a breeze. I find this purée to be more versatile than pesto because it doesn't include cheese. It's also a clever way to conserve fresh basil and other herbs, such as parsley or mint. A small dose of herb purée will liven up a chicken sauté as happily as it will a recipe for steamed vegetables or a plateful of spaghetti. I freeze the purée in fairly small batches to make them usable for individual portions.

*8 cups (packed) fresh basil leaves
(about 1 pound with stems)*
8 to 10 cloves garlic
¾ cup extra-virgin olive oil
Salt and freshly ground black pepper

1. Rinse the basil well and pat it dry. Place the leaves in a food processor.

2. Coarsely chop the garlic (you should have about ¼ cup) and add it to the basil. Process the basil and garlic until the leaves are coarsely chopped.

3. While the processor is running, slowly drizzle in the oil and process until finely puréed. Season to taste with salt and pepper.

4. Line a small baking sheet with plastic wrap, and place 2-tablespoon mounds of the purée on the sheet at 2-inch intervals. Cover with more plastic wrap and pat down lightly (don't worry if some olive oil oozes out of the purée). Freeze until frozen somewhat solid, 1 hour (the herb purées never freeze completely solid).

5. Remove the frozen purée pats and wrap them individually in plastic wrap, then put them in a self-seal plastic bag and freeze for up to 6 months.

VARIATIONS

Parsley Purée: Substitute flat-leaf parsley for the basil.

Mint Purée: Substitute 4 cups mint leaves for the basil, 2 to 3 scallions (white and green parts) for the garlic, and ½ cup vegetable oil for the olive oil. Add the grated zest of 2 lemons. Season with 1 teaspoon salt. This yields 1 cup. Mint purée is delicious in chicken salads.

Cilantro Purée

MAKES: *About 1 cup*
TIME: *15 minutes*

Cilantro purée hints at Thai and Indonesian cuisine and offers a refreshing alternative to the ubiquitous Italian pesto and olivada. The purée is so easy to make that you should always have it on hand in the freezer. Not only is this delicious in stews and soups, but it is fabulous stirred into vinaigrettes or mayonnaises for a chicken salad or sandwich.

*4 cups (packed) fresh cilantro leaves
(about 1 pound with stems on)*
2 cloves garlic
½ cup unsweetened coconut milk
½ cup unsalted roasted peanuts
¼ cup lime or lemon juice
Salt

1. Rinse the cilantro well and pat it dry. Place the leaves in a food processor and add the

DO-IT-YOURSELF COCONUT MILK

If you like Indian, Thai, and other exotic flavors and cannot find unsweetened coconut milk in your part of the country, you can make your own (provided, of course, you can get your hands on a fresh coconut). The coconut is fresh if you can hear the liquid inside when you shake it and if it feels heavy for its size.

To make the milk, first pierce the soft round "eyes" of the coconut with a metal skewer or ice pick. Drain off the liquid and taste a bit: it should taste like sweet water. If it tastes sour, the coconut is rotten—throw it out.

Preheat the oven to 400°F. Place the drained coconut on a baking sheet and bake until it cracks, 10 to 15 minutes. (Don't overbake the coconut or it will taste cooked.)

When the shell cracks, remove the coconut from the oven, wrap it in cloth towels, and tap it all around with a hammer. Then give it a sharp rap with the hammer to crack it in half. The coconut should release from the outer shell. Peel away the thin brown skin and chop the meat into coarse pieces. Purée each cup of chopped coconut with 1 cup of boiling water in a food processor. Remove it to a bowl and let steep for a couple of hours in the refrigerator. Then strain the milk through a couple of layers of cheesecloth, squeezing it well to extract the last drop of milk.

A nice big coconut will yield 4 cups coconut milk. If you don't use the milk right away, freeze it in 1-cup portions.

garlic, coconut milk, peanuts, and lime juice.

2. Process to a fine purée, and season with 1 teaspoon salt or to taste. Divide into ¼-cup portions and freeze.

Coconut Peanut Sauce

MAKES: *About 2½ cups*
TIME: *20 minutes*

Recently I've fallen in love with the flavors of Thai, Vietnamese, and Indonesian cuisines. Tired of endlessly whipping up little seasoning mixtures to satisfy my desire for these flavors, I developed this paste to have on hand so that I could indulge my craving at a moment's notice. It stores for a week or two in the refrigerator and for 2 to 3 months in the freezer. Not unlike the Cilantro Purée, this exotic sauce works magic with beef, lamb, and fish as well as chicken.

1 stalk (about 2 feet) fresh lemongrass
   (optional)
1 cup salted roasted peanuts
2 cloves garlic
1 slice fresh ginger (about the size
   of a quarter)
1 piece lime zest (1 × ¼ inch)
3 tablespoons lime juice
1 tablespoon anchovy paste
1 teaspoon sugar
Salt
½ teaspoon dried red pepper flakes
2 cups (14-ounce can) unsweetened
   coconut milk
½ cup (packed) fresh basil leaves
2 cups (packed) fresh cilantro leaves

1. Remove the woody outer leaves of the lemongrass stalk (if using). Finely slice the tender inner stalk and transfer to a blender. Add the peanuts, garlic, ginger, lime zest and juice, anchovy paste, sugar, salt to taste, and red pepper flakes.

2. Add the coconut milk and blend to a fine purée. Transfer this mixture to a food proces-

LOVELY LEMONGRASS

Lemongrass, one of the miraculous ingredients of the culinary world, brings to food an inimitable citrus fragrance. While similar to lemons and limes, this particular citrus taste is more sweetly aromatic, more perfumed, and vaguely reminiscent of citronella.

Talk about how things have changed! A mere 5 years ago, fresh lemongrass could be found only in markets that catered specifically to a Thai or Vietnamese clientele. Today I can find fresh lemongrass in most of my local produce stores.

Fresh lemongrass looks a bit like a straw-hued, dried scallion. You can usually find it in a market that carries exotic fresh produce, alongside the fresh herbs. To use lemongrass, peel away the tough outer layer and use only the white part. You can steep the tough green parts in boiling water with fresh ginger for a delicious brewed herb tea.

sor and purée with the basil and cilantro leaves. Adjust the seasoning and pack in ½- or 1-cup portions. Store in the freezer.

WAYS TO USE COCONUT PEANUT SAUCE WITH CHICKEN

■ Use the sauce as a condiment to zap the flavor of roasted or barbecued chicken.
■ For soup, stir the sauce into chicken broth, add chunks of leftover cooked chicken, and heat.

OTHER WAYS TO USE COCONUT PEANUT SAUCE

■ Dress up ½ pound of angel hair pasta by tossing it with ¼ cup sauce and 2 tablespoons butter.
■ Create a salad dressing by combining 2 tablespoons sauce with 2 tablespoons plain yogurt or mayonnaise. (Serves 2.)
■ Top a portion of steamed vegetables with 1 tablespoon of the sauce.

Ginger Soy Dipping Sauce

MAKES: *About 1 cup*
TIME: *10 minutes*

This is a great little condiment to have on hand, wonderful drizzled over grilled or roasted chicken or over a plateful of steamed vegetables, or used as a dipping sauce for warm Chinese Chicken Burritos (page 92). This will keep in the refrigerator for a couple of months.

1 tablespoon minced fresh ginger
1 teaspoon minced garlic
1 teaspoon sugar
½ cup chicken broth
¼ cup light soy sauce
1 tablespoon rice vinegar
1 tablespoon Asian sesame oil
Salt
Dried red pepper flakes

1. Place the ginger, garlic, sugar, and broth in a small saucepan and bring to a boil over medium heat. Remove the saucepan from the heat and transfer the liquid to a bowl to cool.

2. When the mixture is at room temperature, combine it with the soy sauce, rice vinegar, and sesame oil. Season to taste with salt and dried red pepper flakes. Transfer to a glass jar, cover, and store in the refrigerator.

Ancho Paste

MAKES: *About 1 cup*
TIME: *15 minutes preparation*
30 minutes no-work soaking time

Dried ancho chiles are used frequently in the Mexican kitchen and are available in the U.S. in many a gourmet store. This seasoning paste with ancho chiles will bring an authentic Mexican flair to many Monday-to-Friday quick dishes. I like to use this with ground beef as well as with poultry.

6 large ancho chiles
1 tablespoon red wine vinegar
½ teaspoon ground cinnamon
¼ teaspoon ground cloves
¼ teaspoon dried oregano
2 cloves garlic, chopped
Salt

1. Heat an ungreased cast-iron skillet over medium-low heat. Add the chiles and toast them for a few seconds, turning them with tongs so they do not burn. The instant they become pliable and smell fragrant, remove them from the skillet.

2. Cut the chiles open and remove the seeds and veins. Tear the chiles into large pieces, transfer them to a bowl, and add just enough hot water to cover. Soak until very soft, 30 minutes; don't soak longer or they will lose their aroma.

3. Drain the softened chiles and pat dry. Transfer them to a blender or small food processor and add the vinegar, ⅓ cup fresh water, the cinnamon, cloves, oregano, and garlic. Blend until smooth, and season with ½ teaspoon salt. Transfer the mixture to a glass jar and keep for 1 week in the refrigerator. Or place small mounds of the purée on a sheet of plastic wrap, top with another piece of plastic wrap, and freeze until solid. When the pats of chile paste are frozen, transfer them to a plastic bag.

WAYS TO USE ANCHO PASTE WITH CHICKEN

- Sauté some ground chicken in oil until crumbled and no longer pink. Stir in Ancho Paste, to taste, along with a can of drained rinsed black beans. Serve over rice, with a dollop of sour cream on top.
- Bring some chicken broth to a boil, and add Ancho Paste to taste. Stir in some thawed frozen corn and diced cooked chicken. Garnish this quick soup with grated sharp Cheddar or Monterey Jack cheese.

OTHER WAYS TO USE ANCHO PASTE

- Mix 1 tablespoon Ancho Paste into 2 tablespoons mayonnaise and spread over hamburgers. Serve on buns.
- For a fabulous salsa, mix some of the paste

into diced fresh tomatoes and avocados. Serve with grilled flank steak or swordfish.

■ Sauté some ground beef until crumbled. Stir in Ancho Paste and tomato paste to taste. Serve in tortillas or over rice.

FEEDING ONE AT A TIME

If late arrivals for dinner are an unavoidable occurrence in your house, solve the problem by turning to soups, sandwiches, and salads. The soups can be made in advance and the individual latecomer can reheat his or her own portion; salads can be served chilled at any hour, and sandwiches can be assembled on an individual basis.

Homemade Tandoori Paste

MAKES: *About ½ cup*
TIME: *15 minutes*

In smaller towns and cities, it can be difficult to find good Indian spices and condiments. Here is a homemade paste of garlic and classic Indian spices that is great rubbed into chicken before grilling or baking. Substitute this when commercially prepared tandoori paste is called

for, or use it in creative ways. It will keep for a week in the refrigerator and indefinitely in the freezer.

4 large cloves garlic, coarsely chopped
1 teaspoon ground cardamom
1 teaspoon ground cinnamon
2 teaspoons ground cumin
½ teaspoon ground coriander
1 teaspoon turmeric
½ teaspoon ground cayenne pepper or
  pure chile powder
1 tablespoon paprika
1 piece (1 inch) fresh ginger, peeled
  and coarsely chopped
¼ cup red wine vinegar
2 tablespoons vegetable oil
½ teaspoon salt

1. Heat a cast-iron skillet over medium heat. When it is hot, add the garlic and stir continuously until slightly golden and toasty, about 1 minute. Add the cardamom, cinnamon, cumin, coriander, and turmeric and stir for a few seconds or until the mixture is aromatic.

2. Remove the skillet from the heat and immediately transfer the spices and garlic to a blender. Add the cayenne, paprika, ginger, vinegar, oil, and salt, and blend until smooth and pastelike. Transfer to a jar and keep in the refrigerator, or divide

into tablespoonfuls, wrap in plastic wrap, and keep in the freezer.

WAYS TO USE TANDOORI PASTE WITH CHICKEN

- Mix a tablespoonful or so into 1 cup plain yogurt and add ¼ cup chopped fresh cilantro. Use as an Indian salsa with grilled or baked chicken.
- Use Tandoori Paste to marinate leftover skinless roasted or other plainly cooked chicken overnight. Then use the chicken in salads or sandwiches.

OTHER WAYS TO USE TANDOORI PASTE

- Omit the vinegar and oil and use as a dry rub to season a whole red snapper before grilling.
- Stir a spoonful into cooked rice.
- Stir a dollop into spaghetti sauce to create an Indian-flavored pasta sauce.

Olive Paste
Olivada

MAKES: *About 2 cups*
TIME: *15 minutes*

There are so many ways to use olive paste that it is a treasure in any Monday-to-Friday pantry. There are many excellent commercial brands of olive paste, or olivada, but it is unavailable in many parts of the country, so here is a quick version to make at home. It is easy to prepare and absolutely delicious, provided you start out with the highest-quality olives. If you are lucky enough to find commercially pitted Kalamata or green "country-style" (they've been marinated in garlic and spices) olives, you'll be able to save some time. If you can't find these, then you'll need to pit the olives first. However, even with commercially pitted olives, be sure you check through them carefully and discard any stray pits (which could damage the blades of your food processor). This mixture keeps nicely in a glass jar for 3 to 4 weeks in the refrigerator. If you think you may not use it up within that time, divide the mixture into ½-cup containers and freeze for 6 to 8 months.

3 cups (20 ounces) pitted black
    Kalamata or "country-style" green
    olives
4 cloves garlic
½ cup extra-virgin olive oil (if the
    olives are packed in olive oil, use
    the oil from the jar)
2 tablespoons lemon juice
Salt and freshly ground black pepper

1. Place the pitted olives and the garlic in a food processor and purée until finely chopped.

2. Add the olive oil, lemon juice, 1 teaspoon salt, and pepper to taste. Purée again and adjust the seasoning. Transfer the olive paste to storage containers.

VARIATION

Sun-Dried Tomato Paste: For the olives substitute 2 cups sun-dried tomatoes packed in olive oil. Reduce the olive oil to ¼ cup.

WAYS TO USE OLIVE PASTE WITH CHICKEN

■ Combine Olive Paste with Basic Vinaigrette (page 64) and use to season chicken salad.
■ Spread some under the skin of a chicken before roasting.
■ Combine the paste with finely chopped cooked chicken and toss over pasta.

OTHER WAYS TO USE OLIVE PASTE

■ Create a delicious topping for steamed vegetables by combining Olive Paste with mayonnaise and chopped tomatoes.
■ Spread some Olive Paste on the bread you're using to make grilled cheese sandwiches.
■ For instant pizzas, spread some olive paste on pita breads and top with grated mozzarella cheese. Bake in a 400°F oven until the cheese has melted.

Roasted Garlic Paste

MAKES: *About ¾ cup*
TIME: *20 minutes preparation*
1 hour no-work roasting time

It's useful to have this paste on hand for several reasons: It's mild enough to use in salad dressings and to spread on bread for sandwiches, and it can give a soup or stew a subtle garlic flavor without your having to cook fresh garlic at the beginning of the recipe. I've added lemon juice to this purée to give it a longer shelf life because the addition of citric acid prevents contamination by botulism bacteria. Keep it in the refrigerator for 2 weeks, in the freezer for 2 months.

5 heads garlic
2 tablespoons extra-virgin olive oil
1 lemon
Salt and freshly ground black pepper

1. Preheat the oven to 425°F.

2. Using a serrated knife, cut ¼ inch off the tops of the heads of garlic to expose the cloves. Drizzle each head with about ¼ teaspoonful olive oil, and wrap each head in aluminum foil.

3. Set the wrapped packages in a baking pan and roast until the garlic cloves are tender, 40 to 45 minutes. Remove the garlic from the oven, unwrap, and let cool until cool enough to handle, 30 minutes. Meanwhile, grate ½ teaspoon lemon zest and squeeze 2 tablespoons lemon juice.

4. Squeeze the soft garlic from the husks into a blender, and blend with the lemon zest, juice, and remaining olive oil. Season to taste with salt and pepper. Transfer to a jar and keep for 2 weeks in the refrigerator, or store for 3 months in the freezer.

WAYS TO USE ROASTED GARLIC PASTE WITH CHICKEN

- Before grilling, spread the paste under the skin of the chicken.
- Spoon a teaspoonful or so into a finished soup or stew.
- Spoon some Roasted Garlic Paste into a raw poultry burger mixture before cooking it.
- Spoon some into a plain vinaigrette dressing.

- Spread some on toast or bread to liven up chicken sandwiches.

OTHER WAYS TO USE ROASTED GARLIC PASTE

- Spoon some garlic paste into a finished side dish of rice, pasta, or mashed potatoes.
- Purée a can of chickpeas with garlic paste to taste, season with salt and pepper, and heat in a double boiler or microwave oven for a great side dish with plain grilled chicken.
- Spoon some garlic paste into olive oil and toss with any plain steamed vegetable.

Tomato Salsa

MAKES: *About 2 cups*
TIME: *20 minutes*

In American Tex-Mex restaurants we have come to expect salsa (which just means "sauce" in Spanish) to be a fiery mix of chopped raw tomatoes, onions, and chiles. This Monday-to-Friday salsa is like restaurant salsa except for one important change: to extend its shelf life, it's made with cooked rather than raw onions. This way the onions don't turn bitter over time and the salsa keeps well (for 1 week) in the refrigerator.

¼ cup olive oil
½ cup finely chopped onions
1 teaspoon minced garlic
1 tablespoon chili powder
2 teaspoons ground cumin
1 tablespoon tomato paste
2 tablespoons red wine vinegar
4 ripe tomatoes
2 fresh jalapeño peppers (optional)
Salt

1. Heat the olive oil in a medium-size skillet over medium heat. Add the onions and cook until tender, about 3 minutes. Add the garlic, chili powder, and cumin and cook, stirring, just to release the flavors, 30 seconds.

2. Add the tomato paste and vinegar and cook for 15 seconds, to evaporate some of the harshness of the vinegar. Remove the skillet from the heat and transfer the contents to a mixing bowl to cool.

3. While the onions are cooling, core and quarter the tomatoes. Remove the juice and seeds with a spoon. Coarsely chop the tomatoes in a food processor and mix them into the onions.

4. Seed and mince the jalapeño peppers, and add them to the tomatoes and onions. Season the mixture to taste with salt, and add a few more drops of vinegar if you need to sharpen the flavor. Transfer to a glass jar and store in the refrigerator for up to 1 week.

WAYS TO USE SALSA WITH CHICKEN

■ For a simple quick dinner, season plain grilled, poached, or microwaved chicken with salsa and serve with a green salad.
■ Cook up some ground chicken or turkey, season with salsa to taste, and fold into warm tortillas.

OTHER WAYS TO USE SALSA

■ Add some to Cheddar cheese sandwiches.
■ Use as a topping on grilled fish or scrambled or fried eggs.
■ Stir some salsa into steamed vegetables.
■ Mix with a plain vinaigrette to dress up every type of salad.

Pretty-Quick Chicken Stock

MAKES: *About 2 quarts*
TIME: *15 minutes preparation*
1 hour no-work cooking time

While there is nothing "exotic" about it, this stock is somewhat different in that it is made more quickly than usual and in an unorthodox way. By browning the chopped onions and chicken parts first, you caramelize the natural sugars, which in turn more quickly releases a deep rich flavor and

PORCINI STOCK

I love the taste of dried porcini mushrooms, but given that they need to soak for 30 minutes before they are soft enough to use, they are not a convenient Monday-to-Friday staple. However, you can create an instant porcini stock to have ready to use when you come home from work: Simply combine 2 ounces dried porcini with a quart of cold water in a quart glass jar. Cover and refrigerate; the mushrooms will soften slowly.

The mushrooms will keep this way (refrigerated) for months, provided that each time you remove some of the mushrooms and their soaking liquid, you use a spotlessly clean spoon and don't contaminate what's in the jar.

To use this as a convenient Monday-to-Friday pantry ingredient, stir some of the soaking liquid and chopped rehydrated mushrooms into chicken soups and stews or to add great flavor to pasta and rice dishes. Here are some more suggestions for uses:

■ Substitute ½ cup of the liquid and chopped rehydrated mushrooms for water when making rice.

■ Use ½ cup liquid and chopped rehydrated mushrooms to deglaze the pan after sautéing chicken breasts.

■ Toss 1 pound cooked pasta with 2 cups liquid and chopped rehydrated mushrooms, plus 2 tablespoons olive oil and ½ cup grated Parmesan cheese.

■ To rehydrate couscous, steep in equal amounts water and drained porcini liquid.

color into the stock. This method yields a decent stock and it is certainly better than anything you get out of a can. Store the stock in the freezer if you are going to keep it longer than 3 days. Always bring the stock back to a boil before using.

2 tablespoons vegetable oil
1 onion, coarsely chopped
2 pounds chicken backs, necks, wing
    tips, gizzards, and/or bones
3 quarts water
1 carrot, chopped
1 rib celery, chopped
2 cloves garlic
1 bay leaf
Salt and freshly ground black pepper

1. Heat the oil in an 8-quart pot over medium-high heat. Add the onion and sauté until golden brown, about 5 minutes.

2. Add the chicken and continue to sauté, stirring frequently, until the pieces are golden, another 5 minutes.

3. Add the water, carrot, celery, garlic, and bay leaf. Bring the water to just below a boil over high heat. As the liquid heats, a beige foam will form on the surface. Remove it with a slotted spoon, taking care not to remove the chopped vegetables.

4. Reduce heat to a simmer, and cook partially covered, for 45 minutes to 1 hour (do not let the water boil, or the stock will become cloudy). Keep the level of the liquid constant by replenishing the water occasionally.

5. Remove the pot from the heat and let the stock cool for 1 hour. Then strain it and discard the solids. When the stock is at room temperature, refrigerate it, covered, overnight, to make it easier to degrease.

6. The next day, remove and discard the congealed fat on the surface. Season the stock lightly with salt and pepper. Pour the stock into 2-cup containers, and store in the freezer for up to 4 months.

CONVERSION TABLE

LIQUID CONVERSIONS

US	IMPERIAL	METRIC
2 tbs	1 fl oz	30 ml
3 tbs	1½ fl oz	45 ml
¼ cup	2 fl oz	60 ml
⅓ cup	2½ fl oz	75 ml
⅓ cup + 1 tbs	3 fl oz	90 ml
⅓ cup + 2 tbs	3½ fl oz	100 ml
½ cup	4 fl oz	125 ml
⅔ cup	5 fl oz	150 ml
¾ cup	6 fl oz	175 ml
¾ cup + 2 tbs	7 fl oz	200 ml
1 cup	8 fl oz	250 ml
1 cup + 2 tbs	9 fl oz	275 ml
1¼ cups	10 fl oz	300 ml
1⅓ cups	11 fl oz	325 ml
1½ cups	12 fl oz	350 ml
1⅔ cups	13 fl oz	375 ml
1¾ cups	14 fl oz	400 ml
1¾ cups + 2 tbs	15 fl oz	450 ml
1 pint (2 cups)	16 fl oz	500 ml
2½ cups	1 pint	600 ml
3¾ cups	1½ pints	900 ml
4 cups	1¾ pints	1 liter

WEIGHT CONVERSIONS

US/UK	METRIC	US/UK	METRIC
½ oz	15 g	7 oz	200 g
1 oz	30 g	8 oz	250 g
1½ oz	45 g	9 oz	275 g
2 oz	60 g	10 oz	300 g
2½ oz	75 g	11 oz	325 g
3 oz	90 g	12 oz	350 g
3½ oz	100 g	13 oz	375 g
4 oz	125 g	14 oz	400 g
5 oz	150 g	15 oz	450 g
6 oz	175 g	1 lb	500 g

OVEN TEMPERATURES

FAHRENHEIT	GAS MARK	CELSIUS
250	½	120
275	1	140
300	2	150
325	3	160
350	4	180
375	5	190
400	6	200
425	7	220
450	8	230
475	9	240
500	10	260

Note: Reduce the temperature by 20°C (68°F) for fan-assisted ovens

APPROXIMATE EQUIVALENTS

1 stick butter = 8 tbs = 4 oz = ½ cup

1 cup all-purpose presifted flour/dried
   bread crumbs = 5 oz

1 cup granulated sugar = 8 oz

1 cup (packed) brown sugar = 6 oz

1 cup confectioners' sugar = 4½ oz

1 cup honey/syrup = 11 oz

1 cup grated cheese = 4 oz

1 cup dried beans = 6 oz

1 large egg = 2 oz = about ¼ cup

1 egg yolk = about 1 tbs

1 egg white = about 2 tbs

Note: All the above conversions are approximate, but close enough to be useful when converting from one system to another.

Index